"*Global Literature and the Environment* is a valuable addition to a growing body of scholarship on the role literature and literary criticism might play in addressing the major environmental challenges of our times. Covering a suitably wide range of literary works and provocatively insisting on the instrumentality rather than singularity of literature, the authors adopt a nuanced eco-materialist approach that avoids the rhetorical excesses of elemental ecocriticism (and other versions of new materialism) and the ideological pieties of world-ecology (and other versions of eco-Marxism). Though it might ruffle a few feathers along the way, the book should appeal to postcolonial and environmental humanities scholars alike, and to all those committed to the continuing pursuit of social and ecological justice in an unevenly developed world."

Graham Huggan, *Professor of Postcolonial and Commonwealth Literatures, Leeds, UK. Co-author of Postcolonial Ecocriticism: Literature, Animals, Environment*

"Matthew Whittle's and Jade Munslow Ong's *Global Literature and the Environment* spans continents in terms of the diverse materialities of soil, oil, ice, air, and life and yet the book brings them together in a brilliant array of textual analyses featuring environmental justice and ecological devastation.

The selection of authors and genres is impressive; the literary insights formidable. I highly recommend this book to anyone working or studying in the environmental humanities, comparative literature, Anglophone literature, and environmental justice studies. The book is informative, well-written, beautifully researched, and a significant contribution to our global understanding of the Anthropocene. It is also eminently readable even as it portrays the sheer brutality of extractivist cultures to our planet and its peoples."

Heather I. Sullivan, *Professor of German and Comparative Literature, Trinity University, US*

Global Literature and the Environment

Global Literature and the Environment analyses literatures from across the world that connect readers to the localized impacts of the climate and ecological emergencies. The book contextualizes ecological breakdown within the history of capitalist-imperialism, exploring how literature helps us to imagine and create a habitable and just world for all forms of life.

The four chapters are organized according to the elements of the climate system that are at risk. 'Earth' examines Caribbean, American, South African, and British literatures that explore how dominant human groups have exploited soils, minerals, metals, and oil in pursuit of economic aims. 'Water' engages with poetic representations of, and responses to, extraction, pollution, and global warming in the fresh- and saltwaters of Nigeria and the icescapes of Alaska. 'Air' analyses prose and poetry that depicts atmospheric pollution caused by gas flaring in the Niger Delta and the production of pesticides in India. 'Life' attends to the ways in which literature contextualizes the drivers of, and proposed solutions to, mass species extinction across North America, Africa, Australasia, and Aotearoa New Zealand.

This accessible and engaging book explores novels, plays, and poetry by writers including Octavia Butler, C.L.R. James, dg nanouk okpik, Ken Saro-Wiwa, Imbolo Mbue, Indra Sinha, Witi Ihimaera, J.M. Coetzee, and Henrietta Rose-Innes, amongst many others. It introduces readers to the concept of the Anthropocene alongside perspectives that challenge the assumption that the climate crisis is caused by an undifferentiated humanity. In doing so, the book draws on, and combines, a range of theoretical approaches, including postcolonialism, Indigenous studies, ecocriticism, cultural materialism, and animal studies.

Matthew Whittle is Lecturer in Postcolonial Literature at the University of Kent, UK. He is the author of *Post-War British Literature and the 'End of Empire'* (Palgrave Macmillan, 2016).

Jade Munslow Ong is Professor of World Literatures in English at the University of Salford, UK. She is author of *Olive Schreiner and African Modernism: Allegory, Empire and Postcolonial Writing* (Routledge, 2018).

Global Literature: Twenty-First Century Perspectives

Series Editors: Claire Chambers, University of York, UK and Shital Pravinchandra, Queen Mary Univerity of London, UK

Global Literature: Twenty-First-Century Perspectives introduces both enduring and cutting-edge debates about literature from around the globe.

The books in this series provide readers with a thorough background to the field, while also offering alternative views and approaches, as well as new research directions. Readers are invited to explore the transnational elements of cultural production and reception, examining texts' critical relationship with colonial history; resistance to (neo-)colonialism; the persistent linguistic hegemony of European languages; identity and equality debates; environments; the body; and the digital age.

Across the series, these accessible books connect key theoretical texts and literary examples to cultural texts and political debates, presenting complex ideas and information in a clear manner ideal for students.

Books in the series

Global Literature and the Environment
Matthew Whittle and Jade Munslow Ong

Global Literature and the Environment

Matthew Whittle and Jade Munslow Ong

LONDON AND NEW YORK

Designed cover image: EXTREME-PHOTOGRAPHER, Getty

First published 2025
by Routledge
4 Park Square, Milton Park, Abingdon, Oxon OX14 4RN

and by Routledge
605 Third Avenue, New York, NY 10158

Routledge is an imprint of the Taylor & Francis Group, an informa business

© 2025 Matthew Whittle and Jade Munslow Ong

The right of Matthew Whittle and Jade Munslow Ong to be identified as author of this work has been asserted in accordance with sections 77 and 78 of the Copyright, Designs and Patents Act 1988.

All rights reserved. No part of this book may be reprinted or reproduced or utilised in any form or by any electronic, mechanical, or other means, now known or hereafter invented, including photocopying and recording, or in any information storage or retrieval system, without permission in writing from the publishers.

Trademark notice: Product or corporate names may be trademarks or registered trademarks, and are used only for identification and explanation without intent to infringe.

British Library Cataloguing in Publication Data
A catalogue record for this book is available from the British Library

ISBN: 9780367145408 (hbk)
ISBN: 9780367373689 (pbk)
ISBN: 9780429353352 (ebk)

DOI: 10.4324/9780429353352

Typeset in Times New Roman
by Taylor & Francis Books

This book is for Julia, Hanna, Louis, Bella, Esmé, and Sebastian

Contents

Acknowledgements		x
Introduction		1
1	Earth	28
	Soil 29	
	Mineral and Metal 47	
	Oil 59	
2	Water	74
	Delta 76	
	Ice 86	
3	Air	103
	Gas Flaring 104	
	Pesticides 114	
4	Life	129
	Commodification 134	
	Game Hunting 154	
	Revival 161	
Conclusion		182
	Glossary of Key Terms	195
	Suggested Further Reading	201
	Index	204

Acknowledgements

Our first thanks go to Claire Chambers and Shital Pravinchandra for inviting us to write for this exciting new series, for their enthusiasm and support, judicious editing, and their great patience and kindness as they steered us to completion. We are also grateful to Karen Raith and Chris Ratcliffe at Routledge for their gentle guidance and expert advice at each stage of the process, and Suzanne Arnold for her exceptional copyediting.

Our friends Chris Vardy and Veronica Barnsley were our most important interlocutors in the early stages of writing, for which we are greatly appreciative. We would also like to thank Scott Thurston, Amy Rushton, Dominic Davies, and Ailise Bulfin, who invited us to speak about the research for this book at the University of Salford, Nottingham Trent University, City University London, and University College Dublin. These talks provided us with invaluable opportunities to develop and refine our thinking.

Matt: This book has been enhanced by the support of, and many meandering conversations with, my colleagues and friends Robbie Richardson, Ben Hickman, Derek Ryan, David Herd, Caroline Rooney, David Stirrup and Shelley Saggar, along with the tireless efforts of Bashir Abu-Manneh and the solidarity of the School of English at the University of Kent. The intellectually rich discussions that I have been a part of with all of the students who took the MA modules 'Postcolonial Writing and the Environment' and 'Writing of Empire and Settlement' have also fed into and helped to refine much of the research and writing.

I am incredibly grateful for the unswerving love and encouragement of my family – Mo, John, Nathan, Isa, Julia, Joe, Rach, and Hanna – and for the sanity and support that has come from my friends Ben Latham, Jared Hamilton, Dan Luck, Suzy Lawlor, Jen Barratt and Andrew Low (plus Annie and Rudy), Dom Davies and Emma Parker, John McLeod, Robert Spencer, John Roache, Johnny Rodgers, and Phil O'Brien. I would like to thank Chris Vardy a second time for always being at the end of the phone, and Goldie for keeping me company at the end of my desk.

This would have been a very different book – and much the poorer for it – had Jade not taken up the challenge with me. Since the early days of our friendship, I'd hoped we would get the opportunity to work together and I'm delighted that this ambitious, wide-ranging, and timely project has allowed us to combine our interests and our strengths.

Jade: I would like to thank my close colleagues Emma Barnes, Sanja Nivesjö, Hannah Helm, Vashti Suwa Gbolagun, and Judy Kendall for their great generosity in sharing their knowledge and resources, and for reading and commenting on drafts. Other of my colleagues at the University of Salford continue to be hugely supportive, and I have particularly benefitted from the encouragement and backing of Glyn White, Tim France, Martin Bull, Allan Walker, Iván García, Jane Kilby, Ursula Hurley, Caroline Magennis, Simon Stanton-Sharma, Scott (again), and indeed all of my colleagues in the English department in recent years. I would also like to thank my students on the modules 'World Literature and the Environment', 'Regional and World Literatures', 'Postcolonial African Literatures', and 'Theory, Text and Writing' for helping to direct and shape my thinking on all things global literature and the environment.

My wonderful family – Gavin, Esmé, Sebastian, Barry, Pauline, Karl, Isobel, Louis, Bella, Sue, and Paul – continue to provide my most important sources and sites of comfort, guidance, and inspiration. Thanks too to friends Katy Bourne, Nick Cameron, Kathy Mair, Michael Durrant, Megan Murray-Pepper, and Anastasia Valassopoulos for their interest in, and support for, this book.

Finally, my most significant and heartfelt thanks goes to Matt. Thank you for inviting me to join you in this endeavour, for your forbearance and compassion beyond all reasonable request and measure, for doing far more than your fair share, and for our uniquely rich, multi-faceted and fulfilling friendship – one of the most important in my life.

***

Every effort has been made to contact copyright holders of material reproduced in this product. We would be pleased to rectify any omissions should they be drawn to our attention.

Introduction

This book introduces students, academic teachers, and other readers to the study of global literature and the environment. Throughout, we use the term 'global literature' to refer to a body of work that is both produced by, and critical of, the structural inequalities engendered by the spread of global capitalism that made globalization, marketization, and neoliberalism possible. Drawing on a range of English-language texts from diverse global locations, we examine how they engage with some of the most pressing environmental issues of the twenty-first century – including the climate crisis, species endangerment and extinction, food and water security, and waste and pollution – via four chapters titled Earth, Water, Air, and Life. These chapter titles are informed by a recognition of the distinct but interacting elements of the climate system that are at risk. Within this framing, we develop a series of case studies that incorporate analyses of established theoretical and literary perspectives alongside marginal(ized) and sometimes unusual or surprising texts. We suggest that in combining synoptic accounts of familiar sources with new explorations of less well-known works, we are better positioned to address the exigencies of the climate and ecological emergencies, which require both expansive and newly creative interpretations of the present and future roles of global literature and literary studies in these contexts. In this way, we endeavour to explore both *how* to read global literature and the environment, and *why* we should read global literature *for* the environment.

As Western environmental science has established during at least the past fifty years[1] – and as Indigenous, (formerly) colonized, and enslaved peoples have known for longer – the activities of dominant human groups are fundamentally changing all interrelated component parts of the world's climate system. These comprise the lithosphere (the earth's crust and upper mantle layer), hydrosphere (water), cryosphere (ice and permafrost), atmosphere (air), and biosphere (living things). The lithosphere has been plundered and degraded for its fossil fuels, minerals, and soils. In the hydrosphere, ocean circulations are slowing, affecting monsoon shifts, whilst aquifers and fresh water sources are depleted and polluted. Cryospheric elements including sea ice, ice sheets, and permafrost are melting, contributing to rising sea levels

DOI: 10.4324/9780429353352-1

and the release of greenhouse gases. The atmosphere is rapidly accumulating heat-trapping greenhouse gases as a result of the burning of fossil fuels and destruction of carbon sinks. And in the biosphere, key threats include deforestation, large-scale coral reef die-offs, biodiversity loss, and new biome susceptibilities to pests, disease, fire, and droughts. As a result, we have now reached a range of key tipping points that will bring about unpredictable, abrupt, and potentially irreversible changes to all elements of the climate system.

In the book, we strive to think about global literature and the environment together using well-known and less well-known theoretical, critical, and literary works. Our discussions are framed by two interlinked lines of argument. Namely, that global literature shapes and facilitates affective engagement with environmental issues, expresses resistance, and envisions solutions; and, that literary studies is uniquely positioned to marshal its vast creative and intellectual resources in support of a liveable planet. We pursue these claims via two simple strategies. First, we read widely. We take an exploratory approach to texts spanning periods and places in recognition of the efforts of global writers to reveal and resist the exploitation of people, animals, and environments, as well as to instigate, support, and justify the protection and improvement of ecosystems threatened with destruction. And whilst truly global coverage remains impossible, we do examine a range of literary and theoretical examples spanning canonical and marginal(ized) politically resonant and aesthetically vibrant theories and texts, so that hitherto under-explored literatures can take their place in the discussions. Second, we propose a simple framing device for use in the study of global literature, one that takes its cue from the components of the climate system, but that is more accessible, flexible, and meaningful across diverse cultural contexts. The book's four interlinked chapters – Earth, Water, Air, and Life – loosely represent the similarly interlinked lithosphere, combined hydrosphere and cryosphere, atmosphere, and biosphere. We suggest that by framing the study of global literature and the environment in this way, we are able to argue for the importance of reading global literature as part of the work towards preventing total climate and ecological breakdown. Our intent, then, is that these topic titles will aid readers in capturing both what is at stake, and what we must work to save.

Why Read Literature in a Burning World?

We begin with this question, though our answer is not new. Our answer is simply that literature cultivates empathy and imagination. Literature, as Robert Eaglestone has it, is 'a living conversation' (2019: 6), able to traverse time and space to bring people together even as they are divided. Literature allows us to inhabit others' lives, impresses feelings, and captures individual and collective responses to real and imagined events. In creation and circulation, it provides a means to overcome barriers imposed by language, nation, race, class, and gender. It tests, and helps us to form, values and beliefs, and develops and promotes understanding, compassion, and creativity. As Robert Spencer and Anastasia Valassopoulos put it, literature 'awakens critical and cosmopolitan sensibilities [...], new ways of organising production as well as new forms of collective life. Today these are achievements of the utmost importance' (2021: 215). We aim then, to show how the prose, poetry, and plays we examine in this book grant us new perspectives on our histories and present moments, supporting us in envisioning and enacting better futures.

Throughout this book, we argue that literature and literary studies are vital players in the efforts to prevent climate and ecological breakdown. We acknowledge at the same time, however, that in content and form, production and circulation, and in its use in education, global literature has also done much to contribute to, and occlude the realities of, the climate and ecological crises. By way of a material example: Amazon, the company that launched as the 'Earth's Biggest Bookstore' in 1995, revealed carbon emissions of 44.4 million metric tons in 2018 alone, amounting to around 85 percent of the total emitted by Switzerland.[2] That same year has been labelled 'a year of climate extremes', with heatwaves, wildfires, flooding, and storms occurring across the globe.[3] We continue to experience new climate extremes every year. And, whilst Amazon sells more than just books, it is also not the only bookseller, and there are multiple individuals, organizations, and associated environmental costs, involved in the workings of the global literary market.

Herein lies one of the key problems that we face as readers and writers. Our book hinges on the case for *reading widely*, but this call for *more* is at odds with the need to reduce consumption and waste if we are to prevent further planetary damage. Imre Szeman explains this problem as follows:

> [T]here is a pervasive, if largely unarticulated, liberal narrative concerning literature that links the expansion of literary culture with the narratives of development that underpin capitalist modernity. This equates more literature with more freedom and more social possibilities [...]. We cannot help but imagine that more literature – and more criticism of this literature – must be better, and yet we tend not to imagine that the material practice of literary production and consumption has any real impact on the environment, at least not by comparison to many other cultural practices.
>
> (2017: 286)

As the production of literature is bound up in the fossil-fuelled world economy, more books means more energy use, more waste, and greater environmental impacts. In her important acknowledgement of this fact, Stephanie LeMenager's *Living Oil: Petroleum Culture in the American Century* presents detailed scholarly analysis of the culture of oil, whilst also making 'a necessary confession' in the form of an appendix authored by Sougandhica Hoysa. This appendix provides a Life Cycle Assessment of LeMenager's book as a way of 'plac[ing] the energy footprint of cultural objects such as books and films into perspective' (2014: 198). Whilst, as both Szeman and LeMenager acknowledge, the production of books has much lower environmental impacts than other sectors of the world economy, their accounts still remind us of the precise environmental consequences of publishing literature. So, though we commit to our call for *more* in the sense of finding, and encouraging engagement with, work by marginal(ized) global writers, we recognize that the consequences of creating and consuming more literature can be only slightly mitigated by actions such as borrowing, regifting, and reselling books, or using libraries and e-resources to minimize the environmental costs of paper production.

One further problem introduced by our call to read widely is that Anglophone literature inhabits a uniquely privileged position in the context of the global literary marketplace.[4] Indeed the creation, production, circulation, and consumption of literature is governed by material conditions ranging from education and accessibility, to language status, costs and networks of publication and distribution, critical and academic reception, even extending to the influence of major book prizes on the consumer public. These contexts and processes embed global inequalities so that, broadly speaking, the dominating literary forms remain those that conform to, and replicate, commercially and critically viable models. In terms of representation, the most saleable literature globally is that which speaks to recognizable 'Africas', 'Asias', 'South Americas', or other continental, national, local, racial, or ethnic constructions familiar to Anglo-American audiences. As the authors of this book, we too are bound by these processes, so that our chosen primary texts are collated from the very narrow range of literature that has made its way to international audiences, and which is available in English.[5]

There is, however, work being done by postcolonial critics to analyse how writers and readers are implicated in, but can also be resistant to, the power dynamics of the literary marketplace. This is exemplified by Graham Huggan's pioneering account of the literary 'postcolonial exotic [...] as a cultural commodity' that 'contemporary postcolonial studies [...] at once serves and resists' (2001: vii); Sarah Brouillette's argument that there are examples of postcolonial literatures that incorporate 'exercises in self-authorization, designed to register the writer's awareness of the political uses or appropriations of his works, appropriations that are intimately related to the market function of postcolonial literatures' (2007: 177); and Caroline Koegler's efforts to 'stimulate *critical* reflection on branding strategies to minimise those that resort to mechanisms directly averse to postcolonial studies' ethical framework, like essentialisation and othering' (2018: 10). These critics remind us that we are always complicit in market forces, though by examining how writers engage with, and are positioned in, the marketplace, we can make visible issues of production and consumption for reflection, resistance, and critique. In this respect, we also take our cue from Aamir R. Mufti, who states that '*wherever English is or goes in the world, it is dogged by various others*' and this in turn provides 'the necessity and possibility of thinking past, around, and *about* it' (2016: 18–19; original emphasis). Our approach in this book, then, is not simply to read widely in an attempt to escape the strangleholds of Anglo-American literary forms and criticisms. Rather, it is to reflect on our own, and our texts', positions in context, to show how diverse Anglophone and translated texts represent, and respond to, environmental concerns.

The contribution of literature to the climate and ecological crises is ideological and aesthetic as well as material. The contents and forms of literature instate and perpetuate what Jennifer Wenzel identifies as particular 'social dynamics and cultural logics that not only *cause* crises but also inflect how crises are experienced and recognized as such, by whom' (2019: 17). In other words, literature establishes particular ideas and attitudes about nature, including and excluding particular lives, lands, skies, and bodies of water, in order to shape who and what we see, and who and what we care about. In *The Great Derangement*, Amitav Ghosh maps cultural responses to climate change in no uncertain terms. He censures 'most forms of art and literature' as 'drawn into the modes of concealment that [prevent] people from recognizing the realities of their plight' (2016: 11), arguing that climate change both resists representation in 'the techniques that are most closely identified with the novel' (63) and poses 'a powerful challenge to what is perhaps the single most important conception of the modern era: the idea of freedom, which is central not only to contemporary politics but also the humanities, the arts, and literature' (119). These problems coalesce, so that Ghosh claims there is a dearth of climate change literature due to both an absence of literary forms able to host its representation, and because there is a stronghold notion of 'freedom' as a literary ideal that promotes a 'way of "transcending" the constraints of material life' (120). In coming up against what Ghosh identifies as 'the individualizing imaginary in which we are trapped' (135), the problem of how to confront, mediate, and resist our various complicities in damaging literary and environmental contexts is important. At the same time, this risks prioritizing an individualizing approach, when micro-consumerist choices (for example, buying only second-hand books from local sellers) have barely perceptible impacts when enacted at individual levels, and risk hindering our abilities to read as widely and creatively as possible. This does not mean that we should stop making individual choices that are better for the environment, but that they need to happen in the context of global structural change. After all, we already know how to save the planet: end the use of fossil fuels. This underpins all other associated actions, such as reducing consumption, including of meat, soya, and non-biodegradables; halting deforestation; adopting sustainable farming practices; and introducing no-fish zones. In short, all of the changes that will allow the planet's natural processes to function. To be effective, these global actions have to happen immediately, though to date nothing at the scale required is occurring. For example, the Paris Agreement on climate change committed to limiting global temperature rises to 2°, with 1.5° the preferred aim, peaking at 2025. This increase would still wipe out whole ecosystems, islands, and nations. Yet the world is far from being on track to meeting even these goals. At the most recent of the United Nations Climate Change Conference of the Parties (COP27), various countries tried to renege on the 1.5° goal, and abolish the ratchet intended to strengthen international commitments to cutting emissions. Though they failed, the 2025 commitment was removed, once again serving to push the planet beyond the tipping points of no return.

Although individuals cannot do the work of governments and industries to halt environmental destruction, key groups and communities are increasingly working together to exert pressure for global action. These include various Indigenous activist, charity, NGO, and other grassroots environmentalist movements that have had, and are having, global impacts. Recent examples include Idle No More in North America; the Movement for the Emancipation of the Niger Delta (MEND); Extinction Rebellion; and Greta Thunberg's Skolstrejk för Klimatet (School Strike for Climate). As the urgency of the situation becomes ever more apparent, environmentalists are increasingly looking towards radical and revolutionary strategies to force change. William E. Connolly provides one such example, making a provocative case for 'a politics of swarming' enabled by 'militant citizen alliances [...] to challenge the priorities of investment capital, state hegemony, local cronyisms, international organizations, and frontier mentalities' (2017: 12, 9). Importantly, however, precedents for bringing about meaningful change have not only been set by pressure groups and mass movements working to challenge government inaction and harmful industrial practices; they have also been demonstrated by national leaders from all over the world who instigated rapid emergency measures to tackle the 2020 Covid-19 crisis through extended national lockdowns, relief funds, and the mass mobilization of medical, pharmaceutical, and other industrial responses. The climate and ecological emergencies require similarly rapid and even larger-scale actions, because ecological breakdown created the context in which Covid-19 was able to become a planetary crisis and poses an *even greater* threat to life.[6] As Gerardo Ceballos et al. (2020) point out, our current rate of extinction is comparable to that which wiped out the dinosaurs around 66 million years ago.

Given the exigencies of the current crises, it may not be immediately clear what literature can do to help, when, as Ghosh claims, literature tends to prioritize the individual and individual freedoms over planetary concerns. For Ghosh, this is

> another form of resistance, a scalar one, that the Anthropocene presents to the techniques that are most closely identified with the novel: its essence consists of phenomena that were long ago expelled from the

territory of the novel – forces of unthinkable magnitude that create unbearably intimate connections over vast gaps in time and space.

(2016: 63)

We disagree with this point. First, because as Spencer and Valassopoulos point out: 'there is no reason to think that novels cannot portray these things, not least because they have long been doing so' (2020: 204). Second, because what Ghosh identifies as a weakness of literature – an emphasis on the individual – is also, paradoxically, its strength. We therefore argue that literature does not suffer the struggle over representation that Ghosh suggests; rather, it is uniquely able to bring close large-scale ideas. Kathleen Jamie exemplifies this beautifully in her creative essay, 'The Reindeer Cave', in which she describes a rock dislodged by melting ice in order to illustrate the deathly consequences of climate breakdown: '[a]t your cave-mouth, you wonder if the ice will ever return, a natural cycle, or if we've gone too far with our Anthropocene', muses Jamie, '[b]ut who can answer that? We just can't grasp the scale of our species' effects. But the single falling stone which could smash our brains out – that we understand' (2019: 4). It is precisely because literature can zoom in and out from planetary concerns to individuals and their emotions that it is able to bridge the gaps between what the climate scientists and activists are saying, what governments and industries are *not* doing, and the effects of environmental destruction for all of our own, unique lives.

In much the same way that reading and writing allows us to move and think across scales, so too does much of the exciting work being done in contemporary literary studies. Some prominent examples include the work of Ursula K. Heise, who 'explore[s] what new possibilities for ecological awareness inhere in cultural forms that are increasingly detached from their anchorings in particular geographies' (2008: 13); and Wai Chee Dimock, who restores American literature 'to a *long durée*, a scale enlargement along the temporal axis that also enlarges its spatial compass' (2006: 4). Another key example is Rob Nixon's brilliant and highly influential study of 'slow violence', in which he explains that the climate and ecological crises, and associated environments and environmentalism of the poor, are discounted because the violence enacted against them is 'incremental and accretive, its calamitous repercussions playing out across a range of temporal scales' (2011: 2). For Nixon, slow violence poses 'rhetorical and visual challenges' (5) that are not always accommodated by dominant – though Nixon uses the term 'visible' – cultural forms. To redress the balance, Nixon finds multiple examples of work by diverse and multinational writer-activists that reveal and resist the operations of slow violence. Wenzel too is keenly aware of the ability of literature to move between scales from, for example, a stream of consciousness, to a community, to the world at large. She models a 'multiscalar reading practice' that can accommodate these shifting perspectives by 'reading from near to there: between specific sites, across multiple divides, at more than one scale [...] shuttl[ing] between the microscopic and the world-historical, in four dimensions, across space and time – reading (and rereading) as a dynamic process of *rescaling*' (2019: 2). As both the literature and analysis of that literature enable us to make and see these moves, so too are we, as readers, supported in thinking beyond the limits of our own selves, communities, and cultures.

As has been established by the critics named above (as well as many others), literature and literary studies enable affective, creative, ethical, active, and critical conversations and responses to variably integrated global crises relating to issues of race, gender, politics, economics, and the ecological. We follow their lead here, whilst contributing a further, and likely more contentious, claim, which is that literature does, and can be further instrumentalized to, support efforts to halt the destruction of global environments. We realize that this provocation may be met with hostile response. As a standalone claim it lies open to accusations of ideological scientism, reductivism, and as enabling ideology-hunting at the expense of both the literature itself and the discipline of literary studies. To be clear, then, our approach takes a cue from Derek Attridge's warning against reading literature 'with the hope or the assumption that it can be instrumental in furthering an existing project, and responding to it in such a way as to test, or even produce, that usefulness' (2004: 7). As such, we adopt what Attridge calls 'a responsible textual instrumentality' that 'rest[s] only on readings that are themselves responsible' (13). In recognizing Attridge's point that literature 'has had a role to play in significant, and frequently laudable, social changes, like the ending of slavery or the reduction in the use of capital punishment in some parts of the globe' so that it 'functions, and is made to function, as a powerful and invaluable instrument of individual and social advancement' (8), we aim to promote, advance, and *responsibly instrumentalize* literature and the discipline of English Studies in support of a habitable planet. This involves paying close attention to what Attridge describes as the 'invention' and 'singularity' (2) of the literary, as 'effective' (4) in the context of a burning world, even as the forms, functions, politics, and philosophies of a work or body of works are unique and multiple, irreducible to single meaning or interpretation, and grapple in uneven and contradictory ways with the shaping effects of globalization.

We fully recognize then, that not every text or reading can be tasked with tackling environmental issues, and yet even when writing and reading are used only to pass the time, or for pleasure, or for escape, they operate still as techniques for survival that are essential in times of multiple crises. Turning again to leading scholarly work on this subject, we suggest that Ghosh's particularly narrow perspective on the forms of literature equipped to respond to the climate emergency is therefore wrong in both claim and sentiment. He suggests that climate change novels are niche genre fiction and are therefore 'almost by definition not of the kind that is taken seriously' (2016, 7). Labelling texts as science fiction – or more recently, climate fiction or cli-fi[7] –

thus minimizes their relevance to everyday life, precisely because these texts deal with topics beyond what is traditionally valued in the novel, and because humans are rendered vulnerable to large-scale disasters in ways that undermine ideals of agency and freedom. As Spencer and Valassopoulos point out, however, ample evidence to refute Ghosh's claim can be found in the emerging canons of contemporary literature that address environmental concerns, which now incorporate as standard work by writers including 'Ghosh himself' (2020: 204) as well as Chinua Achebe, Indra Sinha, Henrietta Rose-Innes, Paolo Bacigalupi, and Witi Ihimaera, amongst many others. We would add that it is not only twentieth- and twenty-first century contemporary literatures that deal with issues of climate change – one of the earliest surviving works of literature, *The Epic of Gilgamesh* (c.2100BCE), depicts the destruction of humanity in a great flood. Neither are representations of disaster and destruction the only way to respond to the polycrises. Indeed, Romanticists have in many ways led the charge in developing ecocritical methods for reading literary engagements with nature, and their work has traditionally emphasized the co-constitutive relationship between the environment and imagination/perception.

We therefore suggest that texts from across periods and places, and which do not directly deal with environmental breakdowns caused by fossil fuel consumption, can, and should, be responsibly instrumentalized for the future. An example of how this might work is given by Pulitzer Prize-winning ecopoet Mary Oliver, who has stated in interview: 'I think when we lose the connection with the natural world, we tend to forget that we're animals, that we need the Earth', and where other poets talk 'about this coming devastation a great deal [...] I just happen to think you catch more flies with honey than with vinegar. So I try to do more of the "Have you noticed this wonderful thing? Do you remember this?"' (Shriver, 2011: n.p.). If we endeavour to read across subjects, forms, histories, and locations, we find not only accounts of disasters, consequences, and recoveries, but also evidence of what we have lost, and what more we stand to lose. The answers to our question, 'why read literature in a burning world?', therefore lie not only in genre fiction, contemporary or disaster literature, but in a great expanse of literary forms, modes, and messages. We suggest, then, that reading widely, creatively, critically, actively, and as a technique for survival, will lessen the burdens we place on present and future lives and global environments.

Global Literature

The title of this book, and indeed the series to which it belongs, incorporates the term 'global literature', which has been helpful for us – and so we hope also for readers – in examining diverse texts, geographical contexts, and analytical methods alongside and in relation to one another. It embeds the idea that literary production is the result of the grossly unequal differentials of power and wealth engendered by globalization, whilst at the same time striving to undo the privileging of particular groups, cultures, and forms by viewing connections and networks of exchange beyond the limits imposed by national parameters and circuits of empire. 'Global literature' enables us to attend to the challenge of introducing readers to both the specific preoccupations and aesthetics of individual literary texts *and* a range of discrete and interlinked methodologies, including postcolonial, ecocritical, world-literature, and world-ecological theories and criticism, as well as Indigenous studies and animal studies approaches that we deploy in this book. In brief: postcolonial theory and criticism tends to focus on cultural forms from and about formerly colonized nations; Indigenous studies considers knowledges and cultures from regions across the globe in which humans, nonhuman animals, and environments continue to be dominated by settler colonialism; ecocriticism (with its roots in Anglo-American Romanticism and nature writing) engages cultural depictions of the wilderness; animal studies explores non-anthropocentric relations with, and representations of, animals; world-literature (as conceived by the Warwick Research Collective) offers Marxian analyses of how the combined and uneven development of global capitalism registers in cultural forms; and world-ecology (as formulated by Jason Moore) conceptualizes how global capitalism presses humans and extra-human natures into the service of endless accumulation. No unitary approach would be able to fully address the preoccupations that arise from our range of primary texts, which include but are not restricted to: literary depictions of the oil industry and its environmental effects in prose, poetry, and plays from Nigeria, Alaska, and Scotland; the legacies of the 'Green Revolution' in India; trophy hunting in Kenya and the history of whaling in North America and Aotearoa New Zealand; and species loss in North America, Africa, and Australasia. Across the myriad texts and contexts explored over the course of this book, then, we mobilize key arguments and approaches from each of the theoretical frameworks mentioned above, because in combination they offer the practical vocabularies required to negotiate the richness, complexities, and contradictions engendered by the term 'global literature'.

Our combination of analytical frameworks remains avowedly materialist throughout, underpinned by our understanding that we cannot talk about the relationships between globalization, cultural forms, and the environment without also talking about how the exploitation of the environment by dominant human groups always involves a corresponding exploitation of marginalized societies. In so doing, we take a steer from Pablo Mukherjee's notion of 'eco-materialism', a cultural theory that, he says, is concerned with

> the essential unity of humans and environment, of history and nature; a constant, dynamic and differentiated relation between humans and environment through labour of all kinds; the centrality of material environment in relation to human cognitive processes and the relative

human epistemological passivity before it; finally, the specific enabling condition that the environment offers to all human cultural activities.

(2010: 63)

Thus, what eco-materialism offers us here is a recognition that 'we cannot think of the environmental without the human' nor 'human without the environmental' (62). And if, as Mukherjee avers, we must 'question how exactly the environment enables activities such as writing a novel or a poem, or performing a piece of theatre, cinema, or composing music or painting' (62), then we are impelled to examine just how the localized effects of environmental exploitation and despoliation underpin the emergence of radical cultural responses that are from diverse geographical regions and circulated globally. At the same time, it is in the open, subjective aesthetics of prose, poetry, and drama that the 'indivisibility of humans and [the] environment' (61) can be dramatized without necessarily resorting to a hierarchical worldview that situates *all* humans as dominant over nonhuman animals and the natural world. In this way, eco-materialism enables a meeting point between the traditionally ecological concerns of ecocriticism, the focus on the nonhuman in animal studies, the significance of interspecies kinship in Indigenous studies, the critique of the circulation of capital for world-ecologies, and the traditionally human-centred concerns with the production of racial hierarchies and the ongoing legacies of empire in both Indigenous and postcolonial studies.

In exploring literature that frames localized aspects of the climate emergency within the context of globalization and capitalist–imperial expansion, we remain cognizant too of the contestations that pertain to the 'global turn' in postcolonial studies, initiated in the early 2000s. This turn sought to offer new accounts of, and ways of reading, a world emerging after twentieth-century decolonization. For many, a globalized world in which political, economic, and cultural networks and institutions operate transnationally and on a planetary scale can no longer be accounted for using established postcolonial ideas relating to nations and nationalism, cultural essentialisms, or the centre and the margins.[8] Debates continue to rage as to whether the idea of global literature enables or prevents more productive engagements with the traditional concerns of the field, such as hybridity, capital, and decolonization. On the one hand, the study of global literature is distinctly positive and egalitarian in its aims. As Peter J. Kalliney suggests, globalization offered 'a cure for the ills of postcolonialism' (2002: 51) in dealing with an integrated and multiply interacting world, so that issues of circulation, influence, mass market literature, translation, and global readerships can be discussed without privileging select groups, cultures, forms, or styles. On the other hand, as Eric Hayot notes, '[c]ertain features of globalization studies – its frequent triumphalism; its common US-centrism; its critical methods – have placed it in significant opposition to the political beliefs and intellectual habits of scholars of literature' (2011: 224). Thus, touting globalization as an open and progressive solution to overcome old hierarchies and essentialisms means that it can also act as a homogenizing force to mask sundering social, political, and economic inequalities across, for example, nation, race, class, gender, health, sexuality, and education. Indeed, in theory and in practice, globalization often remains entrenched in Euro-American ideas of capitalist progress.[9]

As we conceive of it here, however, a fundamental aspect of the relationship between 'global literature' and the environmental crises we examine in this book is that they are both product and producer of the very structural inequalities embedded within the ideology of globalization and capitalist 'development'. We are thus cautious in both the selection and analyses of our corpus of primary texts, which we consider as examples of global literature by virtue of their being written (primarily) in English, and because they deal in explicit ways with the processes and consequences of the environmental impacts of the expansion of global capitalism and globalization. This means comparatively analysing prose, poetry, and plays from across the Global North and South, and from, about, and set in the eighteenth- through to the twenty-first centuries. One core concern that binds these transnational and transhistorical comparative analyses together over the course of the book is an interrogation of the dominant, universalizing discourses of both global, capitalist progress, *and* what has been labelled the Anthropocene. For this reason, we turn now to debates over the applicability of the heavily contested term 'Anthropocene', before then providing an overview of the structure of individual chapters.

Setting the 'Cene

The Anthropocene has become one of the most influential, contested, and controversial terms in debates about environmental crises since it entered mainstream academic discourse at the end of the twentieth century. It derives from the Greek *anthropos* (human) and *cene* (from *kainos* meaning now) and is used to describe a new geological epoch – traceable in the strata (series of rock layers) that form over time – and which recognizes the impact of humans on the Earth's ecosystems. Its predecessor, the Holocene – from the Greek *holos* for 'whole' to indicate 'entirely new' – began at the end of the last Ice Age 11,500 years ago, and debates rage over whether the term still incorporates the impact of humans, or whether the latest neologism, the Anthropocene, provides a more appropriate identifier of stratigraphic change. First used in the 1980s and passing into wider usage through the work of the Nobel Prize-winning chemist Paul Crutzen, the Anthropocene has become an incredibly useful concept because, as Jeremy Davies points out, it 'adds human agency' to a 'whole list of geophysical forces – asteroids, ocean currents, volcanoes, and the like' (2016: 10). The term thus foregrounds the way in which '[h]uman societies are now among the most powerful of the ecological forces that operate on, above, and below the surface of the earth' (10). In the environmental humanities, there are two main and interlinked concerns in debates about the deployment of the Anthropocene. The first lies in securing an anthropogenesis narrative (when did the Anthropocene begin?), and the second lies in the precision of the term used, as the concept remains freighted with an unhelpful, even invidious, universalism in which all humans shoulder the blame of environmental catastrophe equally.

The first primary point of contention centres on historical periodization and the establishment of an anthropogenic 'golden spike'. This is because establishing geologic epochs means fixing 'the location of a global marker of an event in stratigraphic material, such as rock, sediment, or glacier ice' (Lewis and Maslin, 2015: 173). Fixing a starting date, moreover, 'will affect the stories people construct about the ongoing development of human societies' (178). Indeed, 'the general rule', according to Davies, 'is that the earlier the proposed starting date for the Anthropocene, the more emphasis its proponents place on human actions themselves, as opposed to the ecological consequences that follow them' (2016: 47). In their foundational 2000 article that proposed the Anthropocene as a new geological epoch distinct from the Holocene, Crutzen and Eugene Stoermer suggested the late eighteenth century as the starting point. This period was chosen because 'data retrieved from glacial ice cores show the beginning of a growth in the atmospheric concentrations of several "greenhouse gases", in particular CO_2 and CH_4', coinciding with James Watt's invention of the steam engine in 1784 (2000: 17–18). Crutzen's subsequent article for *Nature* offers two additional claims: first, that the new epoch has 'been caused by only 25% of the earth's population' (2002: 23), although who this figure refers to is not made clear; and second, that a commitment to 'internationally accepted, large-scale geo-engineering projects' (23) is required as a means of mitigating ecological collapse.[10]

The *Nature* piece has become 'the canonical statement of the first version of the Anthropocene' (Davies, 2016: 44), with several alternatives having been proposed. Crutzen himself has since amended his thinking, arguing (along with Will Steffen and John R. McNeill) for a three-stage development. Stage one, they say, began in the early–mid nineteenth century with the increased reliance on fossil fuels, when the earth's atmosphere noticeably changed beyond previous patterns of fluctuation. Stage two, referred to as the 'Great Acceleration', began after 1945 with the exponential growth in population and petroleum consumption corresponding with the rise in 'greenhouse gases' and the 'sixth great extinction event with rates of species loss growing rapidly for both terrestrial and marine ecosystems' (Crutzen, Steffen, and McNeill, 2007: 617). The third stage, beginning c.2015, looks to a burgeoning self-consciousness whereby humanity is increasingly aware of becoming an 'active agent in the operation of its own life support system' (619). Crutzen, Steffen, and McNeill invest in this third-stage awareness as the driver of geo-engineering solutions, whilst also alluding to the 'ethical questions and intense debate' (620) that such technocratic innovations raise. It is this amended version that was affirmed in May 2019 by the

Anthropocene Working Group (AWG), which consists of over 30 members including Crutzen, Steffen and McNeill.[11] The majority of the group, which was formed in 2008, voted that the Anthropocene 'be treated as a formal chrono-stratigraphic unit' of geological time which has 'intensified significantly since the onset of industrialization', and that 'the primary guide for the base of the Anthropocene be one of the stratigraphic signals around the mid-twentieth century of the Common Era'.[12]

By contrast, Simon Lewis and Mark Maslin accept that the Great Acceleration 'is unambiguously a time of major anthropogenic global environmental impacts', but assert that it cannot constitute a golden spike 'based on the available geological evidence' (2015: 177). Instead, they propose 1610 as the beginning of a new epoch, a date which saw the stratigraphic 'impacts of the meeting of Old and New World human populations – including the geologically unprecedented homogenization of Earth's biota' (175). This trend began with the invasion of the Caribbean and Americas in 1492, which saw the 'globalization of human foodstuffs', such as potatoes, maize, manioc, and sugar, and the cross-continental domestication of animals, resulting in 'a swift, ongoing, radical reorganisation of life on Earth without geological precedent' (174). In addition, colonial genocide, slavery, famine, and disease caused a rapid decline in human population numbers and a dramatic dip in atmospheric CO_2, with the lowest point recorded in 1610. This dip, named the 'Orbis spike', acts as the stratigraphic marker of 'the beginning of the modern "world-system"' when 'humans on the two hemispheres were connected, [and] trade became global' (175). In contrast to the AWG's focus on the stratigraphic legacies of the steam engine and the Industrial Revolution, then, the Orbis spike 'implies that colonialism, global trade and coal brought about the Anthropocene' (177). Our work in this book is aligned to this particular stratigraphic charting, which we find most compelling when mapped onto literary engagements with changing environments. Of particular importance is Lewis and Maslin's argument that the arrival of Christopher Columbus in the Caribbean and introduction of the transatlantic slave trade, the spread of global capitalism, industrialization and urbanization, through to the development of the present global hydrocarbon economy 'highlights social concerns, particularly the unequal power relationships between different groups of people, economic growth, the impacts of globalised trade, and our current reliance on fossil fuels' (177). The exploitation of these differentials of power across human groups enables and enacts global capitalist processes that have world-changing effects on all component parts of the climate system.

Debates on the origins of the Anthropocene remain lively and ongoing and have coincided in more recent years with issues of nomenclature. As theorists and scholars across disciplines have attempted to account for, and come to terms with, specific drivers of geological change, so too have alternative epoch-defining coinages proliferated. In a 2020 article, Franciszek Chwalczyk traces over 80 alternatives to the Anthropocene that extend from the

Technocene (focusing on technology), Econocene (which takes economy as the main episteme of the post-war period), Thanatocene (in which humans master killing and apply this to the environment), through to the Plastocene (how plastics are reshaping the earth) and Pyrocene (the role of fire control in human development), even to the rather flippant Trumpocene (where the former US president is taken as a symbol of climate change denialism) – all of which are designed to account for distinct human activities that have environment-altering effects. The two leading challengers to the Anthropocene label in the context of the environmental humanities are the Capitalocene and Plantationocene. Both terms accept that the Earth's ecology has been irrevocably affected by humans, though they look to distinguish the dominant groups involved in causing climate and ecological degradation, and, by extension, the political, social, and cultural responses needed to tackle it.

Broadly speaking, where formulations of the Anthropocene focus on indicators of chemical changes in the atmosphere, the Capitalocene looks to economic relations, and the Plantationocene to spatial ones. Andreas Malm and Alf Hornborg, who first coined the term Capitalocene, reject the universalist implications of Crutzen's Anthropocene narrative on the grounds that 'species-thinking on climate change is conducive to mystification and political paralysis' (2014: 67). Malm avers that '"the Anthropocene" is an indefensible abstraction at the point of departure as well as the end of the line' and commits instead to 'the geology not of mankind, but of capital accumulation' (2016: 391), whereby 'the historical origins of anthropogenic climate change were predicated on highly inequitable global processes' (2014: 63).[13] It is also the case that a significant proportion of human society 'is not party to the fossil economy at all: hundreds of millions rely on charcoal, firewood, or organic waste such as dung for all domestic purposes', while close to one-third of all humans have no access to electricity (Malm and Hornborg, 2014: 65). One cannot, moreover, regard the invention of the steam engine as the prime mover of climate change without understanding that this new technology was 'geared to the opportunities provided by the constellation of a largely depopulated New World, Afro-American slavery, the exploitation of British labour in factories and mines, and the global demand for inexpensive cotton cloth' (63). Such inequities of power and economic relations are made more pertinent when one considers the use of 'steam-power as a weapon – on sea and land, boats and rails – against the best part of humankind' (64). Jason W. Moore has been a leading proponent and developer of theories of the Capitalocene on the grounds that the narrative popularized by Crutzen et al. excludes the long history of subordination underpinning capitalism and what he refers to as the 'world-ecology of power, capital, and nature' (2016: 6). He observes that '[q]uestions of capitalism, power and class, anthropocentrism, dualist framings of "nature" and "society", and the role of states and empires – all are frequently bracketed by the dominant Anthropocene perspective' (5). For Moore then, the

Anthropocene is insufficiently specific, and fails to explain just how our contemporary environmental crises came about.

Conceding that the term Capitalocene does something that the Anthropocene cannot, Donna Haraway has maintained that it insists on a 'historically situated complex of metabolisms and assemblages', whereby 'slave agriculture, not coal' is the 'key transition' (Haraway et al., 2016: 555). It is this revelation, along with the influence of Lewis and Maslin's conception of the Orbis spike, that has led Haraway and others to consider Plantationocene as a potentially 'better, more descriptive term' (556). Proponents of this nomenclature maintain that 'our current ecological crisis is rooted in logics of environmental modernization, homogeneity, and control, which were developed on historical plantations' (Davis et al., 2019: 1). A shift in focus to the agricultural space of the plantation and its various permutations 'provides a means of decentering the Eurocentric narrative by which coal, the steam engine, and the industrial revolution constitute the epicentre of global environmental change' (4). Adopting a key concept of Marxism, Anna L. Tsing views the plantation as a site of ecological 'alienation' since it 'changes the plants, the animals, and the organisms that become part of the plantation. [...] The people, too, become alienated resources, and it is that move that has allowed the spread of the plantation system' (Haraway et al., 2016: 556). Similarly, for Haraway the plantation is a site of colonization, extermination, appropriation, and the subsequent 'relocation of the generative units: plants, animals, microbes, people' (557). This system of ecological transportation and transformation provided the basis of globalized forms of agriculture and spatial enclosure – such as settler colonialism – that manipulate the environment for the purposes of profit.

Seeking to interrogate and further develop this line of thought, critics have addressed the manner in which 'people' appeared too often as an afterthought in the initial formulation of the Plantationocene. According to Janae Davies et al., '[h]uman labour receives brief attention' in the conversation between Haraway, Tsing, and others, 'and is conceived as only one element within the broader constellation of exploited lifeforms underpinning historical and present-day plantation economies' (2019: 5). The result is that 'matters of Black embodiment and the disciplinary regimes of the slave plantation remain obscured', meaning that 'the racial ideologies that structure ideas of the human and nonhuman are disguised, allowing racial violence and its ecological implications to go largely uninterrogated' (5). We take up precisely this challenge in the first chapter of this book, which draws heavily on Kathryn Yusoff's work on the 'billion black Anthropocenes' to analyse plantation-set texts by C.L.R. James and Arna Bontemps. Yusoff's intervention is allied to Davies et al.'s in the sense that it also emphasizes the obscured racial dynamics of the plantation system and is similarly grounded in an attack on the trope of climate change being caused by humanity as an undifferentiated mass. Yet, in mobilizing Crutzen and Stoermer's original term, Yusoff distances her work from that which constructs 'an alternative or alt-anthro-scene' (2018: 22). Thus she offers a powerful critique of the ways in which 'the origins of the Anthropocene are intensely political in how they draw the world of the present into being and give shape and race to its world-making subjects' (25). If the Anthropocene makes central an imagining of imminent ecological collapse, it does so by ignoring the long history of colonial, genocidal, and ecocidal practices that have decimated non-European populations and ecologies since the invasion of the 'New World'. So, instead of offering a new label, Yusoff's work interrogates how the original and now most widely used and accepted term is bound up with an 'attempt to absolve the positionality of Western colonial knowledge and extraction practices, while simultaneously reinforcing and resettling them in a new territory – a Western frontier of pioneers armed with eco-optimism and geoengineering' (2018: 27). To foreground the violent and apocalyptic plurality of 'a billion Black Anthropocenes' is to view Crutzen, Steffen, and McNeill's technocratic investment in geoengineering as 'a paternalism that is tied to a redemptive narrative of saving the world from harm on account of others while maintaining the protective thick skin of innocence' (27); ultimately, in an ironic allusion to Rudyard Kipling, Yusoff avers that it constitutes the 'white man's overburden' (28).[14]

Where the contestations over the Anthropocene, Capitalocene, and Plantationocene are related to the scale and historicity of the climate crisis, an additional formulation that is less concerned with claiming an anthropogenic 'golden spike' comes from Haraway on the 'Cthulucene'. Haraway's conception of the Cthulucene focuses less on racial and colonial power relations and more on the way in which inter-species connections – or 'kinship' – can provide the basis of a solution to contemporary ecological crises. For Haraway, the Anthropocene should not be regarded as a new epoch but as a boundary event between two epochs. As such, she says, 'our job is to make the Anthropocene as short/thin as possible and to cultivate with each other in every way imaginable epochs to come that can replenish refuge' (2015, 160). To achieve this, Haraway insists that we recognize other-than-human and multiply constituted personhoods, asking: 'when do changes in degree become changes in kind, and what are the effects of bioculturally, biotechnically, biopolitically, historically situated people (not Man) relative to, and combined with, the effects on other species assemblages and other biotic/abiotic forces?' (160). The Cthulucene is an attempt to conceptualize such environmental entanglements across 'myriad temporalities and spatialities and myriad intra-active entities-in-assemblages – including the more-than-human, other-than-human, inhuman, and human-as-humus' (160). In so doing, Haraway insists on the political, social, and cultural significances of kinship and in particular the need 'to make "kin" mean something other/more than entities tied by ancestry or genealogy' (161). She goes on to note that 'making kin and making kind (as category, care, relatives without ties by birth, lateral relatives, lots of other echoes) stretch the imagination and can change the story' (161). Though a useful and compelling claim in that it productively challenges the seemingly compulsory natalism of most human societies and newly imagines egalitarian and equitable cross- and intra-species interactions, it does so without addressing the specifically located differentials of power and agency in situated times and places.

The Cthulucene is ultimately an umbrella term for a diverse range of philosophies and cosmologies of ecological holism, including the Buddhist belief in Naga, the Māori sea god Tangaroa, the Native American figure of the Spider Woman, the Inca's Pachamama, James Lovelock's secular Gaia principle, 'and many many more' (160). A possible problem with Haraway's formulation, however, is that it flattens out a number of culturally and geographically specific belief systems for the benefit of Christian or post-Christian societies in the Global North. It is also open to the charge of claiming and renaming Indigenous cosmologies that have *always* valued kinship relations between human and other-than-human life. For example, the scholar and activist Nick Estes (Lower Brule Sioux) explains that the Lakota and Dakota philosophy of Mitakuye Oyasin translates to 'we are all related' (2019: 15), an assertion that promotes kinship rules between humans and nonhumans alike. 'Indigenous resistance to the trespass of settlers, pipelines, and dams', writes Estes, 'is part of being a good relative to the water, land, and animals, not to mention the human world' (21). As Estes shows, such philosophies are not merely conceptualized forms of ecological holism, but are aligned with a history of land appropriation, Indigenous oppression, anti-colonial resistance, and political activism, and as Naomi Klein puts it, the relationship between Native and non-Native peoples in the fight for climate justice cannot be 'yet another extractive one' (2014, 387). An investment in human and other-than-human kinship cannot, therefore, be detached from colonial aggression towards some of the world's poorest, most marginalized, and disenfranchised communities.

The value of Haraway's Cthulucene lies in the insistence on the significance of the imagination and the positive possibilities of storytelling. '[U]nlike either the Anthropocene or the Capitalocene', writes Haraway, 'the Cthulucene is made up of ongoing multispecies stories and practices of becoming-with in times that remain at stake […] in which the world is not finished and the sky has not fallen – yet' (2016: 59). This, along with the wider conflict over narratives of historicity central to the Anthropocene debate, points to the role of culture in both facilitating an affective engagement with issues of environmental catastrophe and envisioning solutions that look towards preferred futures. It is necessary, moreover, to look at cultural responses from beyond the borders of the primary progenitors of carbon emissions in the Global North.

Earth, Water, Air, and Life

We are convinced that as we face the realities of our burning world, any and all resources must be mobilized to address the vast and various planetary challenges – this means literature and literary scholarship too. Though it is something of a platitude to say that reading builds empathy and imagination, we are not alone in believing in the power of books to change the world. As Jane Kilby and Antony Rowland explain in their own work on reading testimony in/as politics:

> as politicized readers, we read in – and with – hope. [...] There is the risk of narcissism [...] but equally we read in the vain, impossibly stupid hope that reading will spark a revolution, if not in us then in those in whom we invest our reading and our politics: our students. As is generally the case in the academy, we constantly run the risk of overinflating the political effects of texts chosen for study, mixing idealism with justification for our unit of resource. Thus we cannot simply hope to imagine ourselves or our students at our or their very best when reading, but reading is a fevered, blind activity, and for this reason we cannot rule it out. [...] We are moved by what we read and would move heaven and earth for the stories of death and suffering to have been different. We are, indeed, power-crazed in this sense.
>
> (2014: 5)

What Kilby and Rowland capture so brilliantly here are reasons *why* we read, study, and teach literature. While we like to imagine that all teachers of literature feel much the same way, it is striking that our methods, modules, degree programmes, and pedagogies do not always obviously or readily support explanations for *why we read*. Indeed, the categories usually used to organize literary studies seem to emphasize the *whens, wheres, hows*, and *whos* of literature rather than the *whys*, so that we rely on author, period, genre, language, nation, continent, gender, race, class, and other identity components to cluster texts together, even when these groupings reinforce, rather than dismantle, barriers to empathy and imagination.

As the study of global literature and the environment is a world-historical topic, it is not easily broken down into the categories usually used to organize literary studies, nor do these categories help us to address the issue of why we should read global literature in a burning world. 'Instead of divvying up literary works into hundred-year intervals (or elastic variants like the long eighteenth or twentieth century) or categories harnessing the history of ideas (Romanticism, Enlightenment)', Patricia Yaeger asks: 'what happens if we sort texts according to the energy sources that made them possible?' (2011: 305). Answering such a call, according to Yaeger, means developing a reading practice that is 'serious about modes of production as a force field for culture' (308). As such, in the title of her article she proposes that we turn instead to 'the Ages of Wood, Tallow, Coal, Whale Oil, Gasoline, Atomic Power'. Yaeger's prompt helps us to understand the environmental impacts of fuel transitions over time, though we opt for a different organizing device that does not rely on specifically located contexts of use for meaning. We instead strive for wider frames of reference that are more readily meaningful across temporalities and geographies by shifting the focus from energy to environments, from fuels to climate systems. In this, we also take our cue from Christian Moraru's *Reading for the Planet* (2015), Jeffrey Jerome Cohen and Lowell Duckert's collection *Elemental Ecocriticism* (2015), and from a range of works within Indigenous studies, as exemplified by the Iñupiaq filmmaker and activist, Rachel Nutaaq Ayałhuq Naŋinaaq Edwardson's assertion that:

> Our epistemological and ontological truths grow first from our environment and our place in its ecosystem. Like many First Nations peoples, our long-term and complex relationship with our environment fuels our understanding (through a daily lived experience) that we come from/are of the land, ocean/waterways, air/cosmos, and animals.
>
> (2022: 90–91)

Edwardson explains the particular Inuit understanding of humans as coextensive with all component parts of the climate system. Indigenous ways-of-being-in-the-world cannot, therefore, be grasped through methods that are pinned only to colonialist forms of environmental exploitation. In pursuing the ideas that literature can bring to life global-environmental ways of thinking and being, then, we suggest that as critics, teachers, and students, we should endeavour to read as widely (or globally) as possible, with the support of a framework that focuses attention on preserving and protecting the interacting elements of the climate system: earth, water, air, and life.

Using these topics as organizing devices also helps us to overcome the linguistic, temporal, spatial, national, ethnic, gendered, class, and other divides so often reinstated in university teaching as units of study, without eliding the differentials of power and unevenness of experiences associated with the interactions of living things. The book as a whole thus does not promote a single or unified theoretical or methodological approach to the study of global literature and the environment. Rather, we seek to introduce a range of global theories, critical and historical writings, and literary texts, to test whether and how they can be turned towards the issues at stake. This means that we make familiar postcolonial and ecocritical textual selections alongside less well-known and geographically and historically diverse sources, homing in on situated case studies and testing methods that can take in a wide range of transnational and transhistorical materials. This approach, we argue, is essential, as by directing our analyses of distinct and disparate literatures and theories towards the protection and preservation of components of the climate system, we strive to underscore the role of literature in the struggle to save the planet, and better equip ourselves to work towards liveable futures.

Chapter One, 'Earth', is divided into three subsections: 'Soil', 'Mineral and Metal', and 'Oil'. These subsections focus on key components of the lithosphere that humans have exploited, altered, and extracted in pursuit of economic aims, and loosely map on to a developmental narrative of global capitalism. This moves from the agricultural revolution and mercantilism of the fifteenth through to the eighteenth centuries in which European powers colonized foreign soil, deforested huge swaths of the Americas, and established monocultural plantations, to the steam-powered empires and mineral and metal mining of the nineteenth and twentieth centuries, and finally to the development of the oil-fuelled global economy of the twentieth- and twenty-first centuries. In 'Soil' we analyse C.L.R. James's play, *Toussaint Louverture: The Story of the Only Successful Slave Revolt in History* (written 1934, performed 1936), Arna Bontemps' novel, *Black Thunder, Gabriel's Revolt: Virginia, 1800* (1936), and Octavia Butler's dystopian novels, *The Parable of the Sower* (1993) and *The Parable of the Talents* (1998). These texts are examined in order to explore the environmental and human costs of monoculture plantations; the meaningful changes brought about by slave-led resistance and revolt; and the use of Indigenous and translocated African knowledges in establishing the roots of recovery and liveable futures. Moving from the 'sugar rush' of the sugarcane and cacao plantations of the Americas to the gold and diamond rushes of nineteenth- and twentieth-century colonial South Africa in the section 'Minerals and Metals', we consider how Olive Schreiner's *Undine* (1929) and Peter Abrahams' *Mine Boy* (1946) illustrate the destructive consequences of the mining industries for Black Africans and settler women. The novels present anti-colonial, workers union, Pan-Africanist, and feminist resistance to the forms of extractivism practised and sanctioned under colonialism. The last section of the chapter turns to the 'oil rush' of the twentieth century, and provides a close reading of John McGrath's play *The Cheviot, the Stag and the Black, Black Oil* as a pre-eminent example of 'world literature' and 'petro-drama' in its staging of land dispossession, monocultural farming, extractive capitalism, and the operations of the petroleum industry in Scotland.

Chapter Two, 'Water', engages with poetic representations and responses to pollution and global warming in the hydrosphere and cryosphere. In the first section, 'Delta', we analyse poems from and about the Niger Delta by writers Ken Saro-Wiwa, Tanure Ojaide, Nnimmo Bassey, Ibiwari Ikiriko, Obari Gomba, Niyi Osundare, and Ogaga Ifowodo. We use these texts to establish key connecting forms, ideas, and politics of Niger Delta petro-poetry, arguing that the poems serve as collective testimony to the extreme levels of violence, corruption, and pollution in the Niger basin, and are forceful examples of literary activism that have real-world impacts in the ongoing struggles for social and environmental equity and justice in the region. In the second section, titled 'Ice', we demonstrate the significant contribution that literary analysis and Indigenous knowledges can make to environmental science concerning the threats that melting icescapes pose both for communities that rely on ice for their survival and for the global patterns of water and air circulation that sustain life on Earth. To do this, we explore how

Alaskan Native poets Cathy Tagnak Rexford and dg nanouk okpik depict the ways in which oil drilling and global warming are transforming the Alaskan Arctic, causing the disappearance of social, cultural, and ecological ways of life. In moving from the heat of the swamp forests located close to the equator to the frozen northernmost points of the globe, from the frontier zones of oil extraction to the frontlines of global warming, the chapter endeavours to illustrate the truly global impacts of fossil fuel reliance for global environments.

In Chapter Three, 'Air', we expand upon our earlier examination of the relationship between ecological despoliation, agriculture, and health with an analysis of prose and poetry that depicts atmospheric pollution caused by oil extraction in the Niger Delta and chemical gas leaks linked to the production of pesticides in India. We concentrate first on how Helon Habila's *Oil on Water* (2011), Christie Watson's *Tiny Sunbirds Far Away* (2011), and Imbolo Mbue's *How Beautiful We Were* (2021) depict the damaging impacts of gas flaring, which is a widely used technique of burning off the excess gases that are released during oil extraction. A shared concern across these novels is with the neocolonial reliance of Nigeria and other African nations on the petroleum industry, and the ecological and health impacts that gas flaring causes in communities forced to live in proximity to petrochemical complexes. Second, we look to the proliferation of pesticides in India to examine how their manufacture and use was integral to the post-war 'Green Revolution' but has led to the toxification of the atmosphere, along with soils and waterways. Through an analysis of Avaes Mohammad's poem 'Bhopal' (2004), Indra Sinha's *Animal's People* (2007), and Meaghan Delahunt's *The Red Book* (2008) we will explore how this increased reliance on pesticides provided the context for the 1984 Bhopal disaster. We show how the African- and Indian-set novels and poems that are the focus of this chapter can be read as interrogating the structural inequalities concerning class, race, and gender that underpin a language of 'eco-apartheid' in climate justice discourses.

Chapter Four, 'Life', attends to the ways in which literature can contextualize the main drivers of the 'sixth extinction', and is structured around three subsections. The first, 'Commodification', concentrates on the treatment of nonhuman animals as resources. We examine the different ways in which Joseph Conrad's *Heart of Darkness* (1899), Dan Wylie's poem 'Where in the waste is the wisdom?' (2013), and Inua Ellams's poem 'Fuck/Empire' (2020) depict the commodification of elephants in the ivory industry. The emergence of industrial-scale whaling that is depicted in Herman Melville's *Moby Dick or, The Whale* (1851) is contrasted with the forms of kinship between whales and humans in Keri Hulme's 'One Whale, Singing' (1986) and Witi Ihimaera's *The Whale Rider* (1987). The subsection ends by examining representations of the food industry in J.M. Coetzee's *Elizabeth Costello* (2003), Gerald Vizenor's *Griever: An American Monkey King in China* (1987), and Thomas King's *Truth and Bright Water* (1999). The second subsection looks at the centrality of game hunting as an expression of colonial dominance in H. Rider Haggard's *She* (1886) and settler belonging in Karen Blixen's *Out of Africa* (1937), before exploring how Yomi Ṣode's poem 'Untitled' (2019) critiques the connections between colonial-era hunting and the birth of natural history museums. Last, we look to Julia Leigh's *The Hunter* (1999) and Henrietta Rose-Innes's *Green Lion* (2015) as a means of examining literary responses to the controversial initiatives to revive extinct species through de-extinction science. Running through each of these subsections is a discussion of the colonial and post-colonial contexts of the international conservation movement.

We conclude by affirming our commitment to literature as a creative resource that is able to connect readers to the localized impacts of environmental catastrophe, to contextualize today's most urgent instances of ecological despoliation within a long history of capitalist–imperial exploitation and land dispossession, and to envision equitable means of social, political, and ecological organization that are rooted in the protection of all forms of life that are reliant on the Earth's ecosystems for survival. To paraphrase Fredric Jameson, this corpus of novels, plays, and poems pushes us to imagine the end of capitalism before the end of the world. In drawing the book to a close, we assess the investment in literature that depicts end-of-the-world scenarios as the most compelling means of generating mainstream awareness of the existential threats facing humanity if the fossil fuel-burning status quo continues apace. In thinking about the dominance of eco-dystopian narratives in literary responses to climate crises we invite readers to also interrogate the potential for environmental apocalypticism to give a 'green' legitimacy to exclusionary forms of nationalist isolationism that reinforce borders and scapegoat refugees in the name of protecting the delicate socio-ecological balance of individual nation-states.

Notes

1 John Cook et al. identify that 90–100 percent of climate scientists agree that humans are the cause of global warming. The International Union for the Conservation of Nature (IUCN) has been working since 1964 to collate the most comprehensive 'Red List of Threatened Species', identifying 32,000 species or 27 percent of assessed species as threatened with extinction; and they are also currently assessing the risk of collapse of all global ecosystems via the 'Red List of Ecosystems', with full results due in 2025. In his 2019 book *Losing Earth*, moreover, Nathaniel Rich investigates how climate scientists knew conclusively about the existential threat to the planet from climate change as early as 1979. He outlines how coordinated lobbying and propaganda by the oil and gas industries between 1979 and 1989 gave rise to climate denialism.
2 See https://apnews.com/article/dd2368999232425bb5d7d2b9e84604b5 [accessed March 30, 2023].
3 See https://www.wri.org/insights/2018-year-climate-extremes [accessed March 30, 2023].
4 The European Parliamentary Research Service use data from Rudiger Wischenbart's 2014 Global e-book report to identify that over two-thirds of the global

book market is represented by six countries. In order, these are the US, China, Germany, Japan, France, and the U.K. 'The Six Largest Book Markets Globally', *European Parliamentary Research Service Blog* (February 11, 2016), https://epthinktank.eu/2016/02/15/e-books-evolving-markets-and-new-challenges/the-six-largest-book-markets-globally [accessed March 30, 2023].
5 See O'Brien and Szeman's Introduction, special issue 'Anglophone Literatures and Global Cultures'.
6 See Malm (2020).
7 See Gerry Canavan and Stanley Robinson (2014); Trexler (2015); Mehnert (2016); and Milner and Burgmann (2020).
8 See Krishnaswamy and Hawley (2007).
9 Without wishing to rehearse the long, ongoing, and still lively debates about the relationships between globalization and world literature, we will just briefly note here that the study of global literature has a foothold in much older discussions of world literature, which have re-emerged in new forms in recent years. World literature as a discipline has roots in both postcolonial and comparative literary studies, as well as American studies, Marxist analysis, and political theory. Key texts include Moretti (2000), Dimock (2002), Damrosch (2003), Apter (2003, 2013), Casanova ([1999], translated 2004), Prendergast (2004), and the Warwick Research Collective (2015), as well as the journal *World Literature Today* under the editorship of Djelal Kadir.
10 For a critical overview of geo-engineering 'fixes', such as pumping sulphur dioxide into the stratosphere to 'dim the sun' (a solution that might enable the continuation of a fossil fuel economy but would potentially cause droughts across Africa and Asia), see Klein (2014).
11 In July 2023, the Professor of Geography and Environmental Systems Erle Ellis (Maryland) publicly announced his resignation from the AWG. In his statement, Ellis maintains that 'dividing Earth's human transformation into two parts, pre- and post-1950, does real damage by denying the deeper history and the ultimate causes of Earth's unfolding social-environmental crisis. Are the planetary changes wrought by industrial and colonial nations before 1950 not significant enough to transform the planet? The political ramifications of such a misleading and scientifically inaccurate portrayal are clearly profound and regressive' (see Ellis, 2023).
12 It is also noted that, 'The Anthropocene is not currently a formally defined geological unit within the Geological Time Scale; officially we still live within the Meghalayan Age of the Holocene Epoch. A proposal to formalize the Anthropocene is being developed by the AWG.' See http://quaternary.stratigraphy.org/working-groups/anthropocene.
13 For scientific data on per capita CO_2 emissions, see research by the NASA climatologist, James Hansen (2008).
14 Yusoff's core concerns with the terminology of the Anthropocene are echoed by the Métis anthropologist Zoe Todd. In Todd's essay 'Indigenizing the Anthropocene', she contests 'the ways in which well-meaning contemporary artists and academics recreate exploitative patterns from the past' (2015: 251). The Anthropocene, she writes, 'like any theoretical category at play in Euro-Western contexts, is not innocent of such violence' (251), especially that conducted against Indigenous peoples throughout the history of settler colonialism. Contributing to calls to resist 'the hegemonic tendencies of a universalizing paradigm like the Anthropocene', Todd sees 'Indigenous thought and practice – including art – as critical sites of refraction of the current whiteness of Anthropocene discourses' (252).

Bibliography

Apter, Emily. 2003. "Global Translation: The 'Invention' of Comparative Literature, Istanbul, 1933." *Critical Inquiry* 29, no. 2: 253–281.
Apter, Emily. 2013. *Against World Literature: On the Politics of Untranslatability*. London and New York: Verso.
Canavan, Gerry, and Kim Stanley Robinson. 2014. *Green Planets: Ecology and Science Fiction*. Middletown, Connecticut: Wesleyan University Press.
Casanova, Pascale. [1999] 2004. *The World Republic of Letters*. Translated by M.B. DeBevoise. Cambridge MA: Harvard University Press.
Ceballos, Gerardo, *et al.* 2020. "Vertebrates on the Brink as Indicators of Biological Annihilation and the Sixth Mass Extinction." *Proceedings of the National Academy of Sciences of the United States of America PNAS* 117, no. 24 (June 15): 13596–13602.
Cohen, Jeffrey Jerome, and Lowell Duckert, eds. 2015. *Elemental Ecocriticism: Thinking with Earth, Air, Water and Fire*. Minneapolis: University of Minnesota Press.
Connolly, William E. 2017. *Facing the Planetary: Entangled Humanism and the Politics of Swarming*. London: Duke University Press.
Cook, John, *et al.* 2006. "Consensus on Consensus: A Synthesis of Consensus Estimates on Human-Caused Global Warming." *Environmental Research Letters* 11, no. 4: 1–7.
Crutzen, Paul J. 2002. "Geology of Mankind." *Nature* 415: 23.
Crutzen, Paul J., and Eugene Stoermer. 2000. "The 'Anthropocene'." *IGBP Newsletter* 41: 17–18.
Crutzen, Paul J., Will Steffen, and John R. McNeill. 2007. "The Anthropocene: Are Humans Now Overwhelming the Great Forces of Nature?" *Ambio* 36, no. 8: 614–621.
Damrosch, David. 2003. *What Is World Literature?* Princeton and Oxford: Princeton University Press.
Davies, Janae, *et al.* 2019. "Anthropocene, Capitalocene, … Plantationocene? A Manifesto for Ecological Justice in the Age of Global Crises." *Geography Compass* 13, no. 5: 1–15. https://doi.org/10.1111/gec3.12438.
Davies, Jeremy. 2016. *The Birth of the Anthropocene*. Oakland, CA: University of California Press.
Dimock, Wai Chee. 2006. *Through Other Continents: American Literature Across Deep Time*. Princeton and Oxford: Princeton University Press.
Eaglestone, Robert. 2019. *Literature: Why It Matters*. Cambridge: Polity Press.
Edwardson, Rachel Nutaaq Ayałhuq Naŋinaaq. 2022. "She'll Do What She Needs to Do." In *Risky Futures: Climate, Geopolitics and Local Realities in the Uncertain Circumpolar North*, edited by Olga Ulturgasheva and Barbara Bodenhorn, 89–102. Oxford: Berghahn Books.
Ellis, Erle. 2023. "Why I Resigned from the Anthropocene Working Group". *Anthroecology Lab*, July 13: https://anthroecology.org/why-i-resigned-from-the-anthropocene-working-group/ [accessed July 21, 2023].
Estes, Nick. 2019. *Our History is the Future: Standing Rock versus the Dakota Access Pipeline, and the Long Tradition of Indigenous Resistance*. London: Verso.
Ghosh, Amitav. 2016. *The Great Derangement*. London: University of Chicago Press.
Hansen, James. "*Dear Prime Minister Rudd.*" April 1, 2008. http://www.columbia.edu/~jeh1/mailings/2008/20080401_DearPrimeMinisterRudd.pdf [accessed 2023].

Haraway, Donna. 2015. "Anthropocene, Capitalocene, Plantationocene, Chthulucene: Making Kin." *Environmental Humanities* 6: 159–165.
Haraway, Donna, *et al.* 2016. "Anthropologists are Talking – About the Anthropocene." *Ethnos* 81, no. 3: 535–564.
Heise, Ursula K. 2008. *Sense of Place, Sense of Planet*. New York: Oxford University Press.
Huggan, Graham. 2001. *The Postcolonial Exotic: Marketing the Margins*. London: Routledge.
Jamie, Kathleen. 2019. *Surfacing*. London: Sort of Books.
Kalliney, Peter J. 2002. "Globalization, Postcoloniality, and the Problem of Literary Studies in the Satanic Verses." *Modern Fiction Studies* 48, no. 1: 50–82.
Kilby, Jane, and Antony Rowland. 2014. *The Future of Testimony: Interdisciplinary Perspectives on Witnessing*. New York: Routledge.
Klein, Naomi. 2014. *This Changes Everything: Capitalism vs. the Climate*. London: Penguin.
Koegler, Caroline. 2018. *Critical Branding: Postcolonial Studies and the Market*. New York: Routledge.
Krishnaswamy, Revathi, and John C. Hawley. 2007. *The Postcolonial and the Global*. Minnesota: University of Minnesota Press.
LeMenager, Stephanie. 2014. *Living Oil: Petroleum Culture in the American Century*. Oxford: Oxford University Press.
Lewis, Simon L., and Mark A. Maslin. 2015. "Defining the Anthropocene." *Nature* 519: 171–180.
Malm, Andreas, and Alf Hornborg. 2014. "The geology of mankind? A critique of the Anthropocene narrative." *The Anthropocene Review* 1, no. 1: 62–69.
Malm, Andreas. 2016. *Fossil Capital: The Rise of Steam Power and the Roots of Global Warming*. London: Verso.
Malm, Andreas. 2020. *Corona, Climate, and Chronic Emergency: War Communism in the Twenty-First Century*. London: Verso.
Mehnert, Antonia. 2016. *Climate Change Fictions: Representations of Global Warming in American Literature*. Basingstoke: Palgrave MacMillan.
Milner, Andrew, and J.R. Burgmann. 2020. *Science Fiction and Climate Change: A Sociological Approach*. Liverpool: Liverpool University Press.
Moore, Jason W. 2016. "Introduction: Anthropocene or Capitalocene? Nature, History, and the Crisis of Capitalism." In *Anthropocene or Capitalocene? Nature, History, and the Crisis of Capitalism*, edited by Jason W. Moore, 1–13. Dexter, Michigan: PM Press.
Moraru, Christian. 2015. *Reading for the Planet: Toward A Geomethodology*. Ann Arbor: University of Michigan Press.
Moretti, Franco. 2000. "Conjectures on World Literature." *New Left Review* 1: 54–68.
Mufti, Aamir R. 2016. *Forget English! Orientalisms and World Literatures*. Cambridge MA: Harvard University Press.
Mukherjee, Pablo. 2010. *Postcolonial Environments: Nature, Culture and the Contemporary Indian Novel in English*. Basingstoke: Palgrave Macmillan.
Nixon, Rob. 2011. *Slow Violence and the Environmentalism of the Poor*. Cambridge, MA: Harvard University Press.
O'Brien, Susie, and Imre Szeman. 2001. "Introduction: The Globalization of Fiction / The Fiction of Globalization." *South Atlantic Quarterly* 100, no. 3: 603–626.
Prendergast, Christopher, ed. 2004. *Debating World Literature*. London: Verso.

Rich, Nathaniel. 2019. *Losing Earth: The Decade We Could Have Stopped Climate Change*. London: Picador.

Shriver, Maria. 2011. "*Maria Shriver interviews famously private poet Mary Oliver.*" https://www.oprah.com/entertainment/maria-shriver-interviews-poet-mary-oliver/all#ixzz6m5C5r9TR [accessed 2023].

Spencer, Robert, and Anastasia Valassopoulos. 2021. *Postcolonial Locations: New Issues and Directions in Postcolonial Studies*. London: Routledge.

Szeman, Imre. 2017. "Conjectures on World Energy Literature: Or, What is Petroculture?" *Journal of Postcolonial Writing* 53, no. 3: 277–288.

Todd, Zoe. 2015. "Indigenizing the Anthropocene." In *Art in the Anthropocene*, edited by Heather Davis and Etienne Turpin, 241–254. London: Open Humanities Press.

Trexler, Adam. 2015. *Anthropocene Fictions: The Novel in a Time of Climate Change*. Charlottesville, Virginia: University of Virginia Press.

Warwick Research Collective. 2015. *Combined and Uneven Development: Towards A New Theory of World Literature*. Liverpool: Liverpool University Press.

Wenzel, Jennifer. 2019. *The Disposition of Nature: Environmental Crisis and World Literature*. New York: Fordham University Press.

Yaeger, Patricia. 2011. "Editor's Column: Literature in the Ages of Wood, Tallow, Coal, Whale Oil, Gasoline, Atomic Power, and Other Energy Sources." *PMLA* 126, no. 2 (March): 305–326.

Yusoff, Kathryn. 2018. *A Billion Black Anthropocenes or None*. Minneapolis: University of Minnesota Press.

1 Earth

In this chapter we examine representations of, and engagements with, environmental issues associated with the earth in novels and plays from and about the Caribbean, the US, South Africa, and Scotland. The chapter is divided into three subsections, allied to features of the lithosphere that humans have used, altered, and extracted in pursuit of economic aims, namely: 'Soil', 'Mineral and Metal', and 'Oil'. The order in which they appear also loosely charts the development of global capitalism and major energy transitions. This begins with the colonization of foreign soil and deforestations that fuelled the agricultural revolution, mercantilism and plantation economies of the fifteenth to the eighteenth centuries; followed by the industrial extraction of coal, minerals, and metals as part of the expansion of European empires, industrialization, and urbanization of the nineteenth and twentieth centuries; and finally the emergence of oil as the primary fuel driving the hydrocarbon global economy at present.

In 'Soil', we draw on Kathryn Yusoff's *A Billion Black Anthropocenes or None* (2018) to examine four works of literature by Black Caribbean and American writers, starting with C.L.R James's play, *Toussaint Louverture: The Story of the Only Successful Slave Revolt in History* (written 1934, performed 1936) and Arna Bontemps' novel, *Black Thunder, Gabriel's Revolt: Virginia, 1800* (1936). Both represent slave rebellions – one successful, one unsuccessful – in which the exploitation of soils forms the basis for colonial power, plantation slavery, and mass food production for colonizing nations, while at the same time providing real and symbolic means for resistance, emancipation from slavery, and new forms of community. We then turn to Octavia Butler's dystopian novels, *The Parable of the Sower* (1993) and *The Parable of the Talents* (1998) that imagine a near-future in which the Earth is barely habitable due to climate change, indentured labour and slavery return, and followers of a new religion called *Earthseed* believe that it is humanity's destiny to colonize other planets. We analyse how the heterotemporalities of the *Parables* provide a reverse-historical account of global capitalism, so that Indigenous knowledges and the use value of provision plots of the past provide methods for survival and recovery after ecological collapse.

Digging down then from the plantation topsoils to the underground mines of South Africa, the second section, 'Mineral and Metal', uses Jason Moore's

DOI: 10.4324/9780429353352-2

work on commodity frontiers in the Capitalocene to explore how Olive Schreiner's *Undine* (1928) and Peter Abrahams' *Mine Boy* (1946) represent the damaging socio-ecological effects of the diamond and gold mining industries, and the role played by anti-colonial, feminist, workers union, and Pan-African struggles to resist extractive capitalism. Finally, the chapter turns from the earlier sugar, gold, and diamond rushes to the oil rush of the twentieth century. Using the work of key members of the Warwick Research Collective, Graeme Macdonald and Michael Niblett, we provide a summary account of John McGrath's *The Cheviot, the Stag and the Black, Black Oil* (1973) as a pre-eminent example of 'world literature' and 'petro-drama' that presents a world-historical view of the environmental and human costs of land dispossession, monocultural farming, extractive capitalism, and the hydrocarbon economy.

Soil

In July 2021, the National Institute for Space Research in Brazil published the results of a nine-year study in the journal *Nature*, in which they identify that the Amazon rainforest now emits more CO_2 than it absorbs (Gatti et al., 2021). Though the Amazon basin is often called the 'lungs of the earth' due to its role in producing atmospheric oxygen and regulating climate, around 20 percent of the rainforest now functions as a carbon source rather than a carbon sink. Emissions are predominantly caused by the fires used to clear land, though fewer trees also means reduced evapotranspiration and precipitation leading to drought, increases in temperature causing heatwaves, and degradation of adjacent forested areas resulting in greater vulnerability to wildfires. The primary driver of deforestation in the Amazon is the production of beef and soy, as cleared acreage is turned over to grazing for cattle and soybean crops for use in both livestock feed and cooking. Despite the real and ongoing threats to global lives posed by the denudation of the rainforest, there is no sign that demand will slow. Rather, it looks set to increase, as the dominating markets for beef and soy include the US, China, and Japan, and PricewaterhouseCoopers reports that these nations will form three of the seven largest economies in the world by 2050 (2017: 4).

The burning of forests to meet the consumer demands of the world's superpowers is nothing new. Indeed the global history of deforestation to make way for monocultural farming – both plant and animal – has roots in the fifteenth century, as Raj Patel and Jason Moore explain via the example of the colonization of Madeira: '[o]ne of the earliest flares of the modern world was lit on a small northern African island, where in the 1460s a new system for producing and distributing food took shape' (2018: 14). Patel and Moore explain how in its first phase, the deforestation of Madeira provided Portuguese colonists with lumber for shipbuilding and construction, and land for wheat production. Later came sugar plantations overseen by Portuguese, Genoese, and Flemish owners, as cleared areas were turned over to the cultivation of a crop increasingly in demand from Western Europe. Meanwhile the wood from logged forests provided the fuel needed to turn the sugarcane stalks into sugar. Deforestation and monocultural farming thus provided two key elements of sugar production in Madeira, crucially enabled by a vital third factor: slavery. So, whilst some of the workers on the island plantations were waged staff, others were Guanche (people indigenous to the Canary Islands) and North African slaves.

In 1476 and again in 1478, a Genoese sugar trader visited Madeira, and witnessed the role of enslaved workforces in clearing forests and mass producing crops. This trader, Christopher Columbus, went on to receive financial backing from the Spanish crown to undertake an expedition to Asia. His first voyage across the Atlantic in search of the East Indies culminated on October 12, 1492, when he arrived at Guanahani, an island in the Bahamas, thus marking the first step towards the Spanish colonization of the Caribbean. In the words of Patel and Moore: '[s]lavery didn't begin in Madeira, [...] *modern* slavery did' (30). Indeed, Columbus swiftly implemented the Madeiran slave labour model across the various islands, as Indigenous Taino, Arawak, and Carib peoples were forced to harvest gold and work on plantations. Though wheat and barley did not flourish in Caribbean soils, sugar – which Columbus introduced to Hispaniola on his second voyage – became the primary commodity and basis for the islands' agricultural economy.

In the decade following Columbus's landing, enslaved local populations were decimated by the toll of forced labour, massacres, and the introduction of new European diseases such as smallpox (Crosby 1986). Patel and Moore maintain that

> between his departure from Madeira in 1478 to serve the Spanish crown and his return to Funchal for six days in 1498 as the viceroy of the Indies, Columbus inaugurated a genocide in the Caribbean that would see the death of many of the humans – and civilizations – living there.
> (2018: 36)

At the same time, the arrival of European livestock and pests such as rats irreversibly damaged existing ecosystems through predation, competition, and disease, making it impossible for the remaining Taino and Arawak to recover former ways of life. The death toll was so high that by 1501 the Spanish had a new plan to swell their labour forces and began importing slaves from Africa to work on the Caribbean plantations (Davidson 1992). In so doing, the Spanish colonists laid the foundations for the European colonization of the Americas, the global slave trade, the beginnings of global capitalism, and its associated exploitation of global environments, or what Jennifer Wenzel dubs 'a blueprint for capitalist modernity – a map of the future that [...] bears a complex yet instructive relation to the uneven territory of our present' (2016: n.p.). Across the three centuries following Columbus's landing, huge swaths of the Americas were deforested to make way for monocultural plantations, as cash crops such as sugar, cotton, corn, coffee, indigo, cocoa, tobacco, and rice were mass produced by millions of enslaved Africans and their descendants.

The mass deforestations, genocides, plantations, and transported peoples, plants, animals, diseases, and soils that came in Columbus's wake drastically altered global environments and contributed to a scientifically recognized shift out of the Earth System state typical of the Holocene epoch. As we explained in the Introduction to this book, this new epoch has been dubbed (amongst other things) the Anthropocene (Crutzen), the Capitalocene (Patel and Moore) and the Plantationocene (Haraway).[1] Whilst each of these terms prove useful according to their different contexts of use, it is Yusoff's reworking and racialization of the term 'Anthropocene' in *A Billion Black Anthropocenes or None* that resonates most strongly with our discussion of soil here. She explains her idea as follows: 'invasion, genocide, slavery and settler colonialism [...] presse[d] an inhuman categorization and the inhuman earth into intimacy', and this 'proximity of black and brown bodies to harm in this intimacy with the inhuman is what I am calling *Black Anthropocenes*' (2018: xii). For Yusoff, the racial blindness of the Anthropocene (from *anthropos*, meaning 'human') cannot fully account for the role of slavery and associated extinctions of Black and Indigenous peoples – the 'billion black Anthropocenes' of her book's title. Her concept therefore directly addresses the inextricability of the genocides and ecocides enacted through colonialism and slavery and establishes their effects in geological terms. Through Yusoff, then, it becomes possible to consider the role of plantation slavery in eradicating, damaging, and irreversibly altering humans *and* animals *and* plants *and* soils, in ways traceable in rock strata.

When it comes to reading literature in light of Yusoff's work, things become a little trickier, however, as slave narratives tend to emphasize the humanness and humanity of African people and their descendants in contradistinction to their construction by European colonists and slave owners as inhuman commodity or animal. Treated as commodities or animals, enslaved people could be lawfully and allowably hunted, captured, transported, sold, raped, tortured, and murdered across the centuries and on a global industrial scale. Shipping records reveal that around 10 million African people were transported to the Americas by European slave traders, an additional 1.2–2.4 million people died on the voyage, and millions more were killed in Africa in slave wars, slave raids, and in transit to the coast.[2] Given the sheer scale and brutality of the transatlantic slave trade and plantation slavery, it is hardly surprising that oral and written testimonies and autobiographies by enslaved people and former slaves, as well as various works of fiction on the topic, have challenged European perceptions of slaves as inhuman mass/animal/commodity by emphasizing the personhood and individuality of those who suffered. As a result, slave narratives of the eighteenth and nineteenth centuries by writers such as Olaudah Equiano, Harriet Jacobs, Frederick Douglass, Solomon Northup, Mary Prince, Elizabeth Hobbs Keckley, and many others typically incorporate individual recollections of the horrors and brutalities of the slave trade and life on the plantations, stories of escape, arguments for abolition, and personal journeys towards Christian salvation and progress.

Whilst the human costs of the transatlantic slave trade and plantation slavery remain – for very good reason – at the forefront of most autobiographical slave narratives, there are also examples of fictional works that more explicitly draw out the inextricability of human lives, crops, and soils in the 'billion black Anthropocenes'. Four such texts are James's play *Toussaint Louverture: The Story of the Only Successful Slave Revolt in History*, Bontemps' novel *Black Thunder, Gabriel's Revolt: Virginia, 1800*, and Butler's *Parable of the Sower* and *Parable of the Talents*. All four reveal long historical connections between colonization, slavery, international capitalism, and environmental degradation as a result of the transportation and industrial-scale destruction of humans, animals, plants, and soils. As Yusoff argues, '[t]he Anthropocene might seem to offer a dystopic future that laments the end of the world, but imperialism and ongoing (settler) colonialisms have been ending worlds for as long as they have been in existence' (2018: xiii). As the sixth mass extinction is now well in process, it becomes more important than ever to see – in this case through literature – how historical fights for racial and environmental justice connect across time and space if we are to effectively advocate for the multispecies lives at stake on our planet.

Black Anthropocenes and Anti-Slavery Struggles

For Bontemps, an expanded conception of Black revolutionism as an ongoing historical process was sparked by 'discovering in the Fisk Library a larger collection of slave narratives than I knew existed, I began to read almost frantically' (xxvi). As Arnold Rampersad explains, Bontemps was thus able to '[discover] a link between the slave narratives and the revolutionary social and political goals that in the 1930s were associated almost exclusively with communism' (xii). James similarly sought to link the Haitian revolution to contemporary issues, so that both *Toussaint Louverture* and its partner text, *The Black Jacobins* (James's authoritative history of the revolution), aimed to establish a record of the rebellion in scholarly and public arenas, whilst articulating a Marxist/Pan-Africanist call for an end to colonialism in Africa. Christian Høgsbjerg demonstrates that 'at the heart of James's play was a pioneering recovery of the collective memory of the historic experience uniting people of the African diaspora: the experience of enslavement and the resistance to it' (2013: 3). In this way, both Bontemps and James depart from the generic conventions of earlier individualized slave narratives by imaginatively recreating historical slave rebellions that address longer social, historical, and political views of slavery and the slave trade. Their texts illustrate the importance of collective action, anti-colonialism, anti-racism, and anti-capitalism in the *ongoing* fights for racial justice. In her analysis of Bontemps's *Black Thunder*, Michaela Keck writes:

By interlinking the slave community of Richmond, Virginia, with the French peasant revolution and the Black Revolution of Haiti, Bontemps constructs the South as a marginocentric, that is, peripheral yet with cosmopolitan topography, which inextricably intertwines Gabriel's rebellion with the transnational, multiethnic, and cross-cultural radical political struggles for and discourses about an egalitarian American democracy. At the same time, Bontemps situates the slave rebellion within the class struggle of African-Americans during the 1930s and envisions Gabriel as a proletarian leader of radical social transformation, anticipating future anticolonial and Diasporic intellectual thought.

(2017: 38)

Keck's argument has broader applicability to James's writing, too, as both Bontemps and James link distinct peoples and places from across broad geographical and historical spans as pluralistic revolutionary forces. Michael Bibler and Jessica Adams provide further support for this interpretation, arguing that Bontemps' writing 'insists that we examine the forms and networks of multiracial identities, kinships, and social relations in the Americas, where the political and the genealogical are profoundly linked' (2009: xlvii). In this way, the slave rebellions of the 1790s and 1800s are connected to James and Bontemps's 1930s contexts of writing and beyond.

Here, we extend the reach of these established critical arguments all the way to the work of Butler, though with a new focus on the environment that has hitherto been missing from analysis of all three writers' works. In his discussion of Butler, but equally applicable to James and Bontemps, Kevin Modestino writes that '[s]cholars have frequently and productively placed Butler in dialogue with longer traditions of African American literature but have rarely understood that literature as environmental' (2021: 58). He goes on to explain that 'scholars who have written on Butler's environmentalism have tended to focus on her immediate experience as a Black working-class writer of speculative fiction from Southern California bringing a womanist perspective to environmental science fiction while omitting this longer history' (58). Here, we explore the work of James, Bontemps, and Butler in and as part of the 'longer history' of anti-slavery liberation movements that are embedded in environmental concerns. This involves thinking about the relationships between slavery, deforestation, and monocultural farming, and the associated effects on the integrity of soils, the destruction of ecosystems, and the long-term consequences of plantation capitalism for all forms of life. As such, literary representations of the struggles to (re)claim soils show how reinstating ecologically sound and sustainable interactions between humans and other lifeforms becomes integral to the fights for emancipation, a fair society, racial equality, and justice, and to imagining and creating liveable environments and communities in highly denuded or otherwise inhospitable lands in the Caribbean, US, and worlds beyond.

James's *Toussaint Louverture* was first performed in 1936 in London's Westminster Theatre and marked the first time a play by a Black playwright and featuring Black professional actors appeared on a British stage. The playscript was then presumed lost until 2005 when Høgsbjerg found a 1934 draft in the archives of the Brynmor Jones Library at the University of Hull, and published it with a series of accompanying essays, notes, reviews, photographs, and other associated materials. Though the play took decades to reach reading audiences, James did manage to publish on the slave rebellion in the form of a historical study, and as Robert Spencer explains: 'the play should be read [...] principally as a companion to James's 1938 masterpiece *The Black Jacobins*' (2014: 117). The topic of both texts is the Haitian revolution, the origins of which might be traced as far back as 1517, when the Spanish brought over their first shipment of 15,000 African slaves. It was in 1697, however, when the French took control of the western third of the island, that slave numbers began to grow much more rapidly, so that by 1788 the island population comprised around 25,000 white Europeans, 22,000 'free people of colour', and 700,000 African slaves. The following year, 1789, marked the outbreak of the French revolution, and though news of its progress reached the colonies, the rallying call for *liberté, egalité, fraternité* was not extended to colonial slaves. In 1791, this was set to change, as Haitian slaves and 'free people of colour' staged the uprising that would become the only successful slave rebellion in history.

James's play opens with Colonel Vincent (an officer in the French army) and Monsieur Bullet (President of the Colonial Assembly of San Domingo) listening to Mozart and conversing:

VINCENT: San Domingo – the very name is beautiful. On the boat I was always regretting Paris, and now after forty-eight hours here I have forgotten Paris completely – almost.

(*He walks to the end of the verandah and looks out into the night.*)

BULLET: Colonel Vincent, we produce more sugar here than in Jamaica, Barbados and all the British West Indian Islands put together. In fact, no part of the civilised world produces as much wealth in proportion to its size as the French part of the island of San Domingo.
VINCENT: They tell me the soil is as fertile as the scenery is beautiful.

(Act 1 Scene 1, 2013: 49)

In this opening exchange, James deftly connects Haiti's colonial history, the spread of global capitalism, and environmental concerns. The island is referred to by the Spanish form of its French colonial name (Saint-Domingue) in a gesture to the island's long history of colonization. As was typical of many European colonial narratives, the colonists assert their masculinized authority over new territories by describing colonized land using the feminized terms 'beautiful' and 'fertile', whilst also creating what Wenzel describes as a 'resource aesthetic' in which '[t]he profitable and beautiful are brought into alignment, envisioned as one and the same' (2016: n.p.). For both Vincent and Bullet, the island's greatest value lies in its nutrient-rich soils that are exploited for increasingly intensive modes of agricultural production and economic gain, with the profits then used to bolster France's power and status in the context of an emerging world economy. As such, the play opens with an expression of the idea that colonial economic and environmental networks are indistinguishable, a point also made by Patel and Moore, who suggest that '[c]apitalism is not just part of an ecology but *is* an ecology – a set of relationships integrating power, capital, and nature' (2018: 38).

Though for the colonizers, Bullet and Vincent, the soils of Haiti are life-giving and enriching, for the slaves, the plantation soils are deathly. This idea is also brilliantly evoked by Aimé Césaire in his statement: 'we are walking compost hideously promising tender cane and silky cotton' ([1956] 1969: 61). For both James and Césaire, plantation slavery compresses slaves into the same category as decomposing matter. Slaves are seen and treated as dirt; they die so that crops can grow. This becomes most starkly evident in a scene in which the life-giving and life-sustaining properties of soil are sharply contrasted with its use as a site and method for confinement, punishment, and death:

BULLET: [...] Tomorrow morning I select a slave and set him to dig his own grave. If that runaway is not found in the afternoon, at six o'clock I assemble my thousand slaves in the field. There, before everyone, he buries himself up to the neck. This is a case where honey and molasses will be smeared on his face.
VINCENT: Why?
BULLET: So that the ants and flies will be at him almost immediately. Sometimes we allow the slaves to throw stones at him so as to put him quickly out of his misery. I'll not allow that tomorrow. And every slave looking on will know that perhaps it will be his turn the next day, or the next, or the day after that, as need be. I wager you that the runaway will be found before very long, Colonel Vincent. We have two hundred years of experience behind us. We know how to deal with them.

(53)

This method of putting slaves to death was 'a favourite pastime' in Haiti, according to the fifth article in a five-part series on 'The Horrors of San Domingo', published in *Atlantic Magazine* in June 1863. The article records that plantation owners would select a slave, 'bury him up to his neck, and let the boys bowl at his head. Sometimes the head was covered with molasses, and left to the insects. Pitying comrades were found to stone the sufferer to death' (1863: 770). In James's play, molasses (a product created in the process of refining sugar) draws in the animals that kill the man, allegorizing the

European desire for sweetness that drives the deaths of millions of slaves on the sugar plantations. The body of the man is left to decompose, becoming the dark organic matter that forms as humus, and which will enrich the soils in which the sugarcane grows. As James writes in *The Black Jacobins*: 'on such a soil as San Domingo slavery, only a vicious society could flourish' ([1938] 2001: 22). In both fiction and reality, then, this form of murder makes explicit the deathly symbiosis of soil, sugar, and slavery in the context of plantation economies.

Crucially, however, James plants the seeds of resistance in the opening scene of *Toussaint Louverture* too, via the stage direction: '*All through the scene there is a faint but insistent beating of drums. In moments of tenseness the drums beat louder and with accelerated rhythm, though they remain always in the distance*' (2013: 49). The drums are played by fugitive slaves, meeting secretly in '*the depths of a forest*' (54). There under the cover of indigenous trees and plants not yet cleared for the plantations, they plot rebellion. Here again, the richness of Haiti's soils plays its part, but the plants that grow in the forests are not used to enrich the slave owners, but to shelter and protect the rebelling maroons. In *The Black Jacobins*, James records how the rebellion was hampered by L'Ouverture's 'desire to avoid destruction' of Haiti's environs. He was forced to change this plan in his last, most successful campaign, telling Dessalines 'that we have no other resource than destruction and fire. Bear in mind that the soil bathed with our sweat must not furnish our enemies with the smallest sustenance, [...] burn and annihilate everything' ([1938] 2001: 243). The method of using fire to clear the Caribbean forests was now deployed to raze the crops, towns, and cities established by the colonizers. In burning down hundreds of sugar, coffee, and indigo plantations, and destroying roads and horses alongside their enemies, the rebels effected millions of francs worth of damage and losses. Though L'Ouverture was captured and died seven months before the succeeding rebel leaders issued a preliminary proclamation of independence, 'he had made in ten years an army which could hold its own with finest soldiers Europe had yet seen' (298). This would achieve what Dessalines describes in the play as 'Haiti no colony, but free and independent. Haiti, the first free and independent Negro state in the new world' (2013: 132).

The interactions of humans, plants, and soils that created the context in which the success of the liberation movement became possible is conveyed in *The Black Jacobins* in James's argument that:

> In a revolution, when the ceaseless slow accumulation of centuries bursts into volcanic eruption, the meteoric flares and flights above are a meaningless chaos and lend themselves to infinite caprice and romanticism unless the observer sees them always as projections of the sub-soil from which they came.
>
> ([1938] 2001: xix)

In both *Toussaint Louverture* and *The Black Jacobins*, then, ideas of growth and cultivation, and political awareness and action, are fomented in the environments that remain beyond colonial control and, as such, come from both the soil and the people. This is underscored in the play by Toussaint's final words before his capture: 'Do with me what you will. In destroying me you destroy only the trunk. But the tree of Negro liberty will flourish again, for its roots are many and deep' (2013: 122). For James, this was a message that carried through to the Pan-African and independence struggles of African and Caribbean nations in his own historical moment.

Rising Slaves and Rising Waters in Arna Bontemps' Black Thunder

The Haiti uprisings, and the life of the rebel leader L'Ouverture, also provided the subject matter for Bontemps' 1936 novel *Drums at Dusk* and three chapters of his non-fiction book, *Story of the Negro*, whilst his earlier children's novel co-authored with Langston Hughes, *Popo and Fifina* (1932), represented children's life in Haiti. Here, however, we have chosen to focus on *Black Thunder*, a novel that represents the failed slave uprising in Virginia, US, that took place in 1800 under the leadership of Gabriel Prosser. The story is relayed primarily through dialogue, and the various characters – including plantation owners, slaves, and maroons – are connected in complex webs of relations with each other, as well as with the animals, plants, and soils of their environs.

The catalyst for the uprising is the murder of the old slave Bundy by the slave owner, Master Prosser. Prosser becomes incensed by the sight of Bundy carrying a jug of rum across the corn fields. He views him as '[a] worthless old scavenger […] Not worth his keep. No better'n a lame mule' ([1936] 1992: 14), and attacks him – beating him with his whip, then trampling him to death with his horse. As 'old Bundy was dying', Gabriel is elsewhere on the plantation, tending to the colt, Araby, and talking to him: 'You ain't a horse yet, and you ain't a nigger neither. […] Was you a white colt, I reckon I'd have to call you *mister* Araby', and as he spoke '[h]e took a lump of sugar from the pocket in his coat tail and held it between the crosspieces of the gate. Araby's lips touched the immense boyish hand' (15–16). The hierarchy of life on the plantations in which horses are valued above human slaves is established in these juxtaposed scenes. Although the real Thomas Prosser was in fact a tobacco planter, and the character Bundy is killed in a cornfield, Bontemps makes connections to other monocultural plantations and rebellions by drawing on the real and representational significance of sugar. Where the slaves in *Black Thunder* are denied one of the products of their labour in the form of rum (which is made from cane juice and molasses), the colt is treated to them in the form of a sugar lump. The use of animal language is also important here, because as Graham Huggan and Helen Tiffin point out: 'both human genocide and human slavery have been, and in some cases, continue to be, predicated on the categorization of other people *as* animals' ([2010] 2015: 135). Thus the metaphoric description of Bundy as 'a lame mule' contrasts with the depiction of Master Prosser's horse as the means and method to kill the 'worthless' slave.

Bundy is buried 'in the low field by the swamp'. As his coffin is lowered into the earth, the passage reads:

> Down, down, down: old Bundy's long gone now. Put a jug of rum at his feet. Old Bundy with his legs like knotty canes. Roast a hog and put it on his grave. Down, down. [...] One eye shut and one eye open: down, down, down. Lord, Lord. Mm-mm-mm-mm. Don't let them black boys cover you up in that hole, brother.
>
> They had raised a song without words. They were kneeling with their faces to the sun. Their hands were in the air, the fingers apart, and they bowed and rose together as they sang. Up came the song like a wave, and down went their faces in the dirt.
>
> ([1936] 1992: 52)

The labour of digging – both plantations and grave – is captured in the repetitive, plosive monosyllables; whilst the simile describing Bundy's limbs as like the stems of the plants he cultivated reminds us once again of the inseparability of Black bodies, crops, and organic matter in the context of plantation slavery. As Yusoff argues: 'the human and its subcategory, the inhuman, are historically relational to a discourse of settler-colonial rights and the material practices of extraction' so that 'the categorization of matter is a spatial execution, of place, land, and person cut from relation through geographic displacement (and relocation through forced settlement and transatlantic slavery)' (2018: 2). Though Yusoff here suggests that the transplantation of slaves results in their alienation from the lands on which they are forced to work, *Black Thunder* presents a re-visioning of the relationships between Africans and African descendants with American soils. As Bundy's death provides the prompt for the Richmond rebellion, and as the funereal rites and respect accorded to Bundy in his burial are enacted, new meanings emerge to yoke together human, crop, and earth through ideas of communality, the sharing of resources, and the desire for liberation and social justice. The funeral-goers are united in the musicality of the repeated words and rhythmic murmurings, the bodily movements to express rituals of mourning and blessings 'remembered [from] Africa in 1800' ([1936] 1992: 52), and the tributes of rum and pork. In this way, Bundy's corpse inhabits the earth in a way that he was denied in life. His burial and buried body thus come to represent the future potential for former slaves to claim, inhabit, nourish, and live free with and on the land.

The progression of events in *Black Thunder* is prompted by Bundy's death, so that Gabriel sets out to avenge his murder by leading the slave rebellion that is ultimately betrayed by Ben, one of their recruits. After attending the first planning meeting, Ben has a vision:

> Ben's eyes burned for sleep. He went from window to window raising blinds and throwing open shutters, but there was no sun and the handsome high-ceilinged rooms remained dull and cheerless. Ben was tortured with the vision of filthy black slaves coming suddenly through those windows, pikes and cutlasses in their hands, their eyes burning with murderous passion and their feet dripping mud from the swamp. He saw the lovely hangings crash, the furniture reel and topple, piece by piece, and he saw the increasing black host storm the stairway. In another moment there were quick, choked cries of the dying, followed by wild jungle laughter. Then it occurred to Ben which side he was on, and he covered his eyes with his hand. It was going to be an impossible thing for him to do, a desecrating, sinful thing.
>
> (61–62)

Ben's inherited and internalized colonial perception of Black bodies as dirty, and the zoomorphized descriptions of the rebels as an uncivilized mass, are contrasted with the décor of the colonial homestead that represents civilized living destroyed by the slaves' filth and violence. Like the jungles of Haiti represented in James's play, the swamps of Virginia are uncultivated and undomesticated, and seen as contaminants when trampled into the colonial buildings. The onomatopoeic 'crash', the noise of 'cries' and 'laughter', and the optics of the liberation fighters envisioned as monstrous, uncanny ghouls create highly sensory and evocative representations that create a sense of the soils as brought to life, emerging from the depths to attack the living. In this way, Bontemps reveals the reach of colonial control, which extends deep into the earth as well as into the minds of the slaves. Ben's encompassing fears and engrained servitude lead him to betray his friends.

There is, however, another reading made possible by Ben's premonition, as the scene also reveals the potential for future freedom and ways of living with others that exist in both soils and minds. The name for the type of soil created by the decomposition of plant and animal matter is, as already mentioned, 'humus', which Donna Haraway connects to the 'Proto-Germanic and Old English, *guman* [which] later became *human*, but both come soiled with the earth and its critters, rich in humus, *humaine*, earthly beings as opposed to the gods' (2016: 169–170, n.3). This point forms part of Haraway's argument that all species are part of complex, interpenetrative biotic systems, made with and through one another, and full recognition of this fact provides a means to imagine and build liveable futures. In Ben's premonition, the soils spring to life in intra-action with bodies so that putrefying, composting matter becomes agentive and bound up with human actions. This 'intra-action' – from Karen Barad's work on agential realism – expresses how the continuous formation of the world prevents easy distinctions between the natural and social, material and discursive, and human and nonhuman (2007). In this way, human and nonhuman entities continually act across and through one another, just as the bodies of the liberation fighters, the mud, and marshy soils intra-act in Ben's vision. The earth is no longer comprised of ambivalent, static matter but appears as living beings bent on overthrowing the colonial order. In implicating the soils with the slaves' struggle for emancipation, Bontemps creates a sense of collective ecological reciprocity that suggests new ways of being with and through the earth as alternatives to plantation slavery, whilst at the same time destroying colonial structures and forcing the colonial powers to reckon with the horrors of human and environmental exploitation.

The character Ben is an amalgamation and fictionalization of two real Richmond co-conspirators who tipped off their plantation owners, enabling state militia to act quickly to thwart the Virginia rebellion. The storms and floods depicted in the novel are historically accurate, as torrential rains did indeed lash down on the first day of the planned attack, further hampering the speed and effectiveness of the uprising. Bontemps depicts the aftermath of the failed insurrection in *Black Thunder*, in scenes showing Gabriel attempting to outrun law enforcement whilst slowed by the storm. Deforestation and instatement of monocultural plantations cause unstable soils that are no longer held together by diverse flora and root systems able to soak up excess water. Exhausted, hungry, and desperately striving to continue, Gabriel is then confronted by bodies disinterred by the floods:

> Presently the carcass of a dead animal was under their feet. Buzzards and possums had already cleaned the bones, but shreds of harness were still on the skeleton and the arm of a broken thill lay under the heap. They looked at it briefly, and Gabriel thought of Mingo and of Pharaoh and of Ben.
>
> ([1936] 1992: 159)

Here, the soils resist their colonization by plantation owners, interacting with weather and water to unbury the corpse of the horse on the day of the uprising. Importantly, the skeleton is still attached to a cart, revealing that the horse, like so many slaves, was quite literally driven to death on the plantations. As Gabriel views the carcass he thinks of his deceased comrades, so that the disinterred animal becomes a symbol for the unearthing of the horrors of the plantations. The dead do not stay buried, but return to testify to, and condemn, plantation slavery, and reclaim the earth.

The failed Richmond uprising resulted in the arrests of around 70 men, of which it is estimated that 35 (including Gabriel Prosser) were hanged. In *Black Thunder*, the traitor Ben tries to come to terms with his role in bringing about the deaths of his former friends and feels 'it's a powerful bad thing to sit around waiting for yo' medicine when you know you's sure to get it' (215). He suspects that he is being poisoned, and as he stands in the kitchen of his master's house, his 'hands felt scaly and cold to himself. They were so thin and brittle he imagined they were like the hands of a skeleton' (217). In the final lines of the novel, Ben's premonition of death is realized. He attends

Earth 41

Gabriel's hanging, but leaves before the body is removed to run errands in town. As 'the clouds bore down' and the rain pours:

> Ben could not forget Gabriel's shining naked body or the arc inscribed by the executioner's ax. He could not feel reassured about the knives that waited for him with the sweet brown thrashers in every hedge and clump. For him the rainswept streets had a carnival sadness.
> The little mare's feet played a soothing tune on the cobblestones.
> (224)

The revenge killing of Ben is linked to the other major deaths in the novel through setting and sound. Like Gabriel, he is caught in the stormy weather that contributed to the failure of the rebellion, and like Bundy, the sounds of a horse's hooves echo in his ears as he dies. Ben's betrayal is thus avenged by his former friends and allies, who, along with their descendants, continued to fight for their freedom. It would take another 65 years, however, for the passage of the 13th Amendment to bring about the end of slavery in Virginia.

Provision Plots and Planetary Futures in Octavia Butler's Parables

Butler's dystopian novels, *Parable of the Sower* (1993) and *Parable of the Talents* (1998), depict a twenty-first century US ravaged by the climate and ecological emergencies, corporate greed, a disease known as 'the Pox', racial and religious attacks, and the widespread use of a pyromania-inducing drug that leads to mass burnings of properties and people. *Parable of the Sower* begins in 2024 and depicts the US at the point of near-total social, climate, and ecological breakdown, in which capitalist accumulation, gross economic inequalities, and social divisions have exhausted almost all of the planet's resources. Although the *Parables* move forwards in time, the action unfolds as a reverse history of the development of global capitalism, so that events and figures that appear across the 2024 to 2090 span of the novels find counterparts in historical events and figures reaching back from our present moment to 1492. The heterotemporalities of the novels, which move simultaneously forwards and backwards through time, are used to reveal how lessons from the past and, most particularly, lessons from historically persecuted groups such as Indigenous Americans and plantation slaves, offer strategies for survival, mitigation, and recovery in the present. After all, as Yusoff points out by quoting from Saidiya Hartman's *Lose Your Mother: A Journey Along the Atlantic Slave Route*: 'the end of this world has already happened for some subjects, and it is the prerequisite for the possibility of imagining "living and breathing again" for others' (2018: 12–13).

The first of the two novels, *Parable of the Sower*, is written as a series of diary entries by Lauren Olamina, as she grows up in a gated community in Robledo, California. Although the world outside is lawless and deadly,

Lauren lives in relative safety as part of a community of multi-racial families guided by her father, a Baptist preacher. The group is largely self-sufficient: they grow their own crops and share their resources. Lauren is aware, though, of the temporary nature of their living conditions, recognizing that 'everything was getting worse: the climate, economy, crime, drugs', and she 'didn't believe we would be allowed to sit behind our walls looking clean and fat and rich to the hungry, thirsty, homeless, jobless, filthy people outside' ([1993] 2019: 176). Lauren endeavours to educate herself and prepare for an unknown future beyond the walls, determined 'not [...] to spend my life as some kind of twenty-first century slave' (159). She tries to persuade her friend Joanne to do the same, suggesting they 'bury money and other necessities in the ground' and 'make emergency packs – grab and run packs [...] Money, food, clothing, matches, a blanket' (53). Lauren also asks Joanne if her family has any books that may be of use. When Joanne retorts that '[b]ooks aren't going to save us', Lauren counters with: 'use your imagination. Any kind of survival information from encyclopaedias, biographies, anything that helps you learn to live off the land and defend ourselves. Even some fiction might be useful' (54). Lauren does in fact learn how to cultivate and prepare food crops from the books she reads, and in her diaries records the development of her new 'God-is-Change belief system' that 'will be called Earthseed' (73). She writes:

> I found the name, found it while I was weeding the back garden and thinking about the way plants seed themselves, windborne, animalborne, waterborne, far from their parent plants. They have no ability at all to travel great distances under their own power, and yet, they do travel. Even they don't just sit in one place and wait to be wiped out. There are islands thousands of miles from anywhere – the Hawaiian Islands, for example, and Easter Island – where plants seeded themselves and grew long before any humans arrived.
>
> (73–74)

As Lauren develops her religion, she comes to believe that she must journey to the cooler and wetter north, with the ultimate intention of creating a community that will leave Earth to inhabit other planets. Earthseed is thus founded in soils and vegetation, in the shared knowledge of her family and community, and in learning from books about 'California Indians, the plants they used, and how they used them' (54). Most notably, the staple food of the gated neighbourhood is acorn bread, made using a recipe from Indigenous groups originating from the area. The community's garden plots thus become the grounds in which Lauren is able to grow a religion and way of life that will secure a future for humanity.

Earthseed's method of learning and living also has roots in the real provision plots cultivated by plantation slaves in the Caribbean and US across the fifteenth to the nineteenth centuries. As we described in the earlier parts of this chapter, the plantation system involved the cultivation of monocultural commodities such as sugar, then sold to European markets, and was, according to Sylvia Wynter, 'owned and dominated by external forces' and driven by 'exchange value' (1971: 96). Since the plantation transformed nature into an exploitable resource and, '[s]ince man is a part of Nature', it gave rise to 'a process of dehumanization and alienation' (99) that characterized mass slavery. There were, alongside the plantations, however, plots of land that plantation owners allocated to slaves to cultivate staple foods, such as yam, for personal and communal use. Although granted by the plantocracy to reduce costs, maximize productivity, and discourage desertion, the plots had unintended consequences for the slave owners. Where the plantation was market-driven and involved mass human and ecological exploitation, the plot became, as Wynter describes, an 'indigenous, autochthonous system' (96) driven by 'use value' (97). As a result, the provision plot managed to maintain 'the structure of values that had been created by traditional societies in Africa' (99). For the European plantation owners, the slaves and the land were property; for the transported African slaves, 'the land remained the Earth – and the Earth was a goddess' (99).

A vision of Earth-as-goddess is also realized in the creation of a provision plot in the *Parables*. Lauren's own heritage is important here too, as she explains in *Parable of the Talents* that her ancestors 'were chattel slaves for two and a half centuries – at least 10 generations' ([1993] 2019: 259). When, in *Parable of the Sower*, Lauren's gated neighbourhood is attacked and burned down by pyro addicts, and her family is killed, she takes her emergency pack of seeds, food, clothes, gun, money, and other basics, and journeys north. She is accompanied by two other survivors from her community, Zahra and Harry, and they are later joined by other travellers who become followers of Earthseed. The novel ends with the group establishing a settlement on land owned by Lauren's new lover, Bankole, and they 'decide to call this place Acorn' (311) after their staple crop. In the sequel, *Parable of the Talents*, Earthseed as religion and lifeway is flourishing in Acorn's plot.

In her discussion of Caribbean novels, plots, and plantations, Wynter explains that there was a 'struggle' between a world of 'human need' and 'the market economy world [...] where the product is made in response to its profitability on the market' (1971: 97). Unable to survive on sugar and tobacco from the plantations alone, the plantocracy was reliant on the wide variety of produce cultivated in provision plots. As Elizabeth DeLoughrey notes, this made the plot 'a stepping-stone toward liberation' since 'slaves provided the majority of the region's sustenance and gained significant amounts of currency, autonomy, and even freedom' (2019: 62, 63). So too in *Parable of the Talents*, the Earthseed community trade, share, and sell their excess produce with other nearby individuals, settlements, and groups, using these processes of exchange to enrich their own community with new members, tools, books, weapons, and transport. Though this buys them some autonomy and increased safety, the Acorn community is not able to fully escape the trappings of capitalism, because, as Wynter points out in her discussion of Caribbean slavery, the 'dual relation between plantation and plot' is characterized by an 'ambivalence' that 'is at once the root cause of our alienation; and the possibility of our salvation' (1971: 99). What Wynter means by this is that the brutality of the plantation relied upon the provision plot, but the communal folk culture that sustained, and was sustained by, the plot also offered alternative social orders. In *Parable of the Talents,* Acorn functions as a provision plot and ambivalent space that at once provides a method for resistance and route to freedom, whilst at the same time binding the community to capitalist modes of exchange still practised in the US at large. For Lauren, then, the provision plot functions as an interim measure and essential stepping stone towards a future departure from earth and the fulfilment of 'The Destiny of Earthseed' which 'is to take root among the stars' ([1993] 2019: 209).

In the *Parables*, Butler reverse-narrates an important world-historical shift from systems of slavery to debt bondage labour, so that environmental exhaustion under late capitalism makes possible revived forms of corporate peonage, which then leads to the reintroduction of mass slavery. The first indication of a return to industrial indentured labour appears in *Parable of the Sower*, when Joanne rejects Lauren's suggestion that they journey north together. Instead, she leaves the gated community with her family, who have signed up to work for a company called KSF in the hope it will provide safety and security. Lauren recognizes the KSF labour model as 'an old company-town trick – get people into debt, hang on to them, and work them harder. Debt slavery' (113). It is indeed an 'old trick' because indentured servitude historically provided a primary means for European and Asian migration to British America between the 1630s and 1776; whilst in the broader history of the British Empire, the Slavery Abolition Act that ended slavery in the British colonies in 1833 instigated the start of a major Indian indenture system that involved the transportation of millions of Indian workers to colonial plantations. In *Parable of the Sower*, new recruits to Earthseed, Emery and Tori, reveal that the takeover of their farm by 'a big agribusiness conglomerate' led to wages being paid 'in company scrip, not in cash [...] they could only spend their company notes at the company store. Wages – surprise! – were never quite enough to pay the bills', and 'debt slaves could be forced to work longer hours for less pay, could be "disciplined" if they failed to meet their quotas, could be traded and sold with or without their consent, with or without their families, to distant employers' (273), just as the indentured labourers of the nineteenth century were.

In Lauren's later diary entries that appear in *Parable of the Talents*, slavery is widespread, managed by new technologies such as shock collars, and supported by government-sanctioned institutions, as well as established forms of torture, rape, extreme violence, and threats to life. The election of a new President of the US, the far-right religious fundamentalist Andrew Jarret, is key to these changes. His promise to 'make America great again' (18) recalls the campaign phrase used by Republican President Ronald Reagan in the 1980s, whilst uncannily anticipating the slogan most closely associated with Donald Trump's Presidency. Under Jarret, followers of religions other than his sanctioned 'Christian America' (19) are persecuted, women are forced into traditional and subservient roles, and slavery returns to industrial levels. At the same time, Jarret's Crusaders – a far-right, politically violent group unofficially linked to the President – appear as a twenty-first century Ku Klux Klan, clad in black hoods and gowns adorned with crosses. The Crusaders assault, burn, and kill opponents of the ruling politico-religious regime and others who do not conform to their Christianized and Aryanized vision of America. They eventually attack Acorn, enslaving of all of its inhabitants and forcing them to work as plantation slaves, 'harvesting [...] salad greens, onions, potatoes, carrots, and squashes, all planted and tended by Acorn, of course' (208). The slaves themselves are left with 'bowls of obvious table scraps or boiled up in a watery soup with turnips or potatoes from our gardens' (202). The newly enslaved Acorn inhabitants are controlled by shock collars, are forced to pray to a Christian god, address their captors as 'Teacher' (201), and are routinely punished, raped, abused, and tortured, as in the scene in which they are 'lashed as we were made to kneel and pray [...]. It went on and on for hours with our "teachers" taking turns, trading off, screaming their hate at us, and calling it love' (204). Acorn's plot is thus transformed into the 'Camp Christian Reeducation Facility', imagined by Butler as an amalgamated missionary school/slave plantation/concentration camp surrounded 'with a Lazor-wire fence, so there's no safe entry or exit', in which the slaves sleep in 'bare rooms of shelf beds intended to house 30 people each' and '[use] buckets as toilets' (217). Additional captive slaves are brought to the camp, whilst their children – including Lauren's daughter Larkin – are stolen and given up for adoption to 'good Christian homes' (201).

The downfall of 'Camp Christian' is initiated by the combination of climate change-induced extreme weather, and the destruction of plants and soils that would help to mitigate its effects. Lauren's diary records that '[o]ur teachers had made us cut down the older trees for firewood and lumber and God' though '[w]e begged them to let the hill alone, told them it was our cemetery and they lashed us' (243). Outright contempt for local knowledges, customs, and communities, and the destruction of sacred places along with trees, are familiar stories of empire. Here, however, Butler reveals in microcosm the deadly consequences of epistemicide, ecocide, and the burning of fuels for *all* humans, including dominant groups. When 'a terrible storm' hits Camp Christian, the denuded hillside is no longer held in place by vegetation and root systems, and so 'slumped down into our valley' (243). Slavers and enslaved people alike are buried and killed, but the landslide also has unintended positive effects, as Lauren explains: 'the weather, and our "teachers"' own stupidity freed us' because '*all of our collars* were dead' (244, original emphasis). As in Bontemps's *Black Thunder*, meteorological forces are associated with the struggle for emancipation, but where the storms ultimately hinder Gabriel Prosser's Richmond uprising, here climate change-induced weather frees the slaves from the controlling technology that secured their captivity. They kill their 'teachers', take their weapons and food, and destroy the camp. Lauren records this in her diary as follows:

> We burned Camp Christian so that it couldn't be used as Camp Christian any more. If Christian America still wants the land it stole from us, it will have some serious rebuilding to do. We spread lamp oil and diesel fuel inside the cabins that we built from the trees we cut and the stone and concrete we hauled. [...]
>
> Most of us had seen our homes burn before, but we had not been the ones to set the fires. This time, though, it's too late for fire to be the destroyer that we remembered. The things that we had created and loved had already been destroyed. This time, the fires only cleansed.
>
> (250)

Where historically fires were used to clear forests to make way for the first monocultural plantations worked by slaves, in the reverse-narrative of world history that drives the *Parables*, the burning of Camp Christian marks the *end* rather than the start of plantation slavery, and the beginning of the end of Jarret's Christian America. Over the years, Lauren and Earthseed grow in fame, wealth, and following, and in the 2090 epilogue to *Parable of the Talents*, it is revealed that 'many Earthseed Communities' have been 'established or encouraged in the United States, Canada, Alaska, Mexico and Brazil' (378).

Butler's dystopian vision of ecological collapse, the reintroduction of indentured servitude and then mass slave labour creates novelistic heterotemporalities: the narrative moves forward in time, whilst recounting a reverse history of the development of global capitalism. Butler does not, therefore, hark back to an imagined previous golden age, or otherwise primitivize or exoticize the Indigenous American and African knowledges and methods that define the cosmology and lifeways of Earthseed. Instead, and in line with Wynter's arguments about the twin trajectories of the plantation system and the novel, the supporting plots of both are 'linked to the structure of use-value' (1971: 97). Though also a product of the market economy, Wynter identifies that the novel contains the writer's 'critical and oppositional stance to a process of alienation which had begun to fragment the very human community, without which the writer has neither purpose, nor source material, nor view of the world nor audience' (97). For this reason, the novel form, according to Wynter, contains within it the potential for 'critique of the very historical process which has brought it to such heights of fulfilment' (97). In the *Parables*, then, Butler uses the novel form to both represent and critique the human and environmental costs of global capitalist systems, from the plantation to the hydrocarbon economies. By narrativizing these world-historical developments in reverse, Butler draws lessons from historically persecuted peoples to devise means for survival, mitigation, and recovery in the future we inhabit now.

Lauren's belief, expressed in the opening pages of *Parable of the Sower*, that '[a]s far as I'm concerned, space exploration and colonization are among the only things left over from the last century that can help us more than they hurt us' ([1993] 2019: 20), is finally realized at the end of Butler's second novel. In this way, Acorn's provision plots lay the seeds for saving lives and cultivating ecologically sound communities beyond the ends of the world. In her final diary entry, dated 'Thursday, July 20, 2090', Lauren writes:

> Today's shuttles [...] loaded with cargoes of people, already deeply asleep in DiaPause – the suspended animation process that seems to be the best of the bunch. Traveling with the people are frozen human and animal embryos, plant seeds, tools, equipment, memories, dreams, and hopes. [...] All this is to be off-loaded on the Earth's first starship, the *Christopher Columbus*.
>
> I object to the name. This ship is not about a shortcut to riches and empire. It's not about snatching up slaves and gold and presenting them to some European monarch. But one can't win every battle. One must know which battles to fight. The name is nothing.
>
> (388)

The name of the shuttle roots the destruction of the earth's climate and ecosystem in Columbus's 1492 landing and colonization of the Americas. But the final disavowal breaks from this history of anthropocentric, imperialist exploitation by reclaiming the name as a vehicle to the future.

Mineral and Metal

In the preceding section of this chapter, 'Soil', we explained how capitalist globalization was made possible by the colonization of foreign soils, mass deforestations, ecocides, and genocides, which paved the way for plantation economies based on the transportation, trade, and exploitation of African slaves and their descendants. Tracing this story back to Columbus's landing in the Caribbean, we showed that the development of global capitalism and its devastating effects on global environments grew from select crops planted in colonized soils. Importantly, however, the development of large-scale plantations was not the primary aim of either Columbus, or his Spanish sponsors, King Ferdinand and Queen Isabella. The monarchs had in fact raised funds for Columbus's voyages on the understanding that he would establish trade routes to the East Indies and find new and significant sources of gold that could be used to shore up and extend the political and economic strength of Spain in Europe, and finance religious crusades. This has often been summarized as Columbus's quest for 'gold, God and glory' (Dyson, 1991), and in the opening lines of *The Black Jacobins*, James makes these priorities clear:

> Christopher Columbus landed first in the New World at the island of San Salvador [Guanahani], and after praising God enquired urgently for gold. The natives, Red Indians, were peaceable and friendly and directed him to Haiti, a large island (nearly as large as Ireland), rich, they said, in the yellow metal.
>
> (2001, 3)

During Columbus's second voyage, he identified the gold-bearing area of Hispaniola as Cibao, where he established a fortress and enslaved Taino peoples to work in the mines. Every slave over the age of 14 was required to produce a hawk's bell of gold, or otherwise 25 pounds of spun cotton, at three-monthly intervals. The mines, however, only yielded tiny amounts of the precious metal, which meant that it was impossible for slaves to deliver the required tributes. The Spanish response to quotas not being met was extraordinarily brutal. The hands of many slaves were cut off and they were left to bleed to death, others were murdered outright, and some committed suicide rather than await their fate (Sale, [1990] 2006). After decimating the Taino population, the Spanish colonists then turned to Africa for new mining and plantation workforces, initiating the transnational slave trade that would remain in place for centuries.

The co-determined and co-determining relationships between the development of plantation economies, slavery, and the mining of minerals and metals was, in Yusoff's words, 'established through slaves being exchanged for and as gold' (2018: 5). She goes on to explain that in 'precapitalist economies there was the gold, silver, and copper mining that mobilized the *hunger* for the slavery, and later, the sugar, that fueled the English working classes of the Industrial Revolution in their extraction of coal' (15). Yusoff's pithy summary reveals how the overlapping drivers and factors of the development of global capitalism extend all the way from the first large-scale plantations and mines of the Caribbean and Americas to the period of the greatest expansion of European empires across the globe and associated urbanization and industrialization of the eighteenth and nineteenth centuries. Elsewhere, Jason Moore has theorized the complex and inextricable set of relations between the instatement of plantations, mining of minerals, metals, and fuels, and industrialization as 'capitalism in the web of life' (2015). Though the histories of plantations and mines are indeed inseparable, there was nevertheless a marked shift from the predominantly plantation-based economies established in the fifteenth century to the capitalist–imperialist industrial economies of the nineteenth century. A coincident shift in geographies of power meant that as the Spanish and Portuguese empires receded, a coal-fuelled Britain stepped in to open up new frontiers for resource extraction. As Kenneth Pomeranz explains, 'Europe's overseas extraction' and 'the fruits of overseas exploitation were probably roughly as important to at least Britain's economic transformation as its epochal turn to fossil fuels' (2000: 23). Expounding on the relationships between colonialism and landscape beyond horizontality, Heidi V. Scott writes that 'the dimension of verticality' is 'manifest in practices concerned with the subterranean, such as mining' (2008: 1853). Indeed, the Industrial Revolution altered the balance of world power, which had associated effects on global environments as fuels, minerals, and metals from deep underground began to be extracted on industrial scales. By the nineteenth century, then, colonization extended both *across* landmasses and *down* into the earth.

Diamond Mining in Olive Schreiner's **Undine**

Though the use of steam power in mining was introduced in the seventeenth century, the subsequent centuries saw major technological advances that made larger-scale resource extraction possible. Britain was at the forefront of these activities, as the leading global power with overseas territories that comprised the largest global empire in history. Coal was the primary source of energy production, and the fuel was used in steam-powered water pumps, new forms of transport, and in mills. With the Industrial Revolution accelerating apace, and powered by coal mined on home shores, it was Britain's colonies and dominions that provided a number of new sites for other forms of extraction. From mica and manganese in India, to rubies in Burma (now Myanmar), graphite in Ceylon (now Sri Lanka), copper and gold in mainland Australia, tin in Tasmania, and cobalt and nickel in Canada, Britain extracted a wealth of global mineral and metal resources in the pursuit of capitalist growth (Stokes, 1908). In colonial South Africa, gold and diamond mining proved particularly lucrative, but '[u]nlike many other colonial situations', Daniel Roux explains, 'capital did not simply flow out of the country, but was also deployed to consolidate a cultural and economic infrastructure in South Africa' (2013: n.p.). As a result, he writes, 'a capitalist imaginary was developing right alongside the actual extraction of wealth, which was a process that involved the interlocking devastation of South African lifeworlds and damage to the environment' (n.p.). South Africa's shift from an agrarian to an industrializing nation in the late nineteenth and early twentieth centuries can be described in world-systems terms as the transition from 'periphery' to 'semi-periphery', or what Immanuel Wallerstein dubs 'the *middle* stratum [...] both exploited and exploiter' (1974: 405, original emphasis). As such, South Africa developed key features associated with 'periphery' nations exploited for their raw materials and labour alongside features associated with the industrialized nations that comprised the 'core'. These were divided along racial lines, creating the combined unevenness of economic life required of the semi-periphery.

The story of South Africa's mines begins with the 1867 discovery of a huge diamond at New Rush (now Kimberley), which initiated the Mineral

Revolution and South Africa's transition from a predominantly agricultural nation to an industrializing, urbanizing nation with a resource-based economy. The next few years saw a huge influx of diggers, all keen to claim their own plots of land. Amongst them was a prospector named Theo Schreiner, who arrived at the Diamond Fields in 1870 intent on staking a claim at Du Toit's Pan. He was accompanied by his sister, Ettie, and they were joined in 1873 by another sibling, Olive, who would later become famous as South Africa's first novelist. It was whilst Olive Schreiner was living with Theo and Ettie than she first undertook sustained efforts to write novels, and in her first (abandoned) attempt, *Undine: A Queer Little Child* (published posthumously in 1929), she provides the earliest South African-authored literary account of life in the Diamond Fields.

In the novel, the eponymous protagonist travels to the 'crowded streets' (1929: 203) of New Rush (the camp next to Du Toit's Pan), where she lives in poverty, scraping a living by ironing clothes. One evening as she views 'the camp below [...] aglow with evening lights, and the noise and stir in its tents and streets became louder and stronger', she decides to walk up 'the Kop' (the site of the mine) (204). Surrounded by the 'mountains of gravel' and 'high-piled gravel heaps' of debris dug from the ground, it feels to Undine 'like entering the city of the dead in the land of the living' (204). This is a 'frontier' zone, which Patel and Moore introduce as 'the encounter zones between capital and all kinds of nature' (2018: 18, 22) and Michael Niblett explains 'as zones of extraction or production that reorganize human and bio-physical natures in such a way as to send vast reservoirs of relatively "cheap" food, energy, raw materials and labour-power into the capitalist world-economy' (2020: 3). 'The extension of capitalist power to new, uncommodified spaces' (2015: 63), in Moore's words, is evident in Schreiner's New Rush in its overcrowded, denuded landscapes. New Rush thus appears as both labour frontier and waste frontier, in which 'rising capital intensity' is made possible 'by accelerating the place-specific exhaustion of profitability' (2015: 115). The piles of rubble waste (known as tailings) and rows of hastily assembled and overcrowded tent accommodation in New Rush create a ghostly colonial imitation of the rapidly emerging and expanding industrial cities in core nations such as Britain. As such, the capital intensification represented in the 1870s New Rush setting of *Undine* is marked by both the swelling labour forces and rising towers of waste to create 'the city of the dead'.

The phrase 'city of the dead' also functions as an expression of the very real threats to life in New Rush. Moore explains how frontiers are 'necessary for the commodity-oriented appropriation of unpaid work/energy [...] delivered by humans – women or slaves, for example – or by extra-human natures, such as forests, soils or rivers' (2015: 63). Indeed in the Diamond Fields, it is the exploited majority Black workers as well as soils, minerals, and metals, that are pressed into the service of the accumulation of capital, bringing with it long-term damage to ecosystems, illness, injury, and death. Between 1897 and 1899, 5,368 of 7,853 patients admitted to Kimberley hospital were Black, and 1,144 died. Hospital admissions were mostly due to mining accidents, as well as tuberculosis, pneumonia, scurvy, diarrhoea, and syphilis caused by overcrowding, poor accommodation, the extreme poverty of the precarious labourers, lack of access to (suitable) nutrition, and other associated ill-health effects of land, water, and air pollution caused by open-pit mining.

Undine's first vision of the mine (known locally as the 'Big Hole') is described as follows:

> She walked to the edge of the reef and looked down into the crater. The thousand wires that crossed it, glistening in the moonlight, formed a weird, sheeny, mistlike veil over the black depths beneath. Very dark, very deep it lay all round the edge, but high towering into the bright moonlight rose the unworked centre. She crouched down at the foot of the staging and sat looking at it. In the magic of the moonlight it was a giant castle, a castle of the olden knightly days; you might swear, as you gazed on it, that you saw the shadows of its castellated battlements, and the endless turrets that overcrowned it; a giant castle, lulled to sleep and bound in silence for a thousand years by the word of some enchanter. You might gaze until you almost saw the ivy clinging to its yellow, crumbling walls, till you almost saw the figures of brave knights and lovely ladies, whom the death-like sleep had overtaken as they wandered on the castle terraces, till the motionless horse and the small arched window and the mighty dragon resting in the gateway were all visible.
>
> (1929: 204)

By isolating Undine's view of the Big Hole from the mass of people and noise of the day, Schreiner endeavours to evoke the initial lure of the gem-stones for those drawn to the Diamond Fields. She imagines the 'unworked centre' of the crater as a Medieval or Sleeping Beauty's castle, birthed from the depths of the earth to promise riches. As she falls asleep, this vision slips into a dream. By daylight, however, the spell is broken. Undine is woken by the sound of 'the turning of the wheel overhead', a steam-powered machine used to haul stone and soils out of the mine, and although '[i]t was hardly light, [...] the Kop wakes early, and there were many men at work already among the staging' (205). By daylight, the mine loses its magic and allure: '[i]t was nothing now but a great oval hole in the ground where worshippers of King Gold burrow and scrape and scratch, all in his service' (205). The personification of gold as sovereign and spiritual leader here invokes the combined roles of the British monarch as head of the nation, empire, and Church of England. The hypocrisies of nationalistic pride, patriotism, and the 'civilizing mission' are thus thrown into sharp relief by the all-pervading and unceasing human and environmental costs of capitalist–imperial accumulation; whilst the representation of the diggers as an anonymous mass of zoo-morphized creatures burrowing, scraping, and scratching illustrates in no uncertain terms the dehumanizing effects of extractivist labour on the colonial frontier.

Schreiner also illustrates the deadly consequences of the mining industry in explicit ways, by depicting the decline in health of two male arrivals to the Diamond Fields. Undine first meets Mr Brown on board a ship to South Africa: 'a boy he seemed in his perfect enjoyment of life in spite of his rich brown beard, the only glad, childish thing on board' (154). After a few weeks in New Rush, his 'long arms [...] seemed hardly strong enough to raise themselves, still less to handle sieve or pick' (226), he has 'a long hollow cough', 'heavy eyes' (227), and '[h]e was completely broken down, said the doctor, with hard work and bad living' (229). Although '[t]he doctor did not give much hope of his recovery' (229), Undine is able to nurse him back to health, and sells her Aunt Margaret's diamond ring to buy him passage back to England. Undine's great love, Albert Blair, does not survive New Rush, however. When Undine asks his servant 'What did your master die of?' (243), he replies:

> 'I don't just rightly know. He came here just to have a look at everything, and he took ill, something wrong inside [...] and this six months he's been lying here, and they've been saying he was going to die, but never did till last night'.
>
> (244)

Though the servant claims not to know the reason for Albert's decline, Schreiner makes clear that his death is attributable to the rapidly denuding environs of the Diamond Fields, where overpopulation, strained water and food supplies, inadequate waste disposal, and dust and air pollution generated by increased numbers of people and the processes of open-pit mining caused rapid declines in human and environmental health.

For the young Schreiner, who understood the expansion of empire as an inherently patriarchal pursuit, the alternative to extractive capitalism, masculine competition, environmental degradation, and the exploitation of cheap female labour enacted in the New Rush setting of *Undine* comes in the form of female solidarity, friendship, nurture, and protection. Undine befriends the young, mixed-race disabled child, Diogenes, who has a broken back as a result of a beating by her mother. As one of the authors of this book, Jade Munslow Ong, explains in an earlier publication, Diogenes is named 'after Diogenes of Sinope a key founder of Cynic philosophy' who lived as a dog (2018: 49). So too is Schreiner's Diogenes 'ignored by the other inhabitants of New Rush and treated like a stray dog' because her age and disability mean 'that she is unable to take part in the patterns of economic life in New Rush' (49). Undine, however, takes an interest in the child and, on first meeting, is amazed to find her holding 'the tiniest of rose slips, not half an inch high and crowned with two tiny green leaves' (1929: 208). Undine tells Diogenes that it is 'the first flower I have seen growing here' (209). She begins to visit Diogenes regularly, caring for her by telling her allegories and rubbing her sore back. When a 'deep-bosomed red rosebud' appears on the plant, Diogenes insists that Undine '[p]ick it; it's for you. No – you must not pick it. I will – and fasten it in your hair' (239). Where imperial diamonds are usually given by male to female characters in the form of engagement rings in Schreiner's fiction, thus solidifying the idea of marriage as economic exchange and means of gendered oppression, here a very different kind of earth-borne riches are shared. The exchange of plant life between women expresses inter-racial, cross-generational female friendship and love that come from cultivation rather than exploitative extraction.

By directly addressing the effects of mining and mining economies on women, children, and environments, *Undine* breaks new ground by departing from established representations of masculinized extractivism on the colonial frontier (as exemplified by near-contemporaneous works such as Robert Louis Stevenson's *Treasure Island* (1883), H. Rider Haggard's *King Solomon's Mines* (1885), and Joseph Conrad's *Heart of Darkness* (1899)). And yet, whilst the feminist vision expressed by Schreiner – which was developed at such a young age and with limited resources – is undeniably astounding, *Undine* falls far short of directly and meaningfully addressing the key issues at stake, namely the racist exploitation of labour, the dispossession of land, and the environmental degradation that made the colonial mining industry possible. Indeed, racist representations abound in Schreiner's juvenile text, and – with the exception of Diogenes – *Undine* represents only white lives, animals, and plants as truly valuable and at risk. It was only in later adulthood that Schreiner was able to more fully realize the inseparability of issues of race, capitalism, and the environment in South Africa and beyond. As a result, Schreiner was virtually 'alone' amongst her peers in 'recogni[zing] that the colour question was really the labour question, and that labour, both Black and white, could not be free unless it was united' (1990: 338), write her biographers Ruth First and Ann Scott. And, as 'this African mass organization was beginning only as Olive died' (340), it would take the struggles of the next generations of predominantly Black activists and freedom fighters to bring about the end of colonial/minority rule in South Africa.

Gold Mining in Peter Abrahams' Mine Boy

The intensified diamond speculation that began when Schreiner was writing in the 1870s was increasingly controlled by colonial governments that put in place legislation to end Black ownership of claims. In addition, the increased colonial annexation of land forced the majority population of Black Africans into smaller and smaller 'native reserves', and into a migrant work system that would lay the foundations for the organization and exploitation of Black South African labour in the apartheid years of the twentieth century. By 1872 there were over 10,000 Africans employed at the Fields, and by 1889, when Cecil Rhodes had a monopoly on Kimberley diamonds through the

DeBeers Consolidated Mines, the precarious labour workforce was almost entirely Black, and housed in prison-like compounds. South Africa's transition from an agrarian to a resource-dominated economy in the late-nineteenth century was, Elizabeth Carolyn Miller writes, 'marked by warfare, labor migration, and riotous speculation; after diamonds, gold was discovered in 1869, then coal in 1887', and '[t]he infrastructures of mining, finance and transport meant that one extractible commodity led to another, until the land was overrun with investors and engineers in quest of underground mineral wealth' (2021: 91). The Glen Grey Act of 1894 followed, as did various commissions and provincial legislations, and then the passing of the Native Land Act ensured that by 1913 the Black population of South Africa – which comprised 80 percent of the total population – was only able to legally inhabit 7 percent of the land (later slightly increased to 13 percent).

The racially segregated migrant work structure that had been implemented at Kimberley provided both model and method for the organization of labour on new ore fields, including at Witwatersrand after gold was discovered in 1884. The associated Pass system that was used to direct and monitor the movements of workers in the diamond, gold, and coal mines was expanded over the decades via Pass Laws to become the coercive machinery for labour supply nationwide, which in turn became the basis for the apartheid pass system that came later.[3] These systems for organizing and controlling labour had hugely damaging socio-ecological effects, so that previously small-scale and sustainable indigenous farming and hunting practices were no longer possible with the new division of land. Only able to occupy the least habitable, least fertile, and now overcrowded rural areas, Black South Africans were unable to sustain traditional livelihoods, lifeways, even lives. Without space to graze their cattle, many men were no longer able to provide bride price or set up family homes, and so were forced into indentured labour in the mines. Women, meanwhile, undertook unpaid labour raising children at home, whilst trying to maintain food supplies on eroding soils in ever-decreasing areas of land.

In *Undine*, Schreiner prioritizes discussion of white lives, and introduces feminist ideas as the means to mitigate and counter the effects of patriarchal forms of control, environmental degradation, and the exploitation of women and girls in the Diamond Fields. Yet her understanding and representation of extractive capitalism remain in many ways at surface level. Indeed in her work on other *fin de siècle* literatures, Miller asks: 'Why such narrative resistance to entering the mine or pit itself?' (86). By mid-century, this question was beginning to be answered, including in *Mine Boy* (1946) by South African writer, Peter Abrahams.[4] Abrahams' novel follows the migrant worker, Xuma, who travels to Malay Camp, a township area of Johannesburg, in search of employment. He finds a place to stay in a shebeen run by the formidable Leah, and a job at a nearby mine. His first day at work is described as follows:

> There was the rumbling noise and the shouting and the explosions and the tremblings of the earth. And always the shouting indunas driving the

men on to work. And over all those was the bitter eyes and hardness of the white man who had told him to push the truck when he did not know how. But these were not the worst. These were confusing and frightening. It was the strangeness of it all that terrified him. And the look in the eyes of the other men who worked with him. He had seen that look before when he was at home on the farms. He had seen it when he herded his cattle and when a dog came among the sheep and barked. The eyes of these men were like the eyes of the sheep that did not know where to run when the dog barked. It was this that frightened him.

([1946] 1989: 41)

In this passage, the personification of the 'trembling' earth and a simile in which the workers are described as sheep harried by dogs negates any sense of human exceptionalism or individuality, and breaks down the distinctions between humans, animals, and minerals, so that all are constructed as natural resources. Moore explains that 'capitalism was built on excluding most *humans* from Humanity – Indigenous peoples, enslaved Africans, nearly all women, and even many white-skinned men (Slavs, Jews, the Irish)', and as such, '[t]hey were regarded as part of Nature, along with trees and soils and rivers – and treated accordingly' (2016: 79). This performs, in Moore's words, a 'special kind of "work" for the modern world. Backed by imperial power and capitalist rationality, it mobilized the unpaid work and energy of humans [...] in service to transforming landscapes with a singular purpose: the endless accumulation of capital' (79). In *Mine Boy*, Abrahams reveals the dehumanizing processes of extractive capitalism, what Thuto Thipe describes as 'existential loss and an internal dislocation that wears away at their humanity' (2022: 222) to show how, in the context of the goldmines, white owners and overseers are conceptualized as Human whereas the Black workers are, as Moore indicates, constructed as 'part of Nature'. And so, '[i]nstead of asking what capitalism *does to* nature' writes Moore, 'we may begin to ask how nature *works for* capitalism?' (2015: 12). This in turn enables a shift in thinking towards an understanding of capitalism as 'a world-ecology that joins the accumulation of capital, the pursuit of power, and the co-production of nature in successive historical configurations' (2016: 7).

Goldmining is described by the environmental group Earthworks as 'one of the most destructive industries in the world', and they calculate that the creation of one 18 karat 0.33oz gold ring produces 20 tons of waste.[5] A sense of the processes of goldmining and the scale of waste produced is conveyed in *Mine Boy* in the description of tailing-creating labour:

And one little truck after another, loaded with fine wet white sand, was pushed up the incline to where a new minedump was being born. But as fast as they moved the sand, so fast did the pile grow. A truck load would go and another would come from the bowels of the earth. And another would go and another would come. And another. And yet another. So it went on all day long. On and on and on and on.

[...] Another would come. Another would go.... All day long.... And for all their sweating and hard breathing and for the redness of their eyes and the emptiness of their stare there would be nothing to show. In the morning the pile had been so big. Now it was the same. And the mine-dump did not seem to grow either. It was this that frightened Xuma. This seeing of nothing for a man's work.

([1946] 1989: 41–42)

The repetition of words, anaphora, metrical monosyllables, and short sentences express the relentless, mechanical, and unfulfilling nature of the digging, loading, and shifting of earth in search of gold. The Black labourers move into cavities deeper and deeper underground, as the rocks and sand are elevated from the depths to create huge tailings that rise above the surface level of the earth. As Chris Thurman explains, the mountainous mine dumps in and around Johannesburg 'all too obviously represent exploitation, oppression, inequality and degradation' (2022: 30). This is certainly the case in Abrahams' novel, as the dumps are described as 'huge towering shadowy shapes that reared their heads to the sky' ([1946] 1989: 25), '[a] mountain of white sand made by black men' (26), and '[d]ark, shadowy figures, towering up to the sky' (128). Representing the unearthed evidence of exploited labour, environmental degradation, and barriers to racial equality, and instilling a sense of entrapment and threat, the tailings act as constant reminders that Black oppression and exploitation built, and loom over, the expanding cities. '[M]ine dump aesthetics', writes Thurman, thus collapse 'the binary opposition of rural and urban, of natural and artificial, of transcendent beauty and mundane ugliness, [...] the political (that which has to do with the polis, both the city and the citizens) and the nonpolitical' (2022: 30). At almost any given point in Abrahams' novel, the characters can see both 'the mine dumps towering against the sky, and in the opposite direction they could see the tall buildings of Johannesburg' (171–72). This juxtaposition of the waste-product mountains created through the exploitation of humans and/as Nature, and the city built using mine-generated wealth, creates a sense of the unevenness of life in the semi-periphery, so that the towering tailings become metonyms of the city.

The human and environmental costs of the mining industry are not only educed in the depiction of Johannesburg and its surrounding townships as labour- and waste-frontiers, but in the ill health of the workers. When Xuma first arrives in Malay Camp, he is warned by Leah that '[t]he mines are no good, Xuma, later on you cough and then you spit blood and you become weak and die. [...] To-day you are young and you are strong, and to-morrow you are thin and ready to die' ([1946] 1989: 5). The causes of illness and death in miners are attributable to a range of causes beyond the back-breaking and precarious labour, overwork, undernourishment, poor housing, overcrowding, and poor sanitation experienced by the workers. Cyanide was used to extract gold on the Rand for the first time in 1890 and, as a highly toxic and deadly substance, is a key pollutant – along with arsenic, lead, mercury, copper, zinc, petroleum byproducts, selenium, cadmium, and acids – of mining environs globally. Today, still, the minedumps contain radioactive waste, and Johannesburg is described by water expert Antony Turton as 'the most uranium-contaminated city in the world' (2015: 120). Winds transport dust and toxic substances around a city of 1.5 million people, blanketing huge areas, and causing respiratory and skin disorders amongst the population, most particularly amongst the poorer communities who live close to, even on, the minedumps.

At the end of the novel, Xuma leads a miners' strike – an act of resistance against the exploitation of Black workers. This is prompted by the deaths of his friends, Chris and Johannes, who die to save their escaping colleagues by staying behind to hold up the crumbling walls of a mine as it collapses. After Xuma and the Irish overseer, Paddy, retrieve the bodies of their friends, two engineers declare that the collapse is '[n]othing serious. If those fellows had kept their heads and stayed where they were instead of panicking and trying to keep the place open with their bodies, everything would have been alright' ([1946] 1989: 180). The manager of the mine immediately orders the workers back underground, though Xuma protests: 'We warned you about that thing a long time ago [...] They said it was all right. Now two men are dead! Good men! Let them fix it up first then we will go down!' (180–81). As the manager presses on, Xuma feels 'good suddenly. Strong and free. A man', and shouts in response: 'It does not matter if our skins are black! We are not cattle to throw away our lives!' (181). Now challenging the construction of Black workers as Nature to be pressed into the service of the accumulation of capital, Xuma asserts the humanity of his friends and colleagues. Met with the force of Xuma's strength and leadership, the white manager responds with the threat of violence: 'This is a strike! [...] You will go to jail! I have called the police!' (181).

The context of writing and publication is particularly important here, as *Mine Boy* was published in 1946, shortly after the end of the Second World War and the ground-breaking Fifth Pan-African Congress in Manchester, a city whose cotton industry grew out of the slave trade in the eighteenth and nineteenth centuries. Abrahams co-organized the Congress alongside Caribbean writer and activist George Padmore, Guyanese activists T. Ras Makonnen and Peter Milliard, and future President of Ghana, Kwame Nkrumah; delegates included Jamaican feminist Amy Ashwood Garvey, as well as other future African presidents of independent nations Jomo Kenyatta (Kenya) and Hastings Banda (Malawi). The conference, like Abrahams himself, was internationalist, anti-colonial, and anti-racist in its outlook and aims and helped to set in motion the mass decolonization of Africa in the second half of the twentieth century.

Importantly, too, 1946 was also the year of the first major miners' strike in South Africa.[6] These accelerating decolonial and workers' rights movements overlapped in some ways though, as Megan Jones points out, 'the mismatch of

Marxism and liberalism' in *Mine Boy* 'produces a somewhat tangled politics' (2012: 203). The uneasy combination of political trajectories in the novel is true to the real developments and debates in raising Black consciousness and counteracting the power of the state in the period, and is captured in the imperfect but impassioned cross-racial friendship between Xuma and the Irish overseer, Paddy. Paddy is the first to rise in support of Xuma when he challenges the manager of the mine. Paddy's nickname, 'the Red One' (1989: 35) marks him out, in Jones' words, as 'the fictional equivalent of white socialists involved in African trade unions' (213), who shares with Xuma 'a commonality anchored in shared experiences of (British) colonisation' (212). Paddy declares:

> 'Zuma is right! They pay you a little! They don't care if you risk your lives! Why is it so? Is not the blood of a black man red like that of a white man? Does not a black man feel too? Does not a black man love life too? I am with you!'
>
> (181–182)

Though Paddy's mispronunciation of Xuma's name misses the click sound that accompanies the 'X' in various Southern African languages, thereby expressing a gap in understanding that remains a barrier to cross-racial alliance, the expression here of comradeship founded on socialist principles is asserted as the most effective available class action for challenging capitalist–imperial extractivism in this context.

For Xuma as for Paddy, emerging consciousness and true freedom require thinking outside of the systems of power predicated on categories of race. Xuma thus conceptualizes freedom as being '[s]trong enough to be a man without colour' (181) as '[p]eople were people. Not white and Black people. Just people. Ordinary people' (174). This non-racialized understanding of a shared humanity is Xuma's epiphanic moment, and following one final flight through Malay Camp to tell his lover Maisy of his plans, he declares: 'The Red One's in jail. I must go there too' (183). Xuma explains to Maisy that he

> want[s] to tell them how I feel. [...] It is good that a black man must tell the white people how we feel. And also, a black man must tell the black people how they feel and what they want. These things I must do, and then I will feel like a man. You understand?
>
> (183)

Xuma asserts the humanity of the 'black man', in contrast to the earlier representations of the mineworkers as animals. The point he makes about communication across boundaries of race is offered as a solution to the racist and extractivist interactions represented in the novel. This is an unrealized vision, however, as just like in the real Miners' Strikes that took place in 1946, the workers in the novel are met with police brutality, and forced back into the mines.

Though the focus remains with the workers, whose primary concerns are of course with health and safety, and securing adequate and secured pay for food and shelter for themselves and their families, the environmental consequences of mining are less obviously, but still visibly, intertwined. The human and environmental costs of metal and mineral mining in South Africa, as elsewhere on the continent, continue to proliferate. The Kimberley Process Certification Scheme introduced in 2000 has yet to halt the sales and circulation of conflict or blood diamonds, which fund crimes against humanity, war crimes, and human rights abuses. The use of extreme violence in response to miners' strikes has also continued through the years, and was starkly demonstrated in the 2012 Marikana Massacre in South Africa in which 34 striking miners were shot dead by police. At the same time, the 'slow violence' (2011), in Rob Nixon's terms, of the intensive mining of minerals and metals continues to prove highly damaging and deadly to South African lives and environments, resulting in soil erosion, the forced migration of humans and animals, species endangerment, water overuse, water pollution from acid mine drainage, rising acid water tables, hundreds of huge toxic minedumps containing billions of tonnes of waste, air pollution in the form of toxic dust blown from the tailings, and huge water-filled open-pit mines that give rise to water-borne diseases and provide breeding grounds for mosquitoes carrying disease-causing viruses and parasites. The underground mines that lie buried beneath thus continue to affect the land, water, air, and lives at the surface. In a South Africa in which the 'Big Hole' depicted in Schreiner's *Undine* is now, in Roux's words, 'completely commodified – it is Kimberley's premier tourist attraction' (2013, n.p.), and in which thousands of people continue to live on and amongst the minedumps described in Abrahams' novel, it is as important as ever to return to the lessons of earlier anti-colonial, feminist, workers' union, and Pan-African struggles to resist extractive capitalism, and find ways to realize liveable futures.

Oil

In this final section of our chapter 'Earth', we examine how John McGrath's play *The Cheviot, the Stag and the Black, Black Oil* (1973) dramatizes in focalized and localized ways the effects of shifting commodity frontiers and changing forms of extractive capitalism for the Scottish Highlands, Highlanders, and Scottish diaspora across the eighteenth through to the twentieth centuries. The play shows how processes of capitalism profoundly reconfigure humans and animals as resources in order to dispossess Indigenous peoples of their land, enable mass monocultural farming and hunting of select species, and establish hydrocarbon industries that together and cumulatively cause extensive socio-ecological damage in Scotland and beyond. The play spans the period from the Highland Clearances of the 1750s–1860s, to the rise of empire, wars, and blood-sports of the leisure classes in the nineteenth century, the emerging Scottish tourism sector of the twentieth century, and finally to the 1962 discovery of oil in the North Sea and development of the oil industry in Scotland. Though we touch briefly on the stages of Scottish history represented by the 'Cheviot' and 'Stag', our analysis here concentrates most closely on the play's representation of the mid-twentieth century energy transition to oil, which also serves as the title of this chapter section. In this way, we follow Macdonald in reading *The Cheviot* 'as an important text of world theatre' (2015: 62) that illustrates the combined and uneven development of global capitalism in the world-system, and as 'petro-drama' (54) that moves us as readers/audiences across and between linked commodity frontiers: from soil to oil.

Over the last 20 years or so, leading figures such as Macdonald, as well as Imre Szeman, Dominic Boyer, Stephanie LeMenager, and Michael Niblett have greatly expanded our awareness and understanding of literary representations of what Amitav Ghosh dubs the 'Oil Encounter' (1992: 29). Now, the increasing number of works gathered under the sign of 'petroliterature' include novels, short stories, poems, comics, ficto-criticism, and various other mediums that demonstrate wide-ranging global literary investments in representing the operations, inequalities, and consequences of the oil economy.[7] It has taken some effort on the part of those working in the literary strand of the energy humanities to conceptualize, compile, group, and revive well-known, marginal, and marginalized works as petro-texts, however, because as Macdonald explains, 'oil secrecy' has been expertly 'managed by the occlusion tactics of state-corporate alliances' (2015: 45), and as Szeman and Boyer elucidate further, oil's pervasive-yet-invisible presence has enabled it 'to hide in plain sight/site, evading inclusion in our economic calculations as much as in our literary fiction' (2017: 6). Even as early as 1929 Bertolt Brecht expressed this struggle over representation in the phrase: 'petroleum resists the five act form; today's catastrophes do not progress in a straight line but in cyclical crises' (1964: 30), thus deploying petroleum as an icon to evoke the challenge of trying to represent in writing and performance the boom–bust cycles of capitalist modernity.

The Cheviot, however, offers a response to this challenge, answering what Lara Stevens calls a 'need' created by our 'globally industrialised world' for 'theatrical forms that can show how conflict and power struggles over petroleum also fuel widespread class-based social, economic and political inequalities and injustices' (2016: 28–29), to which we add here: environmental inequalities and injustices too. McGrath multiply integrates genres and forms that combine dialogue, dramatic speech, dance, chorus, storytelling, song, poem, historical records, the alienation effects of Brecht's Epic Theatre, and generic conventions from music hall, Ceilidh, anti-naturalism, pantomime, and Variety, to create political theatre that 'fulfil[s] the role of agitation on an ideological level within the working class' by paying 'a certain amount of attention to working-class forms of entertainment' (2002: 118). The hybrid, multi-generic forms and methods deployed in *The Cheviot* make capitalist frontiers (including the oil frontier) visible in their operations, enabling what Macdonald describes as the play's '"shocking" plot moves'

(2015: 21). These are both effective and affective 'precisely because the experience it relates *is* shocking and unsettling. This is a story of displacement and cultural dissonance rendered dramatically; a theatre of displacement that intends to register the distress and uprooting consonant with capitalist modernity itself' (21). The play thus brings to life what Macdonald has elsewhere called 'an aesthetics of oil' that 'can be uncovered by comparing the recurring motifs, systemic connections and structures of feeling produced by oil modernity' (2017: 291). This is evidenced in *The Cheviot* by the songs, phrases, images, and ideas that are returned to and repeated throughout, theatrically constructing the rise–fall patterns, 'crises', and 'catastrophes' of capitalist modernity that both Brecht and McGrath consider unrepresented in, and unrepresentable by, traditional theatre forms.

Clearances and Colonialism: the Cheviot and the Stag

The Cheviot opens during the Highland Clearances, when landowners in Scotland, most notably the Duke and Duchess of Sutherland, evicted their tenants to make way for mass monocultural farming of the cheviot sheep. In discussing the play's development, McGrath explained that he 'wanted to write a specific piece about the clearances, and at that time the whole monstrosity of the oil exploitation in the north of Scotland, particularly the onshore developments connected with oil' (2002: 54). The cheviot, stag, and oil thus figure as icons of connected resource frontiers. This is made clear in the closing statements, delivered by alternating members of the Company, to show how processes of capitalism associated with the three title topics are interconnected, repeat, and replicate across the broad historical and geographical spans represented in the play:

> Then it was the Great Sheep
> Now it is the black black oil.
> Then it was done by outside capital, with the connivance of the local ruling class and central government.
> [...]
> Now it is being done by outside capital, with the connivance of the local ruling class and central government.
> [...]
> When the Cheviot came, only the landlords benefited.
> When the Stag came, only the upper-class sportsmen benefited.
> Now the Black Black Oil is coming.
>
> (2015: 162)

McGrath's mapping of the repeating patterns of capitalist frontiers means that oil emerges in the final part of the play as merely the next and newest twentieth-century economic base for recurring, accelerating, and accumulating struggles relating to land, animals, and people in the Highlands and British colonies.

The interconnected loss of forested areas, introduction of monocultural farming, land dispossession, and extreme violence that characterized the soil-based commodity frontiers we earlier discussed in relation to the Caribbean and US are again evident in the first part of *The Cheviot*, as eighteenth and nineteenth century landowners pursued agricultural wealth at the cost of human suffering, displacements, deaths, and environmental denudation in the Highlands. The second part of the play then shows how the expansion of the British Empire in the nineteenth century meant that many displaced Highlanders became displacing forces themselves through imperial emigration to colonies such as Canada. Here they worked on farms and ranches, in the timber and construction trades, on railways and in mines, contributing to environmental degradation abroad whilst reducing First Nations peoples 'to the same state as our fathers […] defeated, hunted, treated like the scum of the earth, their culture polluted and torn out with slow deliberation and their land no longer their own' (2015: 114). The profits generated by colonialism in turn enabled the British elite to extend their blood-sports across species and locations, including to great estates in the Highlands where they fished and hunted pheasant, grouse, trout, salmon, and red deer. The first two parts of the play, then, show how in Highlands and British colonial history, people were repeatedly replaced by more 'valuable' resources: by the animals killed for meat, wool, sport, and trophies, or by other human populations better positioned to accumulate wealth for the Empire. At the same time, *The Cheviot* attests to how resistance to these forces of global capitalism came from below in the form of the Glen-Calvie, Strathoykel, Sollas, Greenyards, Knockan, Elphin, and Coigeach women who fought their evictors during the Clearances (95–98); the successful rent strikers in the Braes (115–122); and the Sutherland tenants who refused conscription to the Crimean War, telling the Duke that 'We have no country to fight for. You robbed us of our country and gave it to the sheep' (133).

The introduction of lucrative mass farming of sheep was in part made possible because of deforestation – Scotland's woodland cover reached historic lows as the Clearances began. We know now too that sheep farming has significant ecological impacts: a single sheep creates around 30 litres of methane per day, intensive grazing leads to soil erosion and landslips, sheep displace other species leading to decreased biodiversity, and their excrement pollutes land and water leading to the eutrophication of water systems. The extent of the damage they cause has led environmental journalist George Monbiot to describe the British Isles as 'sheepwrecked' (2014: 153), to which 'deerwrecked' may be added for a specifically Scottish context. As we also showed in our case studies on South African literature earlier in this chapter, Britain's increasing reliance on coal for energy generation in the eighteenth and nineteenth centuries enabled steam-powered industrial and technological advancements that supported, and were supported by, capitalist extraction of minerals and metals in the colonies. In John Mackenzie's 1974 BBC TV film adaptation of *The Cheviot*, performed by the original 7:84 Theatre Company, nineteenth-century imperial wealth is shown to have disastrous effects on home soils too, as an overhead shot of running deer is accompanied by the voiceover: 'And then suddenly: the stag. Thousands of herds of red deer were reared to provide sport for the gentry. The Highlands became Queen Victoria's own, and in her wake came the upper classes of Europe intent on slaughter' (44:00). Still today, less than 500 people own 50 percent of Scotland's private land, and deer stalking is worth over £100 million annually. Deer management therefore remains a major concern in Scotland. The animals trample vegetation underfoot and strip bark from trees, inhibiting woodland expansion and damaging peatlands and moorland ecosystems, whilst also causing vehicle accidents and collisions, and increasing risk and incidence of Lyme disease.

Tourism and Petrocapitalism

Though the environmental impacts of the cheviot and stag in the Highlands are not always made explicit in the play, they provide the context for the third stage of Scottish history that it represents, which focuses on the socio-ecological ravages wrought by the hydrocarbon economy in the twentieth century. *The Cheviot* shows how, over the eighteenth and nineteenth centuries, Scottish peoples, animals, and plants were profoundly reconfigured as either resource or waste, and so were divested of land or habitat, displaced and eradicated to enable various and connected processes of capitalist extraction and degradation to take place. As the play moves into the twentieth century, 'an Academic' arrives on stage to outline how the 'Highlands and Islands Development Board' then sought to advertise Scotland as 'a land of solitary splendour – mountains, lochs and glens of unrivalled beauty add a sharper poignancy to the scattered stones of the ruined crofting townships' (2015: 134–135). Now emptied of its Indigenous peoples, animals, and culture, 'the tragedy of the Highlands has become a saleable commodity' (135), explains the Academic. The play still manages to keep multiple frontiers in view, however, so that the rise of the tourism industry, represented by the comedic and stereotyped '*Glasgow Property-operator's man*' (135) Andy McChuckemup, overlaps and coincides with both the old imperial regimes and emerging petrocapitalism. McChuckemup attempts to buy land from an inebriated Lord Vat (whose name recalls both tax and barrels of whiskey), to which Lord Vat replies:

LORD VAT: No amount of money could compensate for the disruption of the couthie way of life that has gone on here uninterrupted for yonks. Your Bantu – I mean your Highlander – is a dignified sort of chap, conservative to the core. From time immemorial, they have proved excellent servants – the gels in the kitchen, your sherpar – I mean your stalker – marvellously surefooted on the hills, your ghillie-wallah tugging the forelock, doing up your flies – you won't find people like that anywhere else in the world, I wouldn't part with all this even if you were to offer me half a million pounds.

(136–137)

Lord Vat betrays his entrenched colonial racism in the slippages between the African Bantu and/as Highlander, the Himalayan sherpas and/as deer stalkers, and the conflated 'ghillie-wallah' that combines the Gaelic term for an attendant on a hunting expedition with a Hindi word used by English colonists to refer to manual labourers and servants. In so doing, he reveals the workings of complex and connected commodity chains that stretch across time and place, so that even as ascending frontiers of capital introduce new socio-ecological pressures, existing systems of power can facilitate their rise and remain in place to sustain long-standing pressures of their own.

McChuckemup announces the advent of the tourism industry in the Highlands by taking the microphone to declare 'the motel' as 'the thing of the future' (135). He goes on:

ANDY: So – picture it, if yous will, right there at the top of the glen, beautiful vista – the Crammem Inn, High Rise Motorcroft – all finished in natural, washable, plastic granitette. Right next door, the 'Frying Scotsman'.

All Night Chipperama – with a wee ethnic bit, Fingal's Caff – serving seaweed-suppers-in-the-basket, and draught Drambuie. And to cater for the younger set, yous've got your Grouse-a-go-go. [...] So – picture it, if yous will – a drive-in clachan on every hill-top where formerly there was hee-haw but scenery.

(135)

The plant and animal species required to maintain healthy ecosystems in Scotland are now not only threatened by sheep and deer, but by new buildings, increased human traffic, and activities that bring with them land, water, air, noise, and light pollution. McChuckemup shows how Highlands culture, names, and animals are appropriated and falsified as marketable symbols, just as the (fictional) petroleum product 'plastic granitette' captures the inauthenticity of the version of the Highlands being sold to tourists by imitating the appearance of local granite traditionally used for building. 'Highlandism', writes Macdonald, thus 'became an eminently commodifiable identity' (2015: 44), 'strik[ing] a resonant chord with the vicissitudes of the property-fuelled, service-economy of neoliberalism, the market-sovereign form of political and economic governance slowly stirring into life as McGrath was composing the play in the 1970s' (9). As petroleum product, moreover, the 'plastic granitette' also provides a hint of the effects of the oil industry to come.

The point that the international networks of the tourism industry are interconnected with the international networks of the oil industry is further established later in the play, as members of the Company (M.C.1–4) step out of character to explain:

M.C.4: Question: What does a meat-packer in the Argentine, a merchant seaman on the high seas, a docker in London, a container-lorry driver on the motorways, have in common with a crofter in Lochinver?

M.C.: Nothing at all.
M.C.4: Wrong. They are all wholly-owned subsidiaries of the Vestey Brothers.
M.C.: Ah! The Vesteys – owners of over 100,000 acres in Sutherland and Wester Ross! – and directors of approximately 127 companies, including:
M.C.4: Red Bank Meatworks
Monarch Bacon [...]
International Fish
Norwest Whaling
Commercial Properties
Albion Insurance
Assynt Minerals
Assynt Trading
Lochinver Ice and Scottish-Canadian Oil and Transportation
(2015: 145)

The effect of this list 'is to publicize and politicize the extent to which domestic "public" resources are controlled by agencies outwith the national/public domain', writes Macdonald, in ways that clearly identify 'the incipient world of privatization and the step-change in economic forms of globalization that the neoliberalization of various national economies would help facilitate' (2015: 10–11). As the exchange shows, farming, fishing, meat processing and packaging, mineral mining, property, tourism, trading, and finally the oil industries all combine to serve the capital interests of major landowners in Scotland.

Interestingly, the televized version of *The Cheviot* includes collages of vox pops in which local Aberdonians offer first-hand accounts of the effects of the burgeoning oil industry on their everyday lives. Couples Agnes and Laurie McGeough, and Iain and Pat Read, explain that they have been priced out of housing in Aberdeen by landlords renting to oil workers, and have been forced to move out of their home city, in a move that Macdonald describes as 'a contemporary "petro" form of marginalization and clearance' (55). Interviews with oil riggers then reveal difficult and dangerous working conditions, experiences of delayed and inadequate medical treatment following accidents at work, long hours, unpaid shore- and sick leave, precarity, risk of job losses, and inability to provide for their families on the wages paid by Shell, BP, Esso, and other multinationals, whose logos, rigs, and equipment also appear on screen. As Robin Nelson argues, 'in the theatre, the live collective audience is invited to be persuaded by the directness of the performer address, underscored by the sentiment of a Gaelic song of Mary MacPherson, cementing the sense of "communitas"', whereas '[i]n the television adaptation, the Vox Pops technique [...] lends conviction', and 'serves to authenticate the narratives and political implications of *The Cheviot*' (2002: n.p.). In both cases, the focus stays on the local people.

The entrance of Texas Jim, a gun-toting American in a ten-gallon hat who represents US petro-capital interest in Scotland, marks the key turning point in *The Cheviot*. Jim combines appeal with threat, just as the 'oil culture' he represents 'registers a rather contradictory mix of excitement and dread' that is 'fantastic and emancipatory' on the one hand, and 'ecologically disastrous and economically maldistributed' (2015: 59) on the other, as Macdonald has it. This is captured in Jim's close association with music and song. He repeats and refashions a number of pieces that appear earlier in the play, including folk songs 'For these are my mountains' and 'Bonnie Dundee', as well as the hymn 'Lord of the Dance', and by shouting out square-dance calls during a hoe-down. His comical performances include these parodic adoptions and reworkings of traditional, familiar, and religious songs to echo at the level of form the appropriation, remodelling, and destruction of the Highlands and Highlands culture by external capital. His entrance is accompanied by folk music forms, beginning with '*Grannie's Hielan' Hame on accordion*' (2015: 145), as he lays claim to Scottish heritage. The music then changes to the keynote song of the play, 'For these are my mountains', but this time played on guitar, in an American '*Blue grass* [...] *country style*' (146). This is accompanied by a shift in attitude as '*He changes from nostalgia to a more aggressive approach*' (146) and '*he fires [a] pistol as oil rigs appear on the mountains*' (146) on the pop-up book set behind. The shot and rigs serve as a warning, connecting the gun's immediate threat to life to the deadly threat of oil. Now, too, Jim further modifies the traditional meanings of the songs he sings by introducing his own lyrics. So, when the music changes once more, this time to a '*hoe-down*', Jim calls out as the company dance:

TEXAS JIM: I'll bring work that's hard and good –
　　　　　A little oil costs a lot of blood
　　　　　[...]
　　　　　So leave your fishing, and leave your soil,
　　　　　Come work for me, I want your oil.
　　　　　Screw your landscape, screw your bays
　　　　　I'll screw you in a hundred ways –
　　　　　Take your partner by the hand
　　　　　Tiptoe through the oily sand
　　　　　[...]
　　　　　I'm going to grab a pile of dough
　　　　　When that there oil begins to flow.

(146–148)

By now fully substituting Scottish folk song for American hoe-down, Jim enacts through music and song the effects of US oil capital in Scotland. As the lyrics indicate, this comes at the cost of people's health and traditional livelihoods, and with extensive pollution of earth, water, and air.

The Cheviot shows how the US takeover of oil revenue from the North Sea was made possible by the close collusion of American magnates with the British government, represented by the character Whitehall and a character based on the real Lord Polwarth, Governor of the Bank of Scotland (1966–72) and

Minister of State (1972–74). The second performance of a version of the folk song 'Bonnie Dundee' to appear in the play is sung as a duet between Jim and Whitehall. The first was sung by actors representing two overseers of the Clearances, Patrick Sellars and James Loch, and included the lines:

> There's a many a fine shoal of fish in the sea
> All waiting for catching and frying for tea –
> I'll buy the surplus then sell them you see
> At double the price that you sold them to me.
> (92)

Jim and Whitehall's *'souped-up version'* (151) includes the lines:

> There's many a barrel of oil in the sea
> All waiting for drilling and piping to me
> I'll refine it in Texas, you'll get it, you'll see
> At four times the price that you sold it to me.
> (151)

In both cases, the lyrics convey the operations of capitalism, whereby humans, animals, and environments are pressed into the service of a contempt-filled, mocking, and outside minority elite. This is a cycle repeated again and again under conditions of capitalist modernity, and always in pursuit of the endless accumulation of profit, which rises across the songs from 'double' to 'four times'. In Jim's final musical contribution, 'Texas Jim *and* Whitehall *turn* Lord Polwarth *into a puppet by taking out and holding up strings attached to his wrist and back*' as the three sing:

> Oil, oil underneath the sea,
> I am the Lord of the Oil said he,
> And my friends in the Banks and the trusts all agree,
> I am the Lord of the Oil – Tee Hee
> (156)

This 'hymn of an emergent carbon democratic and increasingly financialized capitalism' (14), in Macdonald's words, ends abruptly: Polwarth collapses, and Jim and Whitehall each announce: 'And the West is next in line' (157, 158).

The cultural losses and environmental exhaustion of the Highlands cumulatively caused by capitalist processes associated with cheviot, stag, and oil, are most fully realized in a tragicomic scene featuring a late-twentieth-century Highlands couple, the Crofter and his wife, who, Macdonald asserts, 'are forced to become bed and breakfast performers of a vanquished culture' (2015: 15). Despite all the financial promise of tourism and oil, their only economic opportunity is to mimic 'a Scots/Highland authentic culture [...] in the thin playing out of an over-determined and ersatz depiction of cultural authenticity for uncritical forms of consumption at home and abroad' (14). Thus the wife wears '*a shawl round her head*', the crofter '*a blanket round himself to look like a kilt and* [...] *a tammy*' (2015: 159); they switch off their television to listen to the wireless when their guests arrive; and they hide 'the Marvel milk' because they told their guests 'we had our own cows' (158). As hosts, the crofters are also forced to find ways to sell an increasingly impoverished and denuded landscape to their guests:

The visitors are mimed.

WIFE: Dear heart step forward, come in, come in. (*Clicks fingers to* CROFTER)
CROFTER: (*brightly*) Och aye!
WIFE: You'll have come to see the oil-rigs – oh they're a grand sight, right enough. [...]
CROFTER: Aye, you'll get a much better view now the excavators digging for minerals have cleared away two and half of the Five Sisters of Kintail. [...]
And you'll see all the bonnie big tankers come steaming up the loch without moving from your chair –

(159)

The shifting and overlapping dynamics of capital associated with soil, mineral, metal, and oil are conveyed in this exchange. The couple are associated with their eighteenth century crofter ancestors by their clothing, forms of entertainment, and sustenance, all designed to create the illusion that traditional ways of life are maintained in the Highlands. Outside, whole mountains have been destroyed through excavation, and though the Five Sisters are in fact still standing, gold, silver, iron, limestone, and coal mining did take place in Scotland. Finally, the crofters describe the oil tankers, which travel up the lochs to transport petroleum from the sea to the shores of Scotland. Wenzel explains how usually 'aesthetic judgement serves to legitimate and naturalize appropriation', providing 'ideological cover for appropriation and exploitation' (2016: n.p.). Here, however, this 'resource logic' that 'is also a resource aesthetic' (n.p.), in Wenzel's words, is sharply satirized by the crofters to create a tragicomic scene that throws into sharp relief 'both the progress narrative of accumulation and the narrative of diminishment and decline' (n.p.). The artificial, farcical, comical nature of their setup serves to add deep poignancy to the social, economic, and environmental threats posed to the crofters, thereby enhancing the sense of the impermanency of their situation.

The crofters reveal how the oil industry and military testing have led to pollution and species loss, whilst a telling exchange signals their awareness of a connection to climate change. The 'blizzard' outside is, as Macdonald identifies, 'waste drift from ongoing mineral excavation: gas-flared future "weather"' (2015: 15). The Wife tells the tourists 'Och it's terrible weather for July –', to which the Crofter adds: 'It's not been the same since they struck oil in Loch Duich' (2015: 159). The crofters thus foretell the climate-changing effects of the fossil fuel industries, later reinforced by the Wife's line: 'When the weather clears up, you'll be wanting down to the shore to see the pollution – it's a grand sight, right enough' (160). Forced to recast environmental destruction and climate change as exciting and appealing developments to sustain a now-threatened tourist industry, the crofters then acknowledge that they are being priced out of the area (presumably by landlords seeking accommodation for oil workers). The Crofter's final line is 'One thing's certain, we can't live here', to which the Wife responds: 'Aye, one thing's certain. We can't live here' (161). The lines apply to their particular situation in Scotland, but also to the world at large, as the planet will be rendered uninhabitable with the continued excavation, processing, and burning of fossil fuels.

Macdonald argues that '[f]uture critics will be crucial in discerning *The Cheviot's* comparative international engagements' (2015: 64) – a call that we have offered some pointers to here, as well as (briefly) in the next chapter, 'Water'. *The Cheviot*'s global outlook is made explicit at the close of the play, as the Company summarize a long history of social, economic, political, cultural, and environmental exploitation of the Highlands in the context of a world-system spanning 'Bolivia, Panama, Guatemala, Venezuela, Brazil, Angola, Mozambique, Nigeria, Biafra, Muscat and Oman and many other countries' where 'the same corporations have torn out the mineral wealth from the land' (161). As we have already discussed, the broad geographical, historical, social, and environmental reach of the play is represented through the deployment of techniques from a vast array of generic forms, but also in its creation and performance. Though McGrath's name is on the play, it was co-created, collaboratively devised and assembled by the 7:84 Theatre Company, which McGrath founded alongside Elizabeth and David MacLennan in 1971. Nadine Holdsworth describes how the name of the company came from 'a statistic that appeared in *The Economist* stating that 7 percent of the population of Britain owned 84 percent of the wealth', and this 'made its socialist orientation abundantly clear' (2002: xvi). In his essay 'The Year of the Cheviot' McGrath explains that he sought 'to break down the insane hierarchies of the theatre' by respecting the skills of each member of the company, 'and at the same time lay them open for collective discussion and advice', ensuring that 'we could work as equal human beings, no skill being elevated over another, no personal power or superiority being assumed', and no 'power-seeking or avoidance of responsibility to the collective' (62). Once rehearsed and ready for performance, the company took, in John Bull's words, 'political theatre to non-theatrical venues and, at least in intent, to non-theatrical audiences' (1984: 22). They undertook three tours in Scotland in 1973–74, beginning in Aberdeen and then moving to various small town and village locations across the Highlands, performing '[o]ne hundred shows' to 'over 30,000 people' (2002: 60). As Baz Kershaw argues:

> The geographic progression from the metropolitan centre to the provincial periphery signalled a decisive break, the final stage in a deliberate

shift from the commercial mass-populism of the media, through the subsidised minority-elitism of mainstream theatres, to an ambitious stab at a (to begin with) self-financed popular localism. In moving to Scotland McGrath's aim was to forge a new kind of theatre practice: political community performance.

(1992: 148)

In this way, *The Cheviot* represents a model of collective theatre and action and, in reaching new audiences too, enacts forms of resistance on multiple levels: by challenging the elitism and hierarchies of theatre-making and theatre-going, by introducing new subject matter and maintaining political thrust and critique, and by co-creating an accessible multi-generic and hybrid work underpinned by popular forms. *The Cheviot* has been performed since the original 7:84 version, including by the Dundee Rep and National Theatre of Scotland in 2016 and 2019, because as Macdonald explains, 'the ongoing salience of *The Cheviot* is confirmed by its salient warnings [...] and its attempt to fashion, in both production, performativity, plot and politics, a space of resistance against' the 'cumulative efforts [...] of capitalist ideology and practice' (2015: 66). Even now, 50 years after its first performance, this work of world theatre and petro-drama continues to speak meaningfully for an end to endless capitalist accumulation, land dispossession, fossil energy, and the need for the restoration of global environments.

Conclusion

Over the course of this chapter, we have analysed how plays and novels represent, respond to, and resist, the human and environmental costs of the development of global capitalism and associated energy transitions. We began in 'Soil' by analysing how the Caribbean and American plantation economies of the fifteenth through to the eighteenth centuries were made possible by mass deforestations, the instatement of slave labour monocultural farming, and wood-fuelled production processes that turned cash crops into products such as sugar, molasses, and rum. Using a play by James and novels by Bontemps and Butler, we explored how slave rebellions and translocated African and Indigenous knowledges connect over time to provide methods for resistance, survival, and recovery in the face of extreme violence, exploitation, and environmental destruction. In 'Mineral and Metal' we then examined how Britain's increasing reliance on coal for energy generation in the eighteenth and nineteenth centuries enabled steam-powered industrial and technological advancements that supported, and were supported by, capitalist extraction of diamonds and gold in the colonies, with South Africa serving as a leading example. Novels by Schreiner and Abrahams reveal how feminist, Pan-Africanist, anti-colonial, and workers union resistance to the prevailing inequalities of race and gender that enable mineral and metal extraction in South Africa are aligned to environmental sustainability and restoration. Finally, we showed how McGrath's *The Cheviot, the Stag and the Black, Black Oil* dramatized the next stage in the development of global capitalism, which has been fuelled by the most recent world-changing energy transition to oil. Following Macdonald in reading the play as a work of 'petro-drama' and world literature, *The Cheviot* also illuminates Niblett's argument that 'the experience of frontier-led ecological change is simultaneously locally specific and world historical' (2020: 12). As we continue to grapple with the climate-changing effects of fossil energy, and the accumulating effects of expanding and exhausting global commodity frontiers, we would do well to heed the opening speech of *The Cheviot*, in which we are warned that the global story of land dispossession, cheap labour, extractive capitalism, and environmental destruction is 'a story that has a beginning, a middle, but, as yet, no end –' (2015: 85).

Notes

1 The 'Plantationocene' was coined by Donna Haraway in a conversation with Noboru Ishikawa, Scott F Gilbert, Kenneth Olwig, Anna L Tsing, and Nils Bubandt at an Aarhus University event in October 2014.
2 There was also an Arab slave trade operating out of East Africa and which continued well into the twentieth century, with estimated numbers at around 12–15 million.
3 From 1952, the hated *dompasses* had to be carried by all Black South Africans over the age of 16, and incorporated identifying photograph, fingerprint, and address as well as employer, comments on behaviour by employers, and permissions to enter certain regions. Individuals could be arrested if they failed to show a pass when required by apartheid police.
4 The term 'coloured' has a specific meaning in South Africa, and is used to refer to people of mixed-race descent who predominantly live in the Cape. Although considered offensive elsewhere in the English-speaking world and increasingly debated within South Africa, it is still retained in common usage today.
5 https://earthworks.org/issues/environmental-impacts-of-gold-mining/ https://earthworks.org/resources/how_the_20_tons_of_mine_waste_per_gold_ring_figure_was_calculated.
6 The Miners' Strike of 1946 was preceded by various meetings and smaller strikes over food, but now rallied around a number of core demands, including the recognition of their African Mine Workers Union, a wage of 10 shillings a day, suitable food and family homes, two weeks' paid annual leave, a gratuity of £100 after 5 years of service, and repatriation fees. This was refused, and so the strike took place over August 12–16, and totalled 76,000 striking mine workers – the most significant industrial action by Black workers in South Africa at that point.
7 See, for example, Upton Sinclair's *Oil!* (1927), Edna Ferber's *Giant* (1952), Winifred Sandford's *Windfall and Other Stories* (1988), Susan M. Gaines' *Carbon Dreams* (2001), Cormac McCarthy's *The Road* (2006), Paolo Bacigalupi's *The Windup Girl* (2009), Pablo Neruda's 'Standard Oil Co.' (1940), Italo Calvino's 'The Petrol Pump' (1974), Patrick Chamoiseau's *Texaco* (1992), Ken Saro-Wiwa's *A Forest of Flowers* (1995), Nawal El-Saadawi's *Love in the Kingdom of Oil* (2000), Bessora's *Petroleum* (2004), Robert Alan Jamieson's *Thin Wealth. A Novel from an Oil Decade (1986),* Sina Queyras' *Expressway* (2009), Peter Cizek, Phil Angers, and Marc Tessier's 'OIL: From the bottom of the pit' in *EXTRACTION!: Comix Reportage* (2007), and Reza Negarestani's *Cyclonopaedia* (2008), to name but a

few. Other contributions include the various creative pieces collated by Szeman and Boyer in their remarkable *Energy Humanities: An Anthology*, and the series of oil stories commissioned by *The Guardian* (UK) newspaper in 2011. *The Guardian* short story writers include Tim Gautreaux, Rose Tremain, Joanna Kavenna, China Miéville, Robin Yassin-Kassab, Mohammed Hasan Alwan, Alain Mabanckou, and Simone Lia (see Lea, 2011).

Bibliography

Anon. 1863. "The Horrors of San Domingo." *The Atlantic* (June): 768–785. https://www.theatlantic.com/magazine/archive/1863/06/the-horrors-of-san-domingo/629015/ [accessed 2023].

Abrahams, Peter. [1946] 1989. *Mine Boy*. Oxford: Heinemann.

Barad, Karen. 2007. *Meeting the Universe Halfway: Quantum Physics and the Entanglement of Matter and Meaning*. Durham: Duke University Press.

Bibler, Michael, and Jessica Adams. 2009. "Introduction." In *Drums at Dusk* by Arna Bontemps, vii–lii. Baton Rouge: Louisiana State University Press.

Bontemps, Arna. 1992. *Black Thunder, Gabriel's Revolt: Virginia, 1800*. Boston: Beacon Press.

Butler, Octavia. 2019. *Parable of the Sower*. London: Headline.

Butler, Octavia. 2019. *Parable of the Talents*. London: Headline.

Césaire, Aimé. 2001. *Notebook of a Return to the Native Land*. Translated and edited by Clayton Eshleman and Annette Smith. Middletown, Connecticut: Wesleyan University Press.

Crosby, Alfred W. 2004. *Ecological Imperialism: The Biological Expansion of Europe, 900–1900*. Cambridge: Cambridge University Press.

Davidson, Basil. 1992. "Columbus: The Bones and Blood of Racism." *Race & Class* 33, no. 3: 17–25.

DeLoughrey, Elizabeth M. 2019. *Allegories of the Anthropocene*. Durham: Duke University Press.

Gatti, Luciana V. *et al.* 2021. "Amazonia as a carbon source linked to deforestation and climate change." *Nature* 595: 388–393. https://doi.org/10.1038/s41586-021-03629-6.

Haraway, Donna. 2016. *Staying with the Trouble: Making Kin in the Chthulucene*. Durham: Duke University Press.

Høgsbjerg, Christian. 2013. "Introduction." In *Toussaint Louverture: The Story of the Only Successful Slave Revolt in History: A Play in Three Acts* by C.L.R. James, 1–40. Durham: Duke University Press.

Huggan, Graham, and Helen Tiffin. 2015. *Postcolonial Ecocriticism: Literature: Animals, Environment*. London: Routledge.

James, C.L.R. 2001. *The Black Jacobins: Toussaint L'Ouverture and the San Domingo Revolution*. London: Penguin.

James, C.L.R. 2013. *Toussaint Louverture: The Story of the Only Successful Slave Revolt in History: A Play in Three Acts*. Durham: Duke University Press.

Keck, Michaela. 2017. "Marginocentricity and Cosmopolitan Interconnections of Black Radical Thought in Arna Bontemps' *Black Thunder*." *Atlantic Studies* 14, no. 1: 37–50.

Lea, Richard. 2011. "Can fiction change our view of oil?" *The Guardian* (April 15), https://www.theguardian.com/books/2011/apr/15/oil-stories [accessed 2023].

MacDonald, Graeme. 2015. "Commentary." In *The Cheviot, the Stag and the Black, Black Oil* by John McGrath, 1–71. London: Bloomsbury.

McGrath, John. 2015. *The Cheviot, the Stag and the Black, Black Oil*. London: Bloomsbury.

Modestino, Kevin. 2021. "Octavia Butler's *Parable* Novels and Genealogies of African American Environmental Literature." *Resilience: A Journal of the Environmental Humanities* 9, no. 1: 56–79.

Moore, Jason W. 2015. *Capitalism in the Web of Life: Ecology and the Accumulation of Capital*. London: Verso.

Moore, Jason W. 2016. "The Rise of Cheap Nature." In *Anthropocene or Capitalocene? Nature, History, and the Crisis of Capitalism*, ed. by Jason W. Moore, 78–115. Dexter, MI: PM Press.

Niblett, Michael. 2020. *World Literature and Ecology: The Aesthetics of Commodity Frontiers, 1890–1950*. Cham: Palgrave Macmillan.

Nixon, Rob. 2011. *Slow Violence and the Environmentalism of the Poor*. Cambridge, MA: Harvard University Press.

Patel, Raj, and Jason W. Moore. 2018. *A History of the World in Seven Cheap Things: A Guide to Capitalism, Nature, and the Future of the Planet*. London: Verso.

Pomeranz, Kenneth. 2000. *The Great Divergence: China, Europe, and the Making of the Modern World Economy*. Oxford: Princeton University Press.

PricewaterhouseCoopers report. 2017. "The long view: How will the global economic order change by 2050?" https://www.pwc.com/gx/en/world-2050/assets/pwc-the-world-in-2050-full-report-feb-2017.pdf [accessed 2023].

Rampersad, Arnold. 1992. "Introduction." In *Black Thunder, Gabriel's Revolt: Virginia, 1800* by Arna Bontemps. Boston: Beacon Press.

Schreiner, Olive. 1929. *Undine*. London: Ernest Benn.

Spencer, Robert. 2014. "[Review] *Toussaint Louverture: The Story of the Only Successful Slave Revolt in History: A Play in Three Acts*." *Journal of Postcolonial Writing* 50, no. 1: 116–117.

Stevens, Lara. 2016. *Anti-War Theatre After Brecht: Dialectical Aesthetics in the Twenty-First Century*. London: Palgrave Macmillan.

Thipe, Thuto. 2022. "Photographing Home Life in Alexandra between the 1930s and the 1970s." In *Foundational African Writers: Peter Abrahams, Noni Jabavu, Sibusiso Nyembezi and Es'kia Mphahlele* edited by Bhekizizwe Peterson, Khwezi Mkhize and Makhosazana Xaba, 215–236. Johannesburg: Wilts University Press.

Turton, Antony. 2015. "When gold mining ends: An environmental catastrophe for Johannesburg?." In *New South Africa Review 5: Beyond Marikana* edited by Gilbert M. Khadiagala, Prishani Naidoo, Devan Pillay and Roger Southall, 120–142. Johannesburg: Wilts University Press.

Wenzel, Jennifer. 2016. "Afterword: Improvement and Overburden." *Postmodern Culture* 26, no. 2, n.p.

Wynter, Sylvia. 1971. "Novel and History, Plot and Plantation." *Savacou* 5: 95–102.

Yusoff, Kathryn. 2018. *A Billion Black Anthropocenes or None*. Minneapolis: University of Minnesota Press.

2 Water

In this chapter we examine Indigenous and petropoetic engagements with two elements of the climate system: the hydrosphere (water) and the cryosphere (ice). In the first part, titled 'Delta', we analyse how the operations of the petroleum industry and pollution in the Niger Delta are represented and resisted by poets Ken Saro-Wiwa, Tanure Ojaide, Nnimmo Bassey, Ibiwari Ikiriko, Obari Gomba, Niyi Osundare, and Ogaga Ifowodo. In the second section, 'Ice', we analyse how Indigenous lives, livelihoods, and lifeways are imperilled and destroyed by oil drilling and global warming in poems by the Native Alaskan writers dg nanouk okpik and Cathy Tagnak Rexford. Both groups capture in poetry the existential threats posed by environmental degradation, express resistance and strategies for survival, strive towards environmental reparations and justice, and argue forcefully for an end to the fossil fuel dependencies of global capitalism.

Our foci in this chapter, namely the freshwater courses of the Niger Delta and the melting permafrosts of the frozen north, are perhaps atypical of the topics usually associated with the rapidly expanding, variably named, and overlapping areas of study known as the blue humanities/blue studies, maritime humanities, new thalassology, hydrohumanities/hydro-criticism, and oceanic literary studies. As these titles suggest, and as the ecocritic Steve Mentz explains, '[f]or many ecoscholars in the blue humanities, the most important waters on our planet are the vast interconnected salt-water bodies collectively termed the World Ocean' (2021: 191). Indeed, there have been many exceptional and important contributions made to our understanding of literary oceans and seas over the last ten to 15 years by critics such as Stacy Alaimo, Laura Winkiel, Margaret Cohen, Lowell Duckert, Elizabeth DeLoughrey, Sidney Dobrin, and others. Here, however, we take our cue from Mentz's argument that '[d]espite the overwhelming presence of oceanic literature and oceanic scholarship, not all the water that matters to humans floats in the World Ocean' (193). His work facilitates our directional shift, because '[b]y opening a critical lens onto less familiar forms of water' that he organizes into groupings of 'vapor', 'ice', 'fresh water', and 'salt water', it becomes possible to pursue 'a blue humanities that responds to water's material complexity and imaginative polyphony' (193–195). This quote

DOI: 10.4324/9780429353352-3

provides us with two important steers. First, because we focus here on poetry, which we see as a form uniquely suited to representing the 'material complexity' of liquid ebbs and flows, ice cracks and fissures, and processes of solidifying, melting, and evaporating waters; and second, because both water *and* poetry can host precisely the kinds of 'imaginative polyphony' that range across human and other personhoods, more-than-human voices and concerns that comprise the lifeways and cosmologies of the Ogoni and Alaskan Native writers and writing analysed in this chapter.

Though our primary texts are located at the northernmost points of human habitation on the one hand, and just above the equator on the other, and both at great distance from the Scottish setting of the previous text analysed in this book, John McGrath's *The Cheviot, the Stag, and the Black, Black Oil*, the three regions are connected. As Graeme Macdonald writes of *The Cheviot*: 'the play's themes would equally resonate with those relatively weak communities, from First Nations people of Canada to Nigerian peasants made landless by contemporary mega-oil projects' (2015: 66). Duckert also references the same and additional groups in his analysis of how coal and oil generate stories, outlining that:

> 'Petro-capitalism' and 'petro-imperialism' are tightly linked. Democracies run on hydrocarbons; empires do, too. Their subjugated citizens prosper and perish unequally. It does not take much digging to find examples of rampant exploitation: swathes of Alaska's Beaufort Sea are marked for sale, spurring Gwich'in and Iñupiat activists to protest the inevitable poisons and (failed) promises of oil leases. Then there are First Nations peoples in the tar sands of Alberta, Canada; the Waorani within Ecuador's rainforests; the Ogoni on the Nigerian delta. A global pattern emerges. Indigenous persons, whose lives and cultures are coterminous with the land, are pressured, squeezed, and displaced.
>
> (2021: 215–216)

We suggest that the global patterns of oil-fuelled land dispossession and environmental denudation highlighted by Macdonald and Duckert can be traced in the ripples, waves, and currents of water poetry too. Though geographically distanced and irreducibly specific to place and time, there are recurring and reverberating experiences of land *and* water dispossession and pollution, climate change, species loss, and environmental degradation caused by petrocapitalism in the contexts of the Niger Delta and the Arctic. We argue, therefore, that by reading the work of writers from those groups most threatened and marginalized by oil-fuelled capitalist modernity, we find models and strategies of poetic activism, resistance, and recovery essential for the survival of the lives and environs represented by, and beyond, the poetry.

Our argument extends past frontier zones too. When Jean and John Comaroff counter long-established constructions of Africa as primitive and/or underdeveloped by asking 'whether the West recognizes that *it* is playing catch-up in many respects with the temporality of its others' (2012: 14), the answer is of course implied: the (semi-)peripheral, (post-)colonial, and other frontier regions of the world, including the African and Arctic contexts discussed in this chapter, experience the genocidal, ecocidal, and epistemicidal effects of global capitalism first, where others follow. In this way, the oil-polluted waterways (and lands and skies) of the Niger Delta, and melting glaciers and permafrosts of the Arctic, provide anticipatory evidence of the diminishing futures of even the most wealthy and powerful of the world's nations. The poetic activism, techniques for survival, resistance, and methods for recovery that emerge from these regions, then, are not only comparable across frontiers, but provide the inspiration, influence, and replicable models and strategies required to tackle fossil fuel dependency and structural inequalities engendered by capitalist modernity in the world at large.

Delta

In this section we argue that poems by select Niger Delta writers are pre-eminent examples of 'petropoetry'.[1] Though this term is increasingly gaining currency as a way of clustering together poetic writing that addresses the extractivist and polluting processes of the oil industry, critical interest in petroliterature was initially sparked by Amitav Ghosh focusing on petrofiction in his 1992 review essay of Abdelrahman Munif's novel *Cities of Salt* (1984). In the review, Ghosh lauds Munif's novel 'as a work of immense significance' for 'giv[ing] the Oil Encounter literary expression' (1992: 31). He identifies it as a pioneering text for this reason, claiming that the 'Great American Oil novel' (30) has yet to be produced because '[t]he truth is that we do not yet possess the form that can give the Oil Encounter a literary expression' (31). Ghosh's preoccupation with the novel as the premier form through which to critically engage petromodernity betrays a particular Western bias because of the uniquely privileged place of the novel as the dominant form in the global literary marketplace today (and most particularly when it appears in English). His claim is also not true, as Macdonald points out in his challenge to the widespread and

> strong critical insistence on the general 'invisibility' of oil. […] For the many extraction sites on the (semi-)periphery of the world-system – *and within cultural production from those areas* – oil is or has been overtly visible, even if it is subsequently made 'unseen', either by privatization, securitization and military enforcement *or* by its mediated mystification.
> (2017: 293)

Certainly, many writers from the Niger Delta provide numerous examples of 'Oil Encounter' writing – direct literary engagements with petroleum production and pollution, the workings of the hydrocarbon economy, 'the lived experience of local inhabitants at the sites of extraction' (Aghoghovwia 2014:

61), and the environmental consequences of petromodernity, albeit captured in *poetry* as well as in fiction.

Debates concerning the form and function of the term 'petrofiction' continue to proliferate, revolving around whether the term denotes genre, operates more broadly as critical framework, and/or functions as periodizing signifier. For example, Imre Szeman argues that '[t]he very best petrofictions being produced today understand oil not as a social problem to be (somehow, miraculously) ameliorated, but as a core element of our societies' (2012: 3), and Macdonald proposes that 'all modern writing is premised on both the promise and hidden costs and benefits of hydrocarbon culture' (2012: 31). More recently, however, and prompted by Andrew Pendakis' question '[i]s there an aesthetics of oil or are its cultural manifestations too diverse and localized to be usefully generalized?' (Pendakis and Biemann 2012: 8), Macdonald has developed a comparativist "worlding" approach for analysing the contents, contexts, and forms of petrofiction. Petropoetry certainly shares some of the features that Macdonald identifies, albeit with other and additional distinctive characteristics that can be established through both situated case studies and comparative analysis. In what follows, then, we establish a series of markers – aesthetic, thematic, and political – that recur across Niger Delta petropoetry, and which yet invite comparative global connections to other ecopoetic forms that we explore in this chapter's second case study on Alaskan Native writing. The themes, arguments, and techniques that distinguish the petropoetics of the Delta engender affective and effective forms of literary activism through poetic testimonies, expressions of collective resistance, and shared commitment to social and environmental equity and justice.

Ken Saro-Wiwa and his Afterlives

Oil was first discovered in Nigeria in 1956, four years before the nation gained its independence from Britain after 153 years under colonial control. Since the 1960s, Nigeria has consistently been one of the top 15 oil-producing nations of the world and is the largest economy in Africa, yet suffers from what economists describe as the 'Dutch disease' in which the development of the oil sector happens at the expense of all other industries, such as agriculture and manufacture. Despite the nation's ostensible wealth, successive Nigerian governments have continued to collude with multinational oil corporations, leading to mismanagement, corruption, terror, and conflict in the oil regions, preventing the majority of the population from benefitting from oil revenue. Indeed, as a former colony, Nigeria features as one of the many 'African polities' that Comaroff and Comaroff describe as 'hav[ing] been especially hospitable to rapacious enterprise: to asset stripping, to the alienation of the commons to privateers, to the plunder of personal property, to foreign bribe giving' (2012: 15). Importantly too, Nigeria is one of the most populous nations on the continent, comprising over 140 million people and over 250 ethnic groups, though dominated by three regions associated with three major ethnic groups: the Hausa/Fulani in the north, Yoruba in the west, and Igbo in the south/east. The primary oil fields and wells are located in the Niger Delta basin, which is also host to over 40 ethnic groups, including many minorities. These groups have never been represented by the successive governments and ruling elites that came to power in association with the civil unrest, genocides, war, and military coups that followed decolonization. That said, oil revenue from the area provided, and continues to provide, the source of all political power and corruption. As a result, nearly two-thirds of Nigeria's population survive on less than $2 per day.

The Niger Delta basin is the largest wetland in Africa, spanning nine coastal southern Nigerian states, and comprising swamps, islands, and rainforests. Though the Delta was historically host to some of the highest concentrations of biodiversity in the world, today it is one of the most polluted places on the planet. Bassey, whose many roles include working as the Director of the ecological think-tank, the Health of Mother Earth Foundation (HOMEF), and who was formerly chair of Friends of the Earth International between 2008 and 2012, explains how 'decades of destruction' in Nigeria mean that '[c]reeks, rivers and streams are constantly polluted by oil spills from aged pipelines and faulty equipment. Routine gas flares, illegal since 1984, pump toxic elements into the atmosphere, choking and poisoning the impoverished local people', amounting to 'environmental pollution bordering on ecocide' (2016: 235). There have been over 10,000 oil spills in the Delta since 2006,[2] exposing human and animal inhabitants to lead, chromium, and mercury, and contaminating soils and crops. Simultaneously, perpetual gas flaring causes air pollution and acid rain, as well as carcinogenic, respiratory, and other life-limiting diseases. By way of only one example: a 2019 study on the effects of oil spills on infant mortality in Nigeria found that spills within 10km before conception increased neonatal mortality by around 38.3 deaths per 1000 live births, and identified that oil spills killed around 16,000 infants within the first month of their life in 2012 (Bruederle and Hodler, 2019: 5470). At the same time, the decimation of local agriculture and fishing as a result of the environmental damage mean that oil tapping, illegal refineries, corruption, and gangs provide the new and only means for survival in the basin, creating additional threats to life through the loss of livelihoods and communities, violence, and yet more pollution. The oil industry in the Delta, then, not only affects existing human, animal, and plant lives, but future lives too.

Oil pollution in the Niger Delta came to international attention through the efforts of Saro-Wiwa and the Movement for the Survival of Ogoni People (MOSOP). MOSOP's peaceful protests against the activities of the Royal Dutch Shell oil corporation in Ogoniland garnered a huge following, including for example a January 1993 march that comprised 300,000 people. The Ogoni are one of many ethnic groups in the region, and are the group most closely associated with the pursuit of civil, economic, and environmental rights and reparations, and so became a particular target for government and corporate suppression. In May 1994 Saro-Wiwa was arrested and accused of inciting the murder of four Ogoni chiefs. His poem, 'Keep Out of Prison', which was written during this time, is as follows:

> 'Keep out of prison,' he wrote
> 'Don't get arrested anymore.'
> But while our land is ravaged
> And our pure air is poisoned
> When streams choke with pollution
> Silence would be treason
> Punishable by a term in prison.
> (2014: 159)

The poem provides just one example of the inseparability of Saro-Wiwa's art and activism, with each configured with and through the other in the pursuit of social, economic, and environmental justice. He lays out in no uncertain terms his view that when tackling the combined powerhouses of Big Oil and successive autocratic governments: 'Silence would be treason'. (This was also the title of the posthumously collated collection of his last poetic writings and correspondence in which this poem appears.) Saro-Wiwa was given a death sentence. He was executed on 10 November 1995 along with eight other MOSOP leaders: Baribor Bera, Saturday Dobee, Nordu Eawo, Daniel Gbooko, Barinem Kiobel, John Kpuine, Paul Levera, and Felix Nuate. Yet the record of his resolute struggles against Nigeria's military regimes, political corruption, and the devastating activities of the oil companies remains in his poetry (and elsewhere in his novels, short stories, plays, and essays), which live on after his death.

The literary and political afterlives of Saro-Wiwa's activism and writings can be traced throughout many examples of Niger Delta petropoetry. Critics Udeme Eno Inyang and Mathias Iroro Orhero identify this feature in their analysis of poems by Ojiade and Ikiriko, arguing that the 'influence, legacy and immortality of Saro-Wiwa' appears 'as a motif to thematise ecological devastation, political persecution, Niger Delta activism, and minority politics' (2020: 37). In Ikiriko's 'Remembering Saro-Wiwa' from the collection *Oily Tears of the Delta*, the reader is urged:

> Let's not forget
> that Saro-Wiwa
> was a righter
> a righter
> a righter.
> And let's not forget
> that his hanging
> is still sticking

>   to the remains of our conscience
>   like sludges on mud-flat.
>   ([2000] 2009: 39)

In their analysis of this poem, Inyang and Orhero describe Ikiriko as 'like a town crier' (2020: 49). In many Nigerian cultures, 'town criers' or 'newsmen' play an integral role in systems of communication and information dissemination, and are responsible for significant announcements such as festivals, market days, decrees, war, and peace. Certainly, the poet's message here is one of importance, serving as commemoration, warning, and duty. Rhythmic patterning created by the monosyllabic and disyllabic words and repetition also evoke the drumbeats that often accompany town crier announcements, whilst the repeated homophone righter/writer conveys Saro-Wiwa's persistence in writing for Ogoni rights so that his fight and legacy continue to reverberate over time.

Though not discussed in Inyang and Orhero's article, both Gomba and Ifowodo also refer to Saro-Wiwa in their poems. In Gomba's collection *The Ascent Stone*, 'No Leaf Falls' is dedicated to Saro-Wiwa, and the poem titled 'To Saro-Wiwa' describes how the poet 'Waters the song with his drops of tears' (2014: 175). As 'The voice of pain drowns the cavalcade of hell | And when scores are summed in time | Teardrops quench the fire of the darkheads' (175). Thus Saro-Wiwa is shown as inspiring and sustaining the work of other songwriters or poets with 'his voice' and 'song' (175). This is imagined in more explicitly realized ways as a return from the dead in another poem from the same collection, 'The Spirit of Ogoni'. In this we hear 'The never-dying song: The dead shall rise again' (177). They rise as 'the spirit of Ogoni | The spirit of the people' (177).

The Ogoni Nine also reappear across petropoetry from the Delta. In 'Shell's Love', also from Gomba's *The Ascent Stone*, the poetic voice asks 'why its oil-rigs are festooned with nine corpses?' (2014: 122). Similarly, in 'The Pipes War' and 'Cesspit of the Niger Area' that appear in Ifowodo's poetic sequence *The Oil Lamp* references are made to the 'hanged nine' and 'the famous nine' (2005: 51, 59). Ojaide's *Delta Blues* similarly creates and sustains motifs of the Ogoni Nine and Saro-Wiwa. The collection is dedicated to the 'memory of Ken Saro-Wiwa and the other eight Delta martyrs' (1998: 9), their 'nine mounds' (20, 23) appear in the poems 'Immortal Grief' and 'Delta Blues', and they are remembered as 'nine eaglets' (28) in 'Elegy for Nine Warriors'. Another poem in Ojaide's collection, 'Wails', also appears in elegiac form to grieve and praise the Ogoni Nine:

>   They have murdered a favourite son,
>   this news cannot be a hoax;
>   for the love of terror,
>   they have hanged a favourite son
>   and eight other bearers of truth.

> [...]
> Who will speak to me rotten English,
> the lingua franca of the coastline?
> Who will tell the forest of flowers?
> Who will traverse the darkling plain of the delta?
> Who will stand in front as the *iroko* shield
> To regain the stolen birthright of millions?
>
> (18)

The use of questions as expressions of mourning is common to many African dirge forms, and traditionally used to convey loss. Here, however, the questions also serve a more directly challenging function as calls to action and rallying cries for the next generations of poet-activists for the Delta. A sense of dialogue and conversation is further established through intertextual referents to Saro-Wiwa's *Sozaboy: A Novel in Rotten English* (1985), his short story collection *A Forest of Flowers* (1986), and his account of the events leading to the Nigerian civil war, *On a Darkling Plain* (1989), imbuing the poem with a sense of textual connection, shared experience, and responsibility, and inviting others to engage with the Delta's histories and futures.

Elsewhere in Ojaide's collection, Saro-Wiwa appears as 'the elephant', 'iroko' (deity), 'griot' (historian/storyteller/praise poet), 'chief warrior', and 'true diviner', and in spirit form in the poem, 'My drum beats itself':

> Now that my drum beats itself,
> I know that my dead mentor's hand's at work.
> This sound I lipsing and others think is mine
> could only come from beyond this world –
> [...]
> I bow to the master who never forgot my service.
> [...]
> *Iye iye, iye iye*
> *Iye iye, iye iye*
> *Iye iye, iye iye*
>
> (1998: 10–11)

The repeated '*Iye iye, iye iye*' sees Ojaide imagine Saro-Wiwa as returned spirit, kin, mind, life, mentor, and master, who possesses the poet, speaks through his voice, and thus enables him to continue beating the rhythm of resistance. As Inyang and Orhero explain, the 'Saro-Wiwa motif in Niger Delta poetry [...] reflect[s] the loss and tears that his execution adds to the ruins of the Niger Delta', and repeated returns to his 'execution in the poetry that mourns his death is an eternal indictment to those guilty of his blood [...] and also confirms that Saro-Wiwa remains an undying image of loss, the symbol of struggle and the metaphor of pain' (2020: 50). Ojaide's poems thus provide the space and place for Saro-Wiwa's legacies, authority, art, and activism to retain their provenance and presence, whilst inviting further conversations and actions that extend beyond the lives of humans then, now, and in times to come.

Blood, Oil and Water

An underpinning understanding of human and other persons, and organic and inorganic matter and processes as coextensive, interconnected, vital, agentive, and communicative is one of the most prominent shared features of Niger Delta petropoetry. Again, Saro-Wiwa provides a paradigmatic example in his poem 'The Call':

> Hear the call of the ravaged land
> The raucous cry of famished earth
> The dull dirge of the poisoned air
> The piteous wail of sludged streams
> Hear, oh, hear!
> Stunted crops fast decay
> Fishes die and float away
> Butterflies lose wing and fall
> Nature succumbs to th'ecological war.
> (2014: 158)

Earth, water, and air, here presented as embodied 'land', 'earth', 'air', and 'streams', are grounded in Ogoni understandings that organic forms and inorganic processes are, or contain, other-than-human persons or spirits able to speak and be heard. The poem thus captures a polyphony of elemental voices rising in pain and in search of justice – the 'call', 'cry', 'wail', and 'dirge' addressed to the readers and auditors of the poem. This less human, yet more humane, vision of the world refuses the petrocapitalist construction of the Delta that reduces it to a site of commodities or resources, thereby thwarting and challenging the racist, speciesist, and extractivist structures and logics that facilitate the polluting operations of the oil industry. It introduces a certain ethical provenance too by asserting the rights of those other-than-human persons of the Delta.

Communication is also a key element of Bassey's poetry, which he sees as essential for 'mobilizing resistance, getting people to feel a part of the movement', telling interviewer Vanessa Baird that 'some of my poems are [...] for people to be part of the reading so that there are calls and responses; so, for example, when I say "we thought it was oil" the audience responds "but it was blood"' (2011: 40). The title poem of Bassey's collection *We Thought It Was Oil But It Was Blood* is, as Philip Aghoghovwia outlines, 'modelled on a call-and-response motif of folksongs associated with most Indigenous communities in the Niger Delta' (2014: 66), so that the refrain is twice repeated between stanzas throughout the poem. The poem is intended to rally people to a cause, and so just as with other political writing, there is a premium on accessibility, managed through the use of familiar forms of orature and communication. The use of collective pronouns 'we' and 'our' further suggests shared trauma and invites collective response, as in the examples: 'We danced in the street' until 'We beheld | Red-hot guns', then 'We leapt in fury' as 'we beheld | Bright red pools' (2002: 14).

The rivers of blood that run through Bassey's collection flow through writing by many other of the petropoets. In 'Delta Blues', Ojaide describes the 'dark-veined' rivers of the Delta as 'my lifeblood from the beginning' (1998: 21), and in 'The Pipes War', Ifowodo writes that the 'rivers of blood' in the Delta 'weep' (2005: 53). The blood flow represents the political executions, gang-based violence, and loss of life caused by pollution in the basin, whilst establishing at the same time the impossibility of separating humans from other lives and environs. The Delta is thus imagined as a single body, though comprised of complex and interpenetrative biotic systems. This idea is well captured in Rob Nixon's description of the 'slow violence' of pollution and species extinction, 'the persistence of unofficial hostilities in the cellular domain, the untidy, attritional lethality that moves through the tissue, blood, and bones [...] moving through as well the living body of the land itself' (2011: 200). Ifowodo's 'The Deluge' from his collection *Homeland and Other Poems* provides another example:

> Moments counted by the slowed heart
> of the Delta [...]
> Look how the veins of this malarial belt
> bloated like neglected cow's udders
> spill grief on troubled land and waters!
> It is the curse of oil, hemlock
> Held to lips pocked by acid rain.
>
> ([1998] 2008: 16)

Aerial views of the basin reveal thousands of converging and linked waterways that resemble blood vessels. The simile thus invites the idea of the interconnectedness of all of nature by invoking the repeating patterns of veins and fluvial processes. The oil is to water as poisonous hemlock is to humans and animals: a life-threatening pollutant, forced into unwilling bodies. As a result, the life of the embodied Delta is described as drawing to a close – its heartbeats slow, its blood vessels bloat, and yet the poisons continue to flow. This is not a simple anthropomorphizing strategy as it might perhaps appear to Western readers. Rather, it is an expression of a particular understanding of the coextensive and coterminous relationships between all living things, earth, water, and air.

The blood, water, and oil flows through the Delta are conveyed and enhanced through formal techniques, because, as Macdonald outlines: 'oil has recognizable form, and [...] its mobile, repetitive and relational logics are detectable in petrofictions and other significant representations of petro-development' (2017: 300). The second stanza of Ifowodo's 'A Waterscape' in

The Oil Lamp provides a good example of this: 'Blacker than pear, deeper than soot, | massive ink-well, silent and mute: | water, black water' (2005: xi). The monosyllabic and disyllabic words, trochees, four-syllable phrases, repetition of 'black' and 'water', and half-rhymes 'soot' and 'mute' create the poetic drips, ripples, and streams that suggest the passage of oil through the waterways of the basin.

The petropoetics of the Niger Delta do not only serve to represent, testify to, and mourn the condition of the people and environments of the basin, the loss of traditional lifeways and epistemologies, livelihoods, communities, and lives, they also follow Saro-Wiwa's lead in expressing resistance, confronting corrupt, inept, and cruel governments, and arguing for radical action. The poems analysed here are primarily published with Nigerian presses, and some are difficult to access outside of the country, which is no doubt at least in part due the limitations and biases of the global literary marketplace. Yet the use of poetry rather than the novel form as the medium of choice for testimony and resistance is a political choice too. Poetry resists the colonial/capitalist inheritances of the novel form in creation, production, circulation, and consumption. The texts also appear to be written first and foremost for local audiences, in simple, accessible language to convey the arguments in the clearest ways and inspire support. This choice does not preclude international audiences, of course, but the Delta petropoets do not relinquish local referents or ideas in order to appeal to those wider audiences.

There are many examples, however, of Niger Delta petropoems that directly refer to individuals, bodies, and governments from outside of Nigeria. This address to global audiences can be traced in the writings of internationally renowned petropoets such as Saro-Wiwa and Bassey. Indeed, Sule Emmanuel Egya describes Bassey as one of the most important figures for 'confronting those responsible' because his 'poetry is utterly combative [...] and call[s] on the people to rise against the oppressors' (2015: 9). A clear example of this is Bassey's poem 'I will not dance to your beat', which he recited following his opening remarks at the 2010 World Peoples Climate Conference:

> I will not dance to your beat
> If you call plantations forests
> I will not sing with you
> If you privatize my water
> I will confront you with my fists
> If climate change means death to me but business to you
> I will expose your evil greed
> If you don't leave crude oil in the soil
> Coal in the hole and tar sands in the lands
> [...]
> I will not dance to your beat
> Unless we walk the sustainable path

> And accept real solutions & respect Mother Earth
> Unless you do
> I will not &
> We will not dance to your beat
>
> (2010: 55)³

The poem is a war cry. The repetition, anaphora, monosyllabic and disyllabic words, spondees, and direct address serve up defiant challenge in rhythmic, emphasized, and reemphasized statements and threat. There is no softening or compromise here. Bassey uses his global platform to make clear his position: those in power must act now, or continue to be challenged, confronted, and resisted via any and all means.

Where Bassey addresses the climate and ecological crises at large in 'I will not dance to your beat', Gomba's 'Shell's Love' names and shames the specific nations, individuals, and companies responsible for environmental destruction in the Delta. In Gomba's poem, the seamless shift from British colonial- to neocolonial control enacted by international corporations in Nigeria is captured via anaphora and parallelism, so that 'Royal Britannic Protectorates, Royal Britannic Goldie. | Royal Britannic Killing. Royal Britannic Robbery' turns into 'Royal Dutch Charter. Royal Dutch Shell. | Royal Dutch Disease. Royal Dutch Death' (2014: 122). Other international players are mentioned too. Though in 1995 South African President Nelson Mandela condemned the Abacha regime for killing Saro-Wiwa and called for sanctions against Nigerian oil, Gomba writes that the Shell South African Chairman 'John Drake | Pulls hard wool over Mandela's aged-eyes' (123). This is a reference to the close personal relationships between Shell's senior executives and leading members of the South African government that meant South Africa's involvement in protecting Nigerian people and environments constituted ineffectual and inconsistent (non-)action, if not outright betrayal. Elsewhere in the poem, 'Brian Anderson', Chair of Shell Nigeria between 1994 and 1997, 'works the wreaths' of the Ogoni Nine, as senior figures and generals under Abacha, 'Dauda Komo. Paul Okuntimo. Obi Umahi' are denounced as 'Psychopaths!' (123). Shell's gaslighting (both literally through gas flaring, and metaphorically in the distorting of perceptions of reality) is also expressed in the poem, the latter via the numerous capitalized exclamative interjections: 'SHELL SWEARS!', 'SHELL LOVES!', 'SHELL LOVES THE DELTA! SHELL SWEARS!', 'SHELL SWEARS IT LOVES THE DELTA!' (122–123). Shell's promises of care, recompense, and opportunities are lies, shouted over the truths of the situation. This represents the force and magnitude of oil and the international oil infrastructures that attempt to drown out the testimonies and resistance expressed throughout the poem.

The sheer scale and horror of the corruption, violence, pollution, and destruction of the lives and environs in the Delta means that there is little in the petropoetry to offer visions of a better future. One exception is Osundare's 'Our Earth Will Not Die' from the collection *The Eye of the Earth*. As in some of the earlier examples we mentioned, Osundare's poem begins as an elegy for an embodied Delta, accompanied by *'a solemn, almost elegiac tune'*:

> Lynched
> the lakes
> Slaughtered
> the seas
> Mauled
> The mountains
>   (1986: 50)

The alliteration and offset text create the sense of water flow then interrupted by a clear point of resistance: 'But our earth will not die' (50). In the caesura before the final stanza, there is a shift in tone and style to match this new tone of defiance as the mourning song *'turns festive, louder'* (51), and the poetic voice declares:

> Our earth will see again
> eyes, washed by a new rain
> the westering sun will rise again
> resplendent like a new coin. [...]
> The sea will drink its heart's content
> when a jubilant thunder flings open the skygate
> and a new rain tumbles down
> in drums of joy.
> Our earth will see again
> This earth, OUR EARTH.
>   (51)

Osundare's text is wholly unlike the other petropoems we have examined here in its unrestrained message of hope. The poem imagines a new earth washed clean by a thunderstorm – fresh rather than acidic waters bringing new life and sight where there was previously death and darkness. Here the capitalized 'OUR EARTH' is used to reset and rewrite the planet after its near-death. Though barely conceivable in any real way, Osundare's commitment to a vision of a recovering world remains vital, urgent, and necessary. His poem suggests that even at the very bleakest of times, it is still worth clinging on to the idea of, and fighting for, a better world.

Ice

The Arctic region that we turn to in this section has largely been defined by notions of marginality when viewed in relation to the dominant political, economic, and cultural dynamics of the twentieth and twenty-first centuries.

As Graham Huggan and Roger Norum state in their special issue of *Moving Worlds* entitled 'The Postcolonial Arctic':

> [T]he region continues to be mythologized as an unknown, inaccessible, and forbidden land, a remote, wild, and often 'othered' frontier. As an aggregate territory and a phantasy of the public consciousness, there has been a drive to essentialize this diverse, contested space in a way that heavily glosses over the complex geopolitical, (trans)national, cultural and linguistic distinctions that define it.
>
> (2015: 1)[4]

Olga Ulturgasheva (Eveny, northeast Siberia) and Barbara Bodenhorn affirm this when they write: 'In public discourse, the Arctic has often been associated with a cold, empty, pristine, ambiguous, even liminal land' (2022: 27). This is despite the region being shaped by colonial contestations that have made it integral in the historic trade in whale blubber, timber, and animal furs, as well as diamond mining and oil and gas drilling in the late twentieth and twenty-first centuries. Today, the Arctic region is of particular strategic interest for the US, Canada, Russia, and China as a site of valuable energy resources, as well as being important for the transportation of trade and for food security (Leddy, 2020; McVey, 2022; Stoetman et al., 2023).[5] Adriana Craciun (2009) has labelled this contemporary, late capitalist contestation 'the scramble for the Arctic', drawing a direct comparison to the carving up of Africa by European imperial powers in the late nineteenth century. For Craciun, this scramble predominantly focuses on 'access rights to the rapidly melting Northwest Passage' and is both 'the product of a global environmental crisis unfolding in our lifetime' and 'part of a centuries long struggle to control a transcontinental access point' that connects Asia, North America, and Europe (2009: 104). Rather than being remote and barren, then, the Arctic, say Ulturgasheva and Bodenhorn, is 'a particular cosmo-political zone which continues to register the nineteenth-century colonial footprints of Russia, the US, Canada and Denmark' whilst also remaining a

> global hotspot – politically, economically, and ecologically – with tensions between those who want to exploit its non-renewable resources and those who focus more on the protection of its renewable resources which carry moral and spiritual weight in terms of interspecies sociality.
>
> (2022: 26)

It is in the literary expressions of Native Alaskan poets that this tension is articulated alongside urgent calls to protect and sustain the habitats of people, fauna, and flora reliant upon Arctic ice for their survival.

The creative and sensory interventions offered by both okpik and Rexford on the ways in which oil extraction and mass ice melt are threatening human and other-than-human lives in the Arctic foreground the importance of literary studies in what has been labelled *Etuaptmumk*, or Two-Eyed Seeing. Originating from the teachings of Chief Charles Labrador (Mi'kmaq) of Acadia First Nation, Two-Eyed Seeing advocates for the combination of traditional Indigenous knowledge and experience with Environmental Science. It has been developed for use in Environmental Science education in Canadian university settings by Mi'kmaw Elders Murdena Marshall and Albert Marshall of the Eskasoni First Nation along with the Canadian biologist Cheryl Bartlett. They write that Two-Eyed Seeing involves 'learning to see from one eye with the strengths of Indigenous knowledges and ways of knowing, and from the other eye with the strengths of Western knowledges and ways of knowing, and to using both these eyes together, for the benefit of all' (2012: 335). For this reason, '[t]he scope of relevance for Two-Eyed Seeing is broad' and can be 'place[d] [...] in the context of emerging theory for transdisciplinary research' (331).

A cross-disciplinary, Two-Eyed combination of traditional Indigenous knowledges and Western environmental science has been widely supported by researchers, Indigenous writers, and activists seeking to raise awareness about the catastrophic climatic transformations in the cryosphere. The pioneering environmental scientist David G. Barber, for example, notes that Inuit knowledge 'shows the impacts of changing temperatures on factors such as sea-ice extent, landscapes, wildlife, and wildlife habitat; the accelerated impact of climate change on these factors has been observed by younger generations in recent decades' (Barber et al., 2008: 14). Similarly, Hildegard Diemberger and Astrid Hovden advocate for '[p]erceptions rooted in local day-to-day observations and cosmological frameworks' that can 'blend with a wide range of global scientific narratives and technological infrastructures that reach remote sites in bits and pieces, creating new "assemblages"' (2022: 153). In her book, *The Right to Be Cold*, the Inuk activist and Nobel Peace Prize nominee Sheila Watt-Cloutier argues that 'Inuit are the ground-truthers of climate change' and 'are on the front lines of the cataclysmic environmental shifts that are affecting the world, and we have observed and confirmed the changes in the Arctic for decades' (324). This insistence on the long-standing and present-day impacts of environmental breakdown for Inuit communities contributes to an understanding of the significance of Indigenous perspectives for Environmental Science. As she goes on to affirm: 'We see the local impacts – and help link these observations to global data gathered through satellites or climate models. Our traditional knowledge is holistic but not dated; indeed, it offers cutting-edge insights for science, policy and citizens worldwide' (324).

Although Two-Eyed Seeing has, to date, been applied widely in healthcare, conservation, and education, it has not yet had a significant impact in literary studies. Here we make a claim for its methodological utility by using it to analyse how poetry by Alaskan Native writers bridges the gaps between Environmental Science, Indigenous knowledges, and subjectivities. In discussing the detrimental effects of oil and gas extraction in the Arctic, for instance, okpik herself asserts that the 'specialized, concise, clear, intoxicating language' of poetry 'is much more effective and appealing than prose at conveying this' (Mexina, 2022: n.p.). Similarly, Rexford describes how her poetry expresses her experience of being 'inspired by something bigger than myself', allowing her in turn to develop a sense of spirituality capable of 'grasp[ing] the magnitude and depth of [the Iñupiat] environment' (Harcharek and Rexford, 2015: 10, 17). Both poets also look outwards from individual and community-specific accounts of environmental transformations by identifying the extraction and burning of fossil fuels – and the dominant human groups behind these activities – as the primary cause of environmental ruination across the Arctic, with drastic ramifications for human and other-than-human life both locally and globally. As our discussion of these writers will show, investments in cross-cultural and cross-disciplinary, Two-Eyed research would greatly benefit further engagements with literary depictions of the marginalized lives reliant on Arctic environments where the effects of oil extraction and global warming are most keenly felt. Doing so contributes to the challenge to capitalist–imperial temporalities that place Indigenous peoples in a disappearing past and climate breakdown in the near future.

In what follows, we examine how okpik and Rexford use poetic form to respond to, and challenge, the rapacity and environmentally damaging effects of fossil fuel extraction and use on Arctic icescapes. While much scholarship has been undertaken on Indigenous prose narratives, to date there has been less of a focus on Indigenous poetry. This is noted by Molly McGlennen, who maintains that Indigenous poetry 'has historically taken the back seat to fiction and nonfiction' (2018: 4). Taking poetry seriously, McGlennen argues, means that 'we begin to see poetry's facility to allow for a way of "traveling" in whatever shape it takes – cyclic, back-and-forth, or giant leaps into the seventh generation ahead', whilst 'at the same time the language remains rooted in specific tribal epistemologies and histories' (5). In our analysis of two female Indigenous poets, we follow McGlennen's insistence that it is 'poetry's unique ability to espouse multiple and simultaneous voices, initiate multiple and simultaneous temporal and spatial modes, craft close associations to song and prayer, and support spaces for critical listening' that offers 'a particularly meaningful method for Native women to undo linear colonial and patriarchal narratives' (5).

Our choice to examine the poetry of okpik and Rexford also addresses what McGlennen has identified as the 'potential limitations to literary nationalist framings of Native literatures because of the various types of [...] *dislocations* experienced and expressed by Indigenous women poets' (1, original emphasis). According to McGlennen, 'tribally specific readings of Native literatures' can prove to be inadequate in attending to the 'variety of positionalities that Indigenous poets reveal, such as urbanity, nonrecognition, disenrollment, diaspora and migration, destabilized citizenship, intertribalism, queer identity, and, more broadly, transnational experiences' (1). This is pertinent for our analysis since okpik is of Inuit-Iñupiat heritage but was raised by German and Irish caregivers. She has asserted that, '[b]ecause of the many travels in life at home and abroad, my diction is a composite of these travels and many stories told. [...] My identity in poetics comes from the many places I've lived, visited, or traveled' (Mexina, 2022: n.p.). Similarly, Rexford is of mixed heritage combining Iñupiat, French/German, and English from Alaska, and writing poetry is, for her, an act of ancestral connection and communication. When she began writing aged 17, Rexford says: 'It was the first time I heard the voice that connects me to my lineage' (Harcharek and Rexford, 2015: 10). This voice led her to write 'poems about the beginning of time' based on 'vividly powerful scenes [...] from life as the Iñupiat had been living since our memories began' (10). Rexford and okpik's writing thus offers them a means of working through their own located and dislocated subjectivities to stage the experiential sensation of living in, and relying upon, a rapidly transforming Arctic environment.

We begin our analyses with a focus on oil extraction in the Arctic through a reading of two examples of Alaskan Native petropoetry: Rexford's 'Scripture According to Sila' (2009) and okpik's 'If Oil is Drilled in Bristol Bay' (2012). Then we turn to Rexford's poem 'Migration' (2009) and okpik's 'Anthropocene Years' (2022) to discuss the issue of mass ice melt across the Arctic as a consequence of global warming. These examples demonstrate how close analysis of Indigenous poetry facilitates, and is facilitated by, the method of Two-Eyed Seeing and its investment in combining traditional Indigenous knowledges and Environmental Science as a means of apprehending the interrelated ecological, corporate, and geopolitical drivers threatening human and nonhuman lifeways in the Arctic.

Arctic Oil Extraction in Alaskan Native Petropoetry

In 1989, following the *Exxon Valdez* oil spill in Alaska's Prince William Sound, the Arctic was thrust into the centre of global, environmental discourse. At that time, it was the worst oil spill to occur in an American state, comprising 11 million gallons of oil and causing the mass death of aquatic animals, including approximately a quarter of a million seabirds and almost three thousand otters.[6] *Exxon Valdez* is the worst and most high-profile of the many Alaskan and Canadian oil spills that have occurred since 1970, and its catastrophic impact on the Alaskan environment led to the Oil Pollution Act being passed in 1990, strengthening the remit of the Environmental Protection Agency (EPA) in the US.[7] Since the *Exxon Valdez* spill, oil has remained the 'sacred cow of Alaskan politics' (LaDuke, 2003: 30) with one and a half million barrels being extracted per day.

The expansion of the Alaskan oil industry is directly linked to the colonization and dispossession of Indigenous peoples. As the Anishinaabe writer and activist Winona LaDuke explains:

> When Alaska became the 49th [US] state in 1959, about 85,000 Native people lived there. The discovery of oil prompted the federal government

to address aboriginal title questions in the region, in order to find a tenable legal loophole through which to secure an 800-mile pipeline from the North Slope to Valdez.

(2003: 30)

This loophole was the Alaskan Native Claims Settlement Act (ANCSA), which replicated earlier forms of North American settler colonialism: without consultation with Native communities, the Act extinguished 'all aboriginal land claims', passing jurisdiction over the land on to 'for-profit Alaska Native Corporations, and the people were made shareholders' (30). Alaska has since become one of the most polluted states in the US.

Over the space of four short stanzas, Rexford's poem 'Scripture According to Sila' juxtaposes a series of discrete images that together tell the story of the damaging impacts of oil drilling on the ecosystem and Indigenous lifeways of the Alaskan Arctic. The title refers directly to the epistemologies that structure Indigenous social, political, and ecological relations. According to the Iñupiaq filmmaker and activist, Rachel Nutaaq Ayałhuq Naŋinaaq Edwardson: '[t]here are two fundamental Iñupiaq concepts, common to all Inuit communities – nuna, loosely meaning land, and siḷa, loosely meaning air/atmosphere' (2022: 91). The reference to air and atmosphere, Edwardson explains, does not merely mean that *sila* is a term for the air we breathe. Rather, it refers, she says (quoting the Iñupiaq Elders Fannie Kuutuuq Akpik and Jana Pausauraq Harcharek) to 'anything from the land into the moon, the sun, the stars [...]. In this way, the very life force that is within us is also the weather around us and the life force that fuels the universe' (91). The concepts of *nuna* and *sila* illustrate how 'the complexity of Iñupiaq political and social systems rests in a set of understandings and tools for navigating life in a balanced and respected way together and always in a sustainable way, with our particular ecosystem' (92). 'Scripture According to Sila' places this allusion to social, political, and ecological balance in contrast with imagery that presents the human, nonhuman, and inanimate world of the Iñupiaq as pained and denuded by the rapacious processes of Arctic oil extraction.

Opening with the image of an aquatic bird – specifically an Arctic loon – sitting 'on a lake of black lichen' and 'conversing with Polaris', the poem establishes a communion between the nonhuman Arctic environment and the stars, but it is a communion characterized by despair: the bird 'thinly exhales a round wail' in response to a 'cry' from the 'tongueless' North Star (Rexford, 2009: 48). The source of this despair is indicated by the discoloured, black lichen that surrounds the loon, which acts as the poem's first sign of a natural environment that is being transformed by the oil industry. The bird's 'thin' exhalation emphasizes this, implying that the air it breathes has become dense with pollution. This suggestion is picked up again when the focus shifts in the second stanza to an 'Eskimo' drummer chanting 'with taut scarlet vocal chords | in windfallen alto lament' (48). The mournful cries of the loon, Polaris, and the drummer, we discover, are connected to the arrival of an outsider to this landscape who is prospecting for oil: 'a footstep on sod reddish brown | in land exposed naked | extracted an indigo oil seep' (48). The presence of the prospector thus stages how 'developers' look at the environment and envision a virgin landscape replete with future resources, even though, as Mary Louise Pratt comments, that same landscape is already 'lived as intensely humanized, saturated with local history and meaning, where plants, creatures, and geographical formations have names, uses, symbolic functions, histories, places in indigenous knowledge formations' (1992: 61). When, in the poem, the 'blackened steel' of 'an oilrig' (48) then appears to stake the claim, the scale of the threat of the hydrocarbon industry to Indigenous human and other-than-human lives is keenly felt.

The arrival of the oil industry disturbs the lifeways and sustainable hunting practices of the Indigenous inhabitants by interrupting the coextensive, mutually sustaining, and respectful relationships between the drummer, bird, and stars. The poem's final stanza leaves us with an image of Indigenous hunters sitting on 'a bearded sealskin boat perched | on ice bluish white | expectant of bowhead mist' (48). The hunters are here depicted scanning the waters for the spray of a bowhead whale; yet, when they launch out to sea, they are met with 'silence' (48). As such, there is a noticeable circularity to the poem's imagery, returning as it does to the world of animals. Where the opening stanza stages a communion between the loon and Polaris, however, the final stanza confronts the reader with an *absence* of other-than-human life: the expected whale does not appear on the horizon and the waters are deathly quiet.

The experiential sensation of life in an Arctic environment that is transformed by the oil industry is also captured in okpik's 'If Oil is Drilled in Bristol Bay', which is taken from the 2012 collection *corpse whale*. The poem is addressed to the former Alaska Governor Sarah Palin in response to the 2011 plans to allow drilling in Bristol Bay, which is home to Alaskan Natives with Alutiiq, Dena'ina, and Yup'ik ancestry, as well as numerous threatened species, including seals, otters, and the North Pacific right whale. The Bay also provides the US with around 40 percent of its seafood.[8] In a similar manoeuvre to Rexford, the setting of okpik's poem is established from the vantage point of an aquatic bird, this time a sea cormorant, who shares with humans a dependence on fish for survival. The speaker opens with the question:

> Why is it, in Bristol Bay, a sea cormorant
> hovers, sings a two-fold song with a hinged cover
> for a mouth, teeth set in sockets, with a hissing grind
> of spikelets biting the air? Dip one.
>
> (okpik, 2012: 42)

The question exhibits the speaker's desire to see the Bay from a non-anthropocentric perspective but also to fully understand the motivations behind the bird's movements through the air and water. The language – with its emphasis on the bird's biology and the sound of their song – defamiliarizes both the environment of the Bay and the cormorant, encouraging the reader to see through new (or Two) eyes. The reference to 'Dip one' establishes a pattern whereby the first four, two-lined stanzas are punctuated by the cormorant diving into the water as it hunts for fish. The imagery of the third stanza suggests that the cormorant's movements are directed by its need to find food for its young, and that its future survival is connected to and indivisible from other ecological patterns such as those of Arctic volcanoes: 'The lips of vanished flames in lava coals | glow vermillion as an egg cracks. Dip two' (42). The bird's recurring attempts, however, are indicative of the kind of aquatic emptiness on which Rexford's poem 'Scripture According to Sila' ends; the cormorant repeatedly dives into the water but returns with nothing. In this way, the poem invites the reader, and by implication Palin, the Federal Government, and oil prospectors, to view Bristol Bay from the defamiliarized perspective of another species whose survival is also contingent upon a sustainable relationship with the Bay's fish. Importantly, two years after the publication of okpik's collection, the Obama administration blocked oil drilling in Bristol Bay, and the EPA has since also protected the area from any copper or gold mining projects.[9]

One of the most striking formal aspects of okpik's poetry is her use of the combined pronoun 'she/I'. This is adopted in 'If Oil is Drilled in Bristol Bay' as a means of revealing the lives of both the speaker and the cormorant still hatching from its egg as connected: 'While still in the embryo, separating the body | from death she/I smell/s of arsenic, the Chugach Range | in unnatural bitterness' (42). In this moment, the speaker imagines how toxified air is shared across Indigenous and nonhuman inhabitants of Alaska. This is just one example of how okpik's use of combined pronouns conceptualizes a form of non-anthropocentric selfhood whereby language shapes, and is shaped by, kinships between animals, plants, the land, water, and people, all with distinct but contingent cultures and personhoods. In interview, okpik has commented on her use of pronouns, stating:

> the symbolic meaning of the 'I' of the poems, helps me open the poetry to new curves or slant writing to appeal to the reader, to draw them in in a physical way, to present the internal strife of one, me, she/I, mind. Especially, the 'we' instead of the 'I' is represented as an Iñupiaq way of thinking. […] There is no ego. There is a transformation going on with the internal and external language. So urgent is the writing, but these times require the urgency of language.
>
> (Mexina, 2022: n.p.)

The self that is constructed in okpik's poems is thus defined by a more-than-humanness that stands in opposition to exploitative forms of capitalist greed that can be experienced and expressed as highly individualized *self*ishness.

The repeated use of 'she/I' privileges an Iñupiaq epistemology in which the individual and the environment, the interior and the exterior, are inseparable and mutually impacted by dramatic transformations to shared ecosystems. In 'If Oil Is Drilled in Bristol Bay', the distinction between human and nonhuman that characterizes the poem's opening question is transcended by the inclusion of the 'she/I' pronoun to denote a unified, physical experience of striving to survive in a land that is being transformed by the infrastructure of oil drilling. Importantly, the imagery also alludes to the Chugach mountains, which lie around one thousand kilometres west of Bristol Bay and close to Valdez. Thus, through an evocation of the sense of smell, the poem includes the inanimate environment in this unification, collapsing the distance between disparate Alaskan regions that are vulnerable to the toxic pollutants caused by the oil industry.

In the final moments of 'If Oil Is Drilled in Bristol Bay', the additional pronoun 'they' is introduced, establishing a tension between the unified 'she/I' on the one hand and the perspective of oil prospectors on the other:

> [...] Why is it, man's/woman's nerve scarcely
> stifled and sane, comes to prey? While they swoon
> minerals of crude oil and sea spiders for tricking a way for gold.
> Will they crawl around her/me, sink their eyeteeth in the sea,
> ravaging the ecosphere and the ore gold for fuel. Drill.
>
> (42)

As with the ominous footsteps of the prospector in Rexford's 'Scripture According to Sila', there is conflict staged in this moment between the arrival of a predatory human outsider who envisions the land only as the site of untapped, valuable resources and the Indigenous and environmental victims of their rapacious actions. Distinct from the unity of the speaker, the bird, and the mountains, the land surveyors are characterized by their greed, their eyes transforming into monstrous, vampiric teeth capable of destroying the precarious balance of the Bay. In punctuating the final line with the single word 'Drill', the poem offers an alliterative echo of the cormorant's 'dips' from the opening stanzas, suggesting that the songs of the cormorant are replaced by the mechanical sound of the drills. In so doing, the poem enacts the experience of habitat loss and the extirpative effects of oil drilling in Arctic seas on the region's nonhuman inhabitants.

Ice Melt, Cryocide, and Alaskan Native Poetry

As well as being the site of industrialized oil extraction, the Arctic is also a region that is warming nearly four times faster than the rest of the globe (Rantanen et al., 2022), causing the rapid melting of glaciers, sea ice, and permafrost. In 2021, Markus Rex, the leader of the largest scientific expedition to the Arctic, warned that the Arctic may now be past an irreversible tipping point, and in 2023 a team of climate scientists led by Dirk Notz declared that the region will see ice-free summers as early as the 2030s regardless of any reduction in greenhouse gases.[10] The scale of Arctic ice melt is already altering the Earth's ability to reflect solar energy and is releasing previously trapped greenhouse gases, leading to more global warming. Resultant rising sea levels threaten coastal cities across the globe (Box et el., 2022), and severely modify global patterns of water and atmospheric circulation that are integral to the Earth's capacity to sustain life (Barber et al., 2008). The rapid melting of Arctic ice thus provides stark, undeniable evidence of the reality of climate change (Roe et al., 2016). Across the region, the Arctic Basin has seen the most dramatic decrease in sea ice as a result of global warming, as well as a tendency for ice to melt earlier and freeze later in the year, which has a significant impact on the livelihoods of human and nonhuman inhabitants. 'Longer coastal ice-free seasons', write Barber et al., 'will result in an increase in storm surges and coastal erosion, with important implications for northern coastal communities' (2008: 10). Inuit communities, for example, 'rely upon fast ice (sea ice attached to shore) for transportation, hunting, and cultural traditions' (10), meaning that its reduction severely impacts the ability to harvest fish and to navigate the ocean. The reduction in ice has also meant that 'seals are not able to nurse their pups as much' (15), making them thinner with poor quality pelts, which has a knock-on impact for polar bears 'whose main food source is seals' (15). This in turn affects Inuit communities further as seals provide food and clothing, and pressure on polar bears' hunting patterns has led to them migrating further inland to residential areas where they become a threat.

An awareness of the social and ecological impacts of melting ice across a range of remote but connected Arctic regions is captured in Ulturgasheva and Bodenhorn's term 'cryocide', which refers not only to 'the disappearance of the physical substance, but also to the human and other bio systems that depend on it for their continuity' (2022: 27). Framing Arctic ice melt as 'cryocide' in turn brings to the fore how the despoiling of the region must be understood as a consequence of the exploitative activities of particular human groups. Ulturgasheva and Bodenhorn also affirm that the effects of cryocide are not limited to Arctic regions but will generate new emergencies for human societies across the globe. This includes the potential emergence of 'zombie' viruses akin to Covid-19 but borne of 'the remains of life that once thrived in the Arctic, including microbes, pathogens, viruses, ancient plankton, insects and amphibia' that have been frozen in permafrost as though in 'an ancient refrigerator' (2022: 39). A 'continuous permafrost thaw', they say, will offer these ancient lifeforms 'a chance for a second life' (39). This combination of the drivers of cryocide – namely global warming, the history of colonialism, conflicts between contemporary global superpowers, and possible risks to health across the world – upends mainstream conceptions of the Arctic as marginal and remote and instead makes it a region that is fundamental and central to global geopolitics now.

The connection between the hydrocarbon economy and Arctic ice melt is made explicit in Rexford's petropoem, 'Migration'. The second stanza describes 'a cab driver with cigarette drooping | from his lip, swerves as you stand | in the middle of the street' (Rexford, 2009: 49). The car, as iconic symbol of fossil-fuelled capitalist "progress" and privilege, and driven by a smoke-blowing man, only narrowly misses crashing into the figure in the poem. The deathly effects of the burning of fossil fuels, cigarettes, and dangerous driving are thus united, so that the Indigenous figure can be seen with 'Two Eyes': standing with 'your left foot | on the painted white line, your right | on the edge of a melting polar icecap' (49). The second-person pronoun, although used to paint the image of a pedestrian standing in the road, brings the point home to the reader – *your* life is at risk in a fossil-fuelled world. Though the car might not kill you directly, it is melting the ground beneath your feet. The poem ends with the lines: 'We run into the city, into concrete nightmares; | we fault ourselves into the glass hallway where we stand' (49). The crevices and ice melt caused by global warming merely precede the collapse of urban living too. The play on 'fault' works to capture the climate change-induced faults caused by cracking ice and earth; faulty attempts to look for escape and refuge in man-made structures; and the ideas of fault, criticism, and responsibility when attributing blame for the climate crisis.

The widespread, interrelated, and detrimental effects of Arctic cryocide are also confronted in okpik's poem 'Anthropocene Years', originally published in the 2022 collection *Blood Snow*. The speaker in the poem names a series of marginalized Arctic locations dispersed across Alaska (Cape Lisburne and Kaktovik), Norway (White Island, otherwise known as Kvitøya, and Jan Mayen), northern Russia (Cape Chelyuskin and Novaya Zemlya), Greenland (Disko), and Canada (Baffin Island). In so doing, okpik uses the space of the poem to bring together isolated environments that are divided by national and continental borders but joined by a collective experience of ice melt, global warming, pollution, and coastal erosion. This manoeuvre stages Diemberger and Hovden's assertion that

> [j]ust as island people far removed from one another are increasingly brought together by a shared sense of emergency linked to rising sea levels (and sometimes take joint action on the global stage), people of the cryosphere can be seen as linked by comparable experiences of human responses to vanishing ice.
>
> (2022: 152)

For Diemberger and Hovden, the reality that 'icescapes […] undergoing unprecedented transformations' have quickly become 'local and global proxies for climatic transformations' (151) forges a transnational, transcontinental unity across not only the Arctic but also the icescapes of the Himalayas, Andes, and the Alps. No matter the nationality, culture, or livelihood, there exists a shared experience of 'liv[ing] in places where ice matters and where small differences in temperature have a big impact' (152). Recognizing this means privileging a 'phenomenological' approach that

> revolves around the idea of 'sensing icescapes', exploring the wide range of sensory and conceptual experiences that are involved in knowing ice and snow: glacier views and snow lines, crackling ice and roaring avalanches, as well as the cold breath of crevasses and seracs or the life-supporting taste of unlocked fresh water – all these features are deeply connected to wider cosmological frameworks.
>
> (152)

In okpik's 'Anthropocene Years', the poem's speaker enunciates a unified, phenomenological sensation of rootedness and dislocation that is caused by residing in, and relying upon, an environment that is both known and rapidly transforming. This sensation is created by deploying the repetition of the words 'here' and 'there', as is evinced in the opening lines: 'Here Cape Lisburne | Or maybe not there' (okpik, 2022: 5). Immediately, the reader is located and then dislocated, whilst the inclusion of 'maybe' compounds the sense of dizzying confusion.

The speaker reaches for a 'compass' to set their 'route due north' (5), suggesting a desire to recover a sense of purpose and direction that is intimately tied to the Arctic environment. They are left, however, 'bearing in circles' (5) as they leap east and west, south, and north across different cryospheric regions. The speaker's sense of place only becomes stable when the use of anaphora emphasizes the word 'Here' at the beginning of each of the final four lines:

> Here brilliant colors of pollution so high
> Here in the melt sun, heaving waters of ocean and sea.
> Here start ending double-rate heat to sweat & yet, not yet.
> Here wake-up there not here.
> (6)

The 'here' that the speaker finds themselves in is thus not a fixed location that can be found using navigational devices. Rather, it is a transnational and transcontinental, experiential and phenomenological place of cryocidal destruction that is dispersed across the Arctic. The poem evokes the daily experience of 'people of the cryosphere' (Diemberger and Hovden 2022) forced to live in a state of permanent impermanence. The absence of any identifying pronouns – 'I', 'we' or 'you' – indicates that the speaker is thus neither a specific individual nor are they addressing a regionally specific audience. Rather, the speaker is a synecdochal figure representing the collective 'people of the cryosphere' for whom climate change is happening in the present, but the response of the world's political leaders to preventing its devastating social and ecological impacts is 'not yet'.

Conclusion

In this chapter we have explored the ways in which poetry by Nigerian and Alaskan Native writers draws attention to the burning of fossil fuels and polluting effects of oil across geographically distanced regions of the Niger Delta and the Arctic. The two are connected by the actions of a global petroleum industry, in collusion with national governments, that re-envisage neocolonial Nigeria and settler colonial Alaska as mere repositories of oil to be extracted, traded, and burned. This wreaks staggering damage to local ecosystems and lifeways that are reliant on the present and future sustainability of delta wetlands and Arctic icescapes. The mining activities of the petroleum industry, moreover, put the coastal communities of the Niger Delta and Alaskan Arctic at special risk due to the impact of global warming on rising sea levels. The poetic responses of the Nigerian and Alaskan writers analysed here offer politically conscious and experiential dimensions to the scientific data on ecological issues such as pollution, ice melt, and global warming.

Our analysis of these works contributes to a more varied and complex understanding of the characteristics of contemporary eco-poetry. In Adeline Johns-Putra's productive overview of the ways in which eco-poetry can be thought of as a 'development from nature poetry', she notes that the former involves an 'emphasis on the interconnectedness of human and nonhuman life in a time of unprecedented anthropogenic environmental damage' (2016: 271). This definition, however, is supported by a focus on Anglo-American poetry, including by Mary Oliver, Gary Snyder, and the British Poet Laureates Andrew Motion, Carol Ann Duffy, and Simon Armitage. Drawing on this contemporary Anglo-American context, Johns-Putra asserts that eco-poetry is best defined by

> the use of lyrical descriptions of nature and our place on the planet to promote ecological awareness, the striking of an elegiac or apologetic attitude over damage done (indeed, lament is by far the most dominant tone of climate change poetry), and the use of satire or jeremiad to criticize humans for their careless treatment of the world.
>
> (272)

This is an account of eco-poetry, then, that places it firmly within a tradition that stretches back to the lyricism of nineteenth-century Romantic poetry (perhaps best epitomized by the English writer William Wordsworth) and twentieth-century American nature writing. A paradigmatic feature of these forms of nature writing is a view of the natural world as focalized through a singular, often mournful and nostalgic speaker who frames environmental despoliation as being caused by humanity at large.

The Niger Delta and Indigenous Alaskan poets that we have explored here cannot be read as part of this same generic lineage. As we have shown, the speakers in their poems do not attribute the climate crisis to the actions of an undifferentiated humanity. Instead, they enunciate a criticism of the global oil industry that is rooted in a long history of capitalist–imperial dominance. These speakers, moreover, are distinct from the singular, lyrical speakers characteristic of much Euro-American Romanticism or eco-poetry. In the Nigerian petropoetry we have examined, for example, we find the 'town-crier' voicing a collective message of anti-oil protest to embolden the political consciousness and activism of an assumed Niger Delta audience. In our analysis of Alaskan Native poetry, moreover, we have identified poetic techniques, such as okpik's adoption of 'she/I' and 'they' pronouns, which express a sensory experience of ecological damage that can be seen with 'Two Eyes' and is shared across human and nonhuman inhabitants of Alaskan icescapes. This is sharply contrasted with the extractivist activities of oil prospectors in both Rexford and okpik's poems. In both instances, the poetic form provides the writers with a literary space in which to identify and critique the industrial-scale causes of pollution, species loss, and global warming, whilst also bearing witness to the communal lifeways that are imperilled by the ongoing extraction and burning of fossil fuels.

Notes

1. The rich tradition of ecopoetic writing in Nigeria encompasses the work of the five writers we consider in this chapter, as well as J.P. Clark-Bekederemo (John Pepper Clark), Gabriel Okara, Ebi Yeibo, Odia Ofiemun, Christian Otobotekere, and Adam Usman Garko (amongst others), and these writers stand alongside novelists and short story writers who also address ecological concerns in their work, such as Ben Okri, Isidore Okpewho, Helon Habila, Kaine Agary, Chiemeka Garricks, Chuma-Udeh Ngozi, and Ogaga Oguyade.
2. The Nigerian Oil Spill Monitor is a dedicated website (https://oilspillmonitor.ng) that is intended to raise awareness of the scale of the problem. It calls on the public to report oil spills to NOSDRA through a hotline or by email, but heavily relies on the support of oil companies to provide data. Oil companies reporting to NOSDRA can indicate whether the oil spills are caused by sabotage or theft or by factors that fall under their responsibility, such as operational or maintenance errors, pipeline corrosion, or equipment failure.
3. This was later published in his 2011 collection named after this poem.
4. This special issue emerged out of the HERA-funded project, 'Arctic Encounters: Contemporary Travel/Writing in the European High North'. For more information about this project, see https://heranet.info/projects/hera-2012-cultural-encounters/arctic-encounters-contemporary-travelwriting-in-the-european-high-north [accessed May 10, 2023].
5. In 2007, Russia 'symbolically staked its claim to billions of dollars worth of oil and gas reserves in the Arctic Ocean' by planting a flag on the North Pole seabed (Parfitt, 2007).
6. See https://darrp.noaa.gov/oil-spills/exxon-valdez [accessed May 4, 2023].
7. For a summary of the Oil Pollution Act, see https://www.epa.gov/laws-regulations/summary-oil-pollution-act#:~:text=(1990),or%20unwilling%20to%20do%20so [accessed May 4, 2023].
8. For an overview of the ecological and economic significance of Bristol Bay, see Somander (2014).
9. See 'EPA blocks catastrophic mining project in Bristol Bay, Alaska', https://www.worldwildlife.org/stories/epa-blocks-catastrophic-mining-project-in-bristol-bay-alaska [accessed May 5, 2023].

10 See https://www.sciencealert.com/scientist-suggests-that-we-may-have-already-triggered-the-irreversible-warming-tipping-point [accessed May 31, 2023] and https://www.theguardian.com/environment/2023/jun/06/too-late-now-to-save-arctic-summer-ice-climate-scientists-find [accessed June 19, 2023].

Bibliography

Aghoghovwia, Philip. 2014. "The Poetics and Politics of Transnational Petro-Environmentalism in Nnimmo Bassey's 'We Thought It Was Oil but It Was Blood'." *English in Africa* 41, no. 2: 59–77. http://www.jstor.org/stable/24389456.

Barber, David G., *et al*. 2008. "The Changing Climate of the Arctic." *Arctic* 61, Supplement 1: "Arctic Change and Coastal Communities": 7–26.

Bartlett, Cheryl, Murdena Marshall, and Albert Marshall. 2012. "Two-Eyed Seeing and Other Lessons Learned Within a Co-Learning Journey of Bringing Together Indigenous and Mainstream Knowledges and Ways of Knowing." *Journal of Environmental Studies and Sciences* 2: 331–340.

Bassey, Nnimmo. 2002. *We Thought It Was Oil But It Was Blood*. Ibadan: Kraftgriots.

Bassey, Nnimmo. 2010. "I will not dance to your beat." https://pressbooks.pub/firoze/chapter/i-will-not-dance-to-your-beat [accessed 2023].

Bassey, Nnimmo, 2016. *Oil Politics: Echoes of Ecological Wars*. Wakefield: Daraja Press.

Box, Jason E. *et al*. 2022. "Greenland ice sheet climate disequilibrium and committed sea-level rise." *Nature Climate Change* 12 (August): 808–813.

Bruederle, Anna, and Roland Hodler. 2019. "Effect of oil spills on infant mortality in Nigeria." *Environmental Sciences* 116, no. 12 (March): 5467–5471. https://doi.org/10.1073/pnas.1818303116.

Comaroff, Jean, and John Comaroff. 2012. *Theory from the South, Or, How Euro-America is Evolving Toward Africa*. London: Routledge.

Craciun, Adriana. 2009. "The Scramble for the Arctic." *Interventions* 11, no. 1: 103–114, doi:10.1080/13698010902752855.

Diemberger, Hildegard, and Astrid Hovden. 2022. "People of the Cryosphere: A Cross-Regional, Cross-Disciplinary Approach to Icescapes in a Changing Climate." In *Risky Futures: Climate, Geopolitics and Local Realities in the Uncertain Circumpolar North*, edited by Olga Ulturgasheva and Barbara Bodenhorn, 148–175. Oxford: Berghahn Books.

Duckert, Lowell. 2021. "Coal/Oil." In *The Cambridge Companion to Environmental Humanities*, edited by Jeffrey Jerome Cohen and Stephanie Foote, 214–228. Cambridge: Cambridge University Press.

Edwardson, Rachel Nutaaq Ayałhuq Naŋinaaq. 2022. "She'll Do What She Needs to Do." In *Risky Futures: Climate, Geopolitics and Local Realities in the Uncertain Circumpolar North*, edited by Olga Ulturgasheva and Barbara Bodenhorn, 89–102. Oxford: Berghahn Books.

Ghosh, Amitav. 1992. "Petrofiction: The Oil Encounter and the Novel." *New Republic* 206 (March 2): 30–31.

Gomba, Obari. 2014. *The Ascent Stone*. Port Harcourt: Pearl.

Harcharek, Pausauraq Jana, and Cathy Tagnak Rexford. 2015. "Remembering Their Words, Evoking Kiŋuniivut: The Development of the Iñupiaq Learning Framework." *Journal of American Indian Education* 54, no. 2 (Summer): 9–28.

Huggan, Graham, and Roger Norum. 2015. "Editorial." In *Moving Worlds: A Journal of Transcultural Writings* 15, no. 2, special issue: "The Postcolonial Arctic": 1–5.

Ifowodo, Ogaga. 2005. *The Oil Lamp*. Trenton, New Jersey: Africa World Press.

Ifowodo, Ogaga. 2008. *Homeland and Other Poems*. Ibadan: Kraft Books.

Ikiriko, Ibiwari. 2009. *Oily Tears of the Delta*. Ibadan: Kraftgriots.

Johns-Putra, Adeline. 2016. "Climate change in literature and literary studies: From cli-fi, climate change theater and ecopoetry to ecocriticism and climate change criticism." *WIREs Climate Change* 7: 266–282. doi:10.1002/wcc.385.

LaDuke, Winona. 2003. "Alaska: Oil and the Natives." *Earth Island Journal* 18, no. 3 (Autumn), 30–31.

Leddy, Laura. 2020. "Arctic Climate Change Implications for U.S. National Security." *American Security Project* (Sept).

MacDonald, Graeme. 2012. "Oil and World Literature." *American Book Review* 33, no. 3: 7–31. doi:10.1353/abr.2012.0079.

MacDonald, Graeme. 2015. "Commentary." In *The Cheviot, the Stag and the Black, Black Oil* by John McGrath, 1–71. London: Bloomsbury.

MacDonald, Graeme. 2017. "'Monstrous transformer': Petrofiction and world literature." *Journal of Postcolonial Writing* 53, no. 3: 289–302. doi:10.1080/17449855.2017.1337680.

McGlennen, Molly. 2018. *Creative Alliances: The Transnational Designs of Indigenous Women's Poetry*. Norman: University of Oklahoma Press.

McVey, Robert A. 2022. "Russian Strategic Interest in Arctic Heats Up as Ice Melts." *LSE Ideas: Strategic Update* (Sept).

Mentz, Steve. 2021. "Ice/Water/Vapor." In *The Cambridge Companion to Environmental Humanities*, edited by Jeffrey Jerome Cohen and Stephanie Foote, 185–198. Cambridge: Cambridge University Press.

Mexina, Olga. 2022. "An Interview with dg nanouk okpik." *Southeast Review* (Nov 23) https://www.southeastreview.org/single-post/an-interview-with-dg-nanouk-okpik [accessed May 2, 2023].

Ojaide, Tanure. 1998. *Delta Blues and Home Songs*. Ibadan: Kraft Books.

okpik, dg nanouk. 2012. *corpse whale*. Tucson: University of Arizona Press.

okpik, dg nanouk. 2022. *Blood Snow*. Seattle and New York: Wave Books.

Osundare, Niyi. 1986. *The Eye of the Earth*. Nigeria: Heinemann Educational Books.

Parfitt, Tom. 2007. "Russia plants flag on North Pole seabed." *The Guardian* (Thurs August 2) https://www.theguardian.com/world/2007/aug/02/russia.arctic [accessed 2023].

Pendakis, Andrew, and Ursula Biemann. 2012. "This is Not a Pipeline: Thoughts on the Politico-Aesthetics of Oil." *Imaginations Journal of Cross-Cultural Image Studies* 3, no. 2: 6–16. doi:10.17742/IMAGE.sightoil.3-2.2.

Pratt, Mary Louise. 1992. *Imperial Eyes: Travel Writing and Transculturation*. London: Routledge.

Rantanen, Mika, *et al.* 2022. "The Arctic has warmed nearly four times faster than the globe since 1979." *Communications: Earth and Environment* 3, no. 168 (August): 1–10 https://doi.org/10.1038/s43247-022-00498-3.

Rexford, Cathy Tagnak. 2009. "Scripture According to Sila." In *Effigies: An Anthology of New Indigenous Writing, Pacific Rim*, edited by Allison Adele Hedge Coke. Cromer, Norfolk: Salt Publishing.

Roe, Gerard, *et al.* 2016. "Centennial Glacier Retreat as Categorical Evidence of Regional Climate Change." *Nature Geoscience* 10, no. 2: 95–99.

Saro-Wiwa, Ken. 2014. *Silence Would Be Treason: Last Writings of Ken Saro-Wiwa*, edited by Íde Corley, Helen Fallon, and Laurence Cox. Wakefield: Daraja Press.

Somander, Tanya. 2014. "5 Things You Need to Know About Alaska's Bristol Bay." https://obamawhitehouse.archives.gov/blog/2014/12/16/5-things-you-need-know-about-alaskas-bristol-bay [accessed 2023].

Stoetman, Adája. 2023. "United States taking climate security risks to the military very serious." In *Military capabilities affected by climate change: An analysis of China, Russia and the United States*, 38–47. Clingendael Institute.

Szeman, Imre. 2012. "Introduction to Focus: Petrofictions." *American Book Review* 33, no. 3: 3. doi:10.1353/abr.2012.0079u.

Ulturgasheva, Olga, and Barbara Bodenhorn. 2022. "Activating Cosmo-Geo-Analytics: Anthropocene, Arctics and Cryocide." In *Risky Futures: Climate, Geopolitics and Local Realities in the Uncertain Circumpolar North*, edited by Olga Ulturgasheva and Barbara Bodenhorn, 26–57. Oxford: Berghahn Books.

Watt-Cloutier, Sheila. 2015. *The Right to be Cold: One Woman's Story of Protecting Her Culture, the Arctic and the Whole Planet*. Toronto: Penguin Canada.

3 Air

The ecofeminist writer Greta Gaard remarks that '[o]ne of the most significant contributors to climate change is air pollution, particularly in its contribution of black carbon and its effects on global warming' (2020: 2). Indeed, while the atmosphere has not, to date, garnered as much critical attention in the environmental humanities as other components of the climate system, the World Health Organization (WHO) has declared air pollution as the cause of a global health emergency.[1] The WHO has estimated that '92% of the global population breathes air pollution levels that are unsafe' and over 'seven million lives are lost to indoor and ambient air pollution every year' (Neira and Ramanathan, 2020: 93). This means that 'one in eight of all deaths' are caused by air pollution, 'placing it among the top global risks to health' (94–95).[2] Furthermore, the effects of air pollution are felt more keenly across the Global South, where '98 percent of cities are enveloped by air above the threshold of safety established by WHO' (Wallace-Wells, 2019: 104). A 2023 study by the Environmental Research Group based at Imperial College London affirmed the WHO's research and found that air pollution can cause miscarriages and low sperm counts whilst potentially stunting the growth of children. In later life, it can lead to chronic illness, cancer, and strokes. These impacts, the study says, 'affect our quality of life and have a large cost to society through additional health and social care costs, as well as our ability to learn, work and contribute to society' (Fuller et al., 2023: 3).

Historically, an awareness of air pollution has also played a significant role in legislating against ecological despoliation: it was scientific research into air pollution that underpinned the first environmental laws against coal and the manufacturing of gas in the form of the British Smoke Nuisance Abatement Act of 1821, whilst the prevalence of smog across London at the end of the nineteenth century was acknowledged as a 'climatic phenomenon manufactured by industrial modernity' (Oak Taylor, 2016: 1). Measurements of the fluctuations in atmospheric greenhouse gases, moreover, provide scientific data that is integral to understanding how geologic materials document the impact of humans on the environment. This, as we discussed in the Introduction, is a key aspect in determining the Anthropocene as a new geologic epoch. The 'carbonaceous particles' that enter the atmosphere 'following the high-temperature combustion of fossil fuels', write Simon Lewis and Mark

DOI: 10.4324/9780429353352-4

A. Maslin, are then 'deposited in lakes or the ocean, thereby making their way into geological sediments' (2018: 213). Analysis of the concentration of carbon in these sediments then acts as the baseline for defining the 'golden spikes' of geologic epochs and thus the ecological effects of human activity.

Two of the primary drivers of the current rates of global air pollution are fossil fuel use and the agricultural industry (Neira and Ramanathan, 2020: 93). In this chapter we explore novels and poems that depict, first, gas flaring practices that are an integral part of the extraction of oil, and second, the agricultural use of pesticides and the occurrence of gas leaks that are related to their industrial manufacture. Expanding on our analysis of petropoetry from the Niger Delta that we offered in the previous chapter, 'Water', we look here to depictions of gas flaring in three contemporary novels. Helon Habila's *Oil on Water* (2011), Christie Watson's *Tiny Sunbirds Far Away* (2011), and Imbolo Mbue's *How Beautiful We Were* (2021) reveal how the neocolonial inequities of class, gender, and race in contemporary Nigerian and fictionalized African societies are structured around the extraction, use, and exportation of oil, and are experienced in the act of breathing. Turning to the human and ecological impacts of pesticide use and manufacture, we will then concentrate on India as a country in which the agricultural sector has adopted pesticides under the influence of American-led 'Green Revolution' policies since the 1960s. We show how this instigated 'the world's worst industrial disaster' (Varma and Varma, 2005: 37) at a pesticide-manufacturing plant owned by the American company Union Carbide in the city of Bhopal in 1984. This event informs the narratives of Meaghan Delahunt's *The Red Book* (2008) and Indra Sinha's *Animal's People* (2007), as well as Avaes Mohammad's poem 'Bhopal' (2004).

In depicting the human and ecological effects of air pollution in African and Indian contexts, these texts build on an interrogation of what climate justice activists have termed 'eco-apartheid'. The language of 'eco-apartheid' has been adopted by the Indian environmental activist Vandana Shiva, for example, to describe 'the ecological separation of humans from nature in the mechanical, reductionist worldview, which is resulting in the multiplicity of the eco-crisis that is threatening human survival' (2013: n.p.). Melissa Checker's adoption of eco-apartheid refers 'to the increasingly unequal distribution of environmental benefits and burdens' that worsen the living conditions of 'poor and minority people [who] are most vulnerable to the effects of climate change' (2008: 391).[3] Our analysis here follows Shiva and Checker to examine the socio-economic separations between humans who may well share the same atmosphere, but whose direct exposure to toxified air, and whose access to medicines and livelihoods unaffected by the wider impacts of air pollution, are structured by inequities in class, race, and gender.

Gas Flaring

Whereas oil spills provide one of the most dramatic, locally situated, and immediately impactful examples of environmental damage caused by fossil fuel extraction, a more attritional dimension of this oil drilling is the effect that it has on air quality. In some cases, there is a direct link between oil spills and the toxification of the atmosphere. Abosede Omowumi Babatunde (a Fellow of the Rachel Carson Centre for Environment and Society) has noted, 'where the oil companies attempt to cleanup oil spills, it is often superficial, involving the burning of the crude, leaving behind dangerous chemical fumes' (2017: 48). Much more prevalent than this occasional practice, however, is the persistent flaring of gas (which creates pollutants that cause air pollution, acid rain, biodiversity loss, and carcinogenic and respiratory diseases) and the proliferation of traffic fumes from cars, buses, motorcycles, and trucks. An examination of gas flaring and pollution from traffic fumes in Nigeria reveals that there are demonstrably damaging ecological, socio-economic, and health effects at each stage in the extraction, transportation, and use of the crude oil that is sourced from the Niger Delta region.

Gas flaring is a practice that has been used by Shell and other major oil companies in Nigeria since the beginning of the country's oil boom in the late 1950s.[4] Amanze R. Ejiogu explains that '[w]hen crude oil is brought to the surface it is often accompanied by a blend of gasses' where the 'major component gas is usually methane (natural gas)' which 'must be separated from the oil' before it is exported (2013: 984). Flaring is a method of achieving this by burning off the methane.[5] In 2009, Amnesty International reported that there were 'over two hundred [...] continuous gas flares across Niger Delta' (Babatunde, 2017: 53). In fact, flaring has become such a routine part of the extraction process in the Niger Delta that in 2013 Nigeria was second only to Russia in its extensive use of the practice (Ejiogu, 2013: 984), and to date remains in the world's top seven gas flaring countries according to the World Bank.[6]

The local and global effects of this commonplace feature of oil extraction are significant. According to Gabriel Eweje, the low efficiency of the flares means that 'much of the gas is released as methane rather than carbon dioxide', which 'contributes a measurable percentage of the world's total emission of green house gases' (2006: 39). Some flares, moreover, are 'at ground level and located as close as 250 meters from inhabited houses', while the heat that they release daily has been linked to a rise in temperatures that render whole areas uninhabitable (Ejiogu, 2013: 987). Ogoni leaders, according to Eweje, have argued that 'oil companies have been flaring gas in their villages 24 h[ours] a day since 1958 and it affects plant life, pollutes the air, and the surface water' (2006: 39). In an interview conducted by Babatunde, a youth leader from Ikorigbo, Ilaje, stated that, '[i]n our community, it can be difficult to differentiate between night and day because of the burning light and polluted air' (Babatunde, 2017: 54). Research conducted by Babatunde shows that gas flaring creates acid rain that has 'a huge destructive impact on agriculture' and 'also makes the river uninhabitable to aquatic animals' (53). The impact on fish populations is both ecological and socio-economic as it has rendered Indigenous Nigerian fishermen 'jobless and without income' (44). This ultimately 'erodes their access to basic goods and services, which will invariably affect their well-being and survival' (44). The forced migration of fishermen to neighbouring territories also means that 'claims to fishing areas are a major source of conflict in oil-bearing regions' (39).

As well as affecting the environment and the livelihoods of fishermen, the polluted air and the radioactivity of flaring are known to have serious effects on the health of Indigenous communities, causing 'an emergent trend of carcinogenic diseases' as well as 'bronchial and respiratory diseases', with symptoms and illnesses that include 'respiratory irritation, [...] multiple airway and lung injur[ies], [...] emphysema and chronic bronchitis, [...] immune dysfunction, reproductive disorders and autoimmune rheumatic diseases' (Ejiogu, 2013: 987–998). The despoiling of the air and the trend in illnesses that are linked to gas flaring are intensified further in Nigeria by traffic fumes. This in turn leads to a high prevalence of breathing difficulties, such as wheezing and coughing and problems with phlegm and rhinitis, with studies showing 'associations between respiratory illnesses in children and proximity to busy roads, especially those travelled by large numbers of trucks' (Mustapha et al., 2011: 1481).

The disparities in health and living conditions outlined here align with Esthie Hugo's insistence that, '[a]s a material manifestation of the socio-natures of ongoing forms of coloniality across urban Africa, suffocation gives expression to [Frantz] Fanon's critique of colonialism as Manichaean spatial demarcation' (2021: 4). In making this claim, Hugo reminds us of Fanon's assessment of the zonal features of coloniality, whereby the 'zones' in which the colonizer and colonized live 'follow the principle of reciprocal exclusivity' ([1961] 2001: 30).[7] These zones are alluded to in Habila's novel *Oil on Water*, in which the 'wealthy expatriate oil workers' live in 'colonial-style buildings' that are 'hidden behind a tall, barbed-wire-topped wall' with 'two gates and about half a dozen security men' (2011: 104). The communities of the Niger Delta, by comparison, are forced to live in 'a place for dying' (90) due to their proximity to the infrastructure of oil extraction that contaminates the water and the air, killing people and animals in the process.

Eco-Apartheid in Oil on Water

A key scene in *Oil on Water*'s depiction of gas flaring occurs when a character known only as the Doctor recounts his experience of visiting Niger Delta communities to the protagonist, Rufus. Pointing at 'the faraway orange sky', the Doctor exclaims: 'Those damned flares. There weren't that many of them when I first came here' (90). The Doctor goes on to explain how, for one particular village, the 'orange fire' (91) of the gas flare became the site of meetings, night markets, religious gatherings, and dances. 'At night', he tells Rufus, 'men and women would stand facing it, lost in wonder, for hours, simply staring till their eyes watered and their heads grew dizzy. [...] They said it was a sign, the fulfilment of some covenant with God' (92). This wonderment is soon replaced by distress when toxins in the water start to kill livestock, plants, and then people. The Doctor describes how he has supplied the government with blood samples proving that the flares were causing the deaths, but no action was taken, and the pattern merely spread from one community to the next.

It is through Habila's use of the contrasting imagery of artificial and natural light that we can read how the text's critique of gas flaring is presented alongside a hopeful impulse in socio-ecological rejuvenation. Of central importance to Habila's deployment of this imagery is the island of Irikefe. The character Naman explains that the Irikefe inhabitants have kept the 'island free from oil prospecting and other activities that contaminate the water and lead to greed and violence' (129). Where the villages close to gas flares are 'place[s] for dying' (90), then, the island is 'a place of healing' (216). As part of his journalism assignment on the kidnapping of the wife of a Western oil executive, Rufus passes through communities experiencing ecological decay; yet, on Irikefe, he encounters a space of 'leafy gardenias and acacias' where a priest explains that '[t]he air alone will heal you' (84). In direct contrast to the Doctor's description of communities staring in wonder at the artificial, destructive light of the flare's 'orange fire' (91), the island is peopled by worshippers of natural light who believe that 'the sun rising brings renewal. [...] Whatever goes wrong in the night has a chance for redemption after a cycle' (83). This message is emphasized in the depiction of the island's sculpture garden, which contains statues 'carefully aligned to face east or west. The ones facing east had a happy, ecstatic, worshipful expression, their clumpy, broken-fingered hands open, raised as though to receive the morning sun' (83). Those facing west, meanwhile, 'had their heads bowed, their lips turned down' and looked 'contorted and tortuous' (83). The presence of both east- and west-facing statues points to Habila's ambivalent and open-ended investment in a possible future for the Delta, maybe even Nigeria, Africa, and the world, that is not foreclosed by ecological disaster. Narratives of the future remain available but are grounded in the deeply painful and traumatic present as a way of generating new ideas of family, community, and shared experiences, of and with, animals and environments.

The imagery of light is returned to in the final moments of the novel in a manner that underscores a tentative sense of hope. After Irikefe is suspected of harbouring kidnappers and is attacked by the military, the statues are left damaged, and Rufus is depicted looking out to see 'the flares' in the distance that 'were still sending up smoke into the air' (215). Importantly, however, the unity of the island's sun worshippers is not destroyed; rather, they are last seen regrouping as 'a fragile flotilla, ordinary men and women and babies, a puny armada about to launch itself once more into uncertain waters, braving the darkness in order to get to the light' (216). It is a concluding image of precarious promise that, in contrast to the prevalence of the gas flares, emphasizes the group's continuing belief in the redemptive qualities of the sun. Joining the worshippers is Rufus's sister Boma, who survived a barn fire that saw Rufus's father imprisoned and their mother return to her parents. The unity of the community, along with the healing properties of the island, means that Boma discovers in Irikefe a place where she can heal the literal and figurative scars of the past, and find a renewed sense of belonging outside of her fragmented family unit.

Class, Gender, and Anti-Oil Activism in Watson and Mbue

In the world of Watson's novel *Tiny Sunbirds Far Away*, lower-class Nigerians living close to sites of oil extraction are depicted as experiencing respiratory illnesses, cancer, and miscarriages in a world in which the air is 'thicker' and it is 'difficult to breathe normally' (Watson, 2011: 226). Meanwhile, the predominantly male, upper-class government officials and white, Western oil workers live in 'another world' (67) with access to a clean environment in the air-conditioned, luxury hotels and apartments that the oil companies' wealth affords them. The healthy world of the latter is predicated on their role in the extraction of the combustible resource causing ecological damage and health problems for the former.

The novel is narrated by a young girl named Blessing, who begins her story in the world of insulated privilege due to her father's status and wealth, but soon finds herself exposed to air pollution in the world of the poor. Blessing's father's job as a government accountant enables her, her mother (referred to as Mama), and her brother Ezekiel to live in an air-conditioned apartment in Nigeria's financial centre in Lagos. The control that Blessing has over the quality of the air that she breathes ends abruptly when it is revealed that her father has been having an affair and leaves her mother. Blessing and her family are forced to move to her maternal grandmother's house in the Niger Delta city of Warri, which has been popularly known as 'oil city' since it is 'the location of a major constellation of petrochemical complexes', where '[i]ntensive oil exploration and production takes place' (Mustapha et al., 2011: 1478). As they drive closer to Warri, Blessing explains:

> I saw a flame in the distance. A giant torch, which made the sky look angry.
> 'Pipeline fires', said Zafi [the family's driver]. 'They are burning the gases from the oil'. He started coughing again. [...]
> I looked at the sky but saw nothing except dust and air. [...] Warri even smelled different to Lagos. I closed my eyes and sniffed. The air smelled like a book unopened for a very long time, as though the ground had been on fire.
>
> (Watson, 2011: 16–17)

It is in Warri that Blessing finds her calling and, under the mentorship of her grandmother, trains to be a midwife.[8] Ezekiel, on the other hand, joins a militia group called the Sibeye Boys, while Mama starts dating a white oil worker called Dan who she meets while working at the Highlife Bar situated within the oil company's fortified and gated compound. When describing the world behind the compound gates, Mama states: 'I can't believe that the other side of the wall is another world. One minute you're in an oily swamp, the next, five-star luxury. Cool air-conditioned, five-star luxury' (76). When Mama accepts Dan's marriage proposal, Ezekiel helps the Sibeye Boys to kidnap Dan before joining a plan to sabotage an oil pipeline, an act that ultimately leads to Ezekiel's death when the pipeline explodes. When Dan is released he convinces Blessing's mother to move with him back to London. Mama implores Blessing to join them but, having found her calling as a midwife and fallen in love with a friend of Ezekiel's, she chooses to stay behind to start her own family in Nigeria.

The marked disparity between lives lived on either side of the class divide is established from the outset in the depiction of Blessing's proximity to, but privileged insulation from, the living conditions of lower-class Nigerians, which are characterized by poor housing and sanitation systems. This class disparity is shown to exist even when the family are outside the apartment and stuck in busy traffic jams, referred to as the 'go-slow' (13). Where Blessing is depicted in the backseat of her father's air-conditioned car, and thus protected from contamination, we are told that the family's driver, Zafi, 'coughed all the way out of Lagos' (13). Although Zafi appears only as a minor character at the beginning of the novel, the pointed reference to his health reinforces Watson's preoccupation with how the professions available to lower-class Nigerians involve a heightened exposure to toxic air.

Research into the impact of car fumes on people's health in Nigeria has found strong evidence of 'a causal association' between 'traffic exposure and exacerbations of asthma in children' (Mustapha et al., 2011: 1478). Ezekiel acts as the text's primary means of depicting this association since he suffers from asthma, which first appears when the family are still living in Ikeja, and which causes him regular throat and chest infections. On discovering that they are to move to Warri, Ezekiel proclaims that, 'Warri is not safe. [...] What about my asthma? They burn poisonous chemicals straight into the air! It's not a safe place to live' (Watson, 2011: 11). The depiction of Ezekiel's condition exposes how health is predicated upon at least three socio-economic concerns: one's ability to access services that can diagnose an illness like asthma, one's ability to pay for medicines that ameliorate the symptoms, and one's distance from external factors that might aggravate the illness. Indeed, in their research on the effects of traffic fumes on children's health in Warri, B. Adetoun Mustapha et al. conclude that the priorities for most health centres in the region 'are major tropical and life-threatening infectious diseases such as malaria and tuberculosis, and a diagnosis of asthma is likely to indicate either those with severe disease or those who are richer and better able to access health care' (2011: 1418).⁹

As well as foregrounding the vast disparity between the two worlds of the wealthy and the poor in Nigeria, the family's dramatic change in circumstances stages the precarity of life for women forced to rely on husbands for their security. Women in Nigeria, writes Laine Munir, 'are more likely than men to be in positions of economic need' because of 'divorce, abandonment, widowhood or childcare hindering income-generating activities' (2021: 86). Additionally, the oil industry, which is controlled by predominantly male Nigerian elites and foreign corporations, 'hinder[s] women's economic well-being in the form of environmental damage to agricultural land and diminished governmental attention to small-scale farming that is the bulwark of women's income' (91). The loss of an air-conditioned apartment and car, which allowed Blessing's mother to provide a life for her children that was located far from the infrastructure of oil extraction and protected from traffic fumes, demonstrates what Sule Emmanuel Egya has identified as one of the novel's crucial issues, namely

> the fate of women and children whose victim status is no less than that of the environment, the land, the water, the air [...]. Indeed, Watson consciously weaves into a single narrative the critical conditions of the earth and of females in a society severely ruled by ambitions of men in the forms of the all-male militant groups, all-male government security teams, and the male-favored engineering expertise of the oil corporations.
>
> (2018: 124–125)

The precarious position of women as secondary citizens in the patriarchal ordering of Nigerian society is emphasized further when Mama describes the Executive Club on the oil company's compound. The coupling of male, upper-class power and access to clean air is alluded to in Mama's assertion that 'the Big Men' go to the club to 'sit around in the air conditioning', where they 'drink Remy Martin' and 'watch Sky Sports' whilst boasting about '[w]ho has the best car, the youngest girlfriend, the most wives' (Watson, 2011: 94). In this instant, the executives' air-conditioned environment is predicated on their wealth derived from oil extraction and, within their cloistered upper-class world, their status is bolstered by their acquisition of commodities and their commodification of women.

The novel goes on to depict both the oil industry and the patriarchal ordering of Nigerian society being momentarily challenged by an all-female, peaceful protest at the Western Oil Company gates where women remove their clothes to demand an end to gas flaring. As one unnamed protester cries, 'We want no dangerous gas burnt [...] like our lungs are less important than any other place' (382). It is at the protest that Blessing, under the guidance of her grandmother, is taught to channel the anger and pain she feels following Ezekiel's death in a way that generates an active participation in resistance alongside a wider form of empathy for the lives of women in the poorer villages. Pointedly, as Blessing joins the protest, she is reminded of a 'burnt and dead' (228) village that she visited as a midwife and asserts that

> It was still inside my head. I wanted to ask the women how it felt, to watch the glass buildings [of the oil company] from where they lived in shacks and were hungry. I was so angry. It felt good to be angry. I let it grow inside me. The anger burned my throat.
>
> (378)

The metaphor here demonstrates Blessing's politicization as the anger she feels for the Western Oil Company is felt in her throat, symbolically replacing the toxins she has been forced to breathe daily. In this way, breathing in the novel is not only the most potent means of experiencing the inequities of class, race, and gender, but generates a collective consciousness of exploitation underpinning Blessing's turn to activism. Upon seeing the hundreds of women gathered in protest at the gates of the oil company's compound, Blessing remarks that they were covered in 'fall-out dust from the pipeline fires' but 'looked like flowers in full-bloom, fat and bright. Hopeful' (380). The novel, thus, depicts two divergent forms of activism in response to the ecological and socio-economic effects of oil extraction and air pollution that are clearly gendered: Blessing's activism, in unison with her grandmother and the other women, is a hopeful act of collective non-violence, whereas Ezekiel's involvement in kidnapping and sabotage with the Sibeye Boys sees him break away from his mother and sister and is ultimately the cause of his tragic death.

The novel's depiction of an all-female protest replicates the widely publicized protests that took place in the Niger Delta between 2002 and 2012, when hundreds of women used what has been called the 'curse of nakedness' to protest the oil industry.[10] It must be noted, however, that, according to interviews with protesters conducted by Munir, the nude protests 'would not have come to pass without some degree of politicking by local male elites and were not as gender autonomous as they initially appeared' (2021: 90).[11] Furthermore, the depiction in both *Tiny Sunbirds* and news coverage of the protests of a clearly defined gendered binary between organized male militancy and spontaneous female non-violence potentially elides the long history of women's involvement in organized resistance movements in Nigeria. Munir has shown, for instance, that 'Niger Delta women's oil agitation has not taken only peaceful forms', citing how, in the 1980s, 'women dispossessed of farming land attacked oil industry installations and personnel throughout the Niger Delta with varying degrees of success, including the 1984 Ogharefe women's uprising and the 1986 Ekpan women's revolt in Warri' (2021: 81, 82). More recently, there is evidence of 'women's explicitly violent forms of resistance as part of the efforts of insurgent groups such as the Movement for the Emancipation of the Niger Delta (MEND)' (81), which came together in the mid-2000s after the non-violent campaigns of the 1990s began to wane.

An alternative perspective on class, gender, and activism is offered by Mbue's *How Beautiful We Were*, in which the practice of gas flaring is confronted by the transnational, political consciousness of the enigmatic female character Thula, who organizes a people's movement combining legal action with violent attacks on the infrastructure of the oil industry. The plot revolves around the emergence of a generation of anti-oil activists from the 1970s through to 2020 who are led by Thula. Set in the fictional African village of Kosawa, Thula and her 'age-mates' grow up surrounded by 'oil fields with structures jutting into the air delivering black smoke; pipelines running in all directions; our huts in the distance, undignified and slumped on their knees' (Mbue, [2021] 2022: 264). Located next to Kosawa is an area called Gardens, a suitably ironic name for a site owned by the American oil company Pexton that is dominated by gas flares that turn the air 'heavy', decimating 'whatever life was left in the big river' (32). Overseeing Pexton's oil operations is a corrupt, neocolonial government led by His Excellency, a shadowy totalitarian ruler who executes his political rivals and mobilizes the army to quell unrest in the villages experiencing oil-related environmental degradation. Kosawa is a location that bears many resemblances to the Nigerian settings of *Oil on Water* and *Tiny Sunbirds*, but Mbue's choice to create a fictionalized location opens up an awareness of other neocolonial African countries involved in the oil industry, such as Angola, Ghana, and Algeria.

The narrative of *How Beautiful We Were* reflects on the prevalence of flares in a manner that stages a similar form of 'eco-apartheid' to that seen in the other works explored here. In the chapter narrated by Thula, she notes that, '[f]or reasons we couldn't understand, the smoke always blew in our direction, never in the direction of Gardens and the hilltop mansion of the American overseer', and that the gas flares were 'so savage our skin shriveled and we needed to shout to hear each other over the screaming flames' (Mbue, [2021] 2022: 33). As with *Tiny Sunbirds*, proximity to gas flares is depicted as severely damaging to the respiratory health of Kosawa villagers. In describing one such case, the 'chorus' narrative voice (appearing in alternating chapters recounted by the Children) explains that '[w]hen the cough hit' a child called Wambi, 'his eyes watered, his back hunched out, he had to hold on to something to steady himself', all because the 'dirty air had gotten stuck in his lungs', eventually causing his premature death (7–8). Alluding to the impact of gas flaring on both respiratory health and employment opportunities, the Children note that the Pexton workers are heard 'coughing on the bus' with 'the exact cough Wambi used to have', yet 'for every dead labourer at Gardens, there were ten men in distant villages waiting to replace him, raring to partake in the riches from America' (260). One of the village elders, Thula's uncle Bongo, recounts how he imagines turning himself 'into a fan, blowing away the air over Kosawa, driving it past the hills behind Gardens, dumping it where strong winds will take it afar and bring back to us good air' (83). It is a dream that captures the older generation's desire for change alongside their sense of helplessness in the face of political and corporate power. The story of Thula and her age-mates, on the other hand, stages the text's investment in a widespread, grassroots movement of resistance, a sentiment encapsulated in the communal narrative voice of the Children, who declare: 'the children die on, the gas flares rage on, the pipelines spill on, we're in danger of annihilation, and we're fully capable of freeing ourselves' (102). This belief in the capacity to fight for – as opposed to being granted – freedom ultimately fuels the protest movement that emerges around Thula's activism.

Thula's politicization has roots in three events that occur when she is a child: the disappearance of her father Malabo following his trip to the capital Bézam to campaign against Pexton; the massacre of Kosawa villagers by government soldiers after Pexton spokesmen are taken hostage; and the summary execution of Bongo and three other men charged with the kidnapping. Pursuing her education in America, Thula reads Fanon's *The Wretched of the Earth* and discovers the prevalence of pipelines that deprive Native American 'land of its sanctity' (207). Recognizing an internationalist solidarity with others who 'were made prisoners on their land' (213), she writes home to recount that, '[o]ver here, governments also sit back and do nothing while corporations chain people up and throw them in bondage' (207). These formative experiences of settler colonial, neocolonial, and capitalist power outside of her African homeland inspire Thula to galvanize a grassroots movement in Kosawa by declaring that the government and Pexton 'speak to us in the language of destruction – let's speak it to them too, since it's what they understand' (214). Committed to a form of violent protest that stops short of murder, Thula's followers set to damaging oil infrastructure and intimidating labourers. These forms of organized resistance occur alongside Thula's own campaigning across different communities and her pursuit of a lawsuit in America against Pexton. When the people's movement organize a series of mass protests, however, Thula is ultimately killed by soldiers, the lawsuit fails, Kosawa is burned to the ground, and the next generation to emerge are described as taking up jobs with the government or with European and American corporations.

Despite these defeats, the final image of Mbue's narrative offers a conclusion that is akin to the communal faith in resilience and rejuvenation glimpsed in *Oil on Water*. The collective narrative voice of the Children ends *How Beautiful We Were* by explaining that, when visiting their own now-grown children, they remain attached to their home and to visions of resistance, 'thinking of Kosawa, thinking of Thula' and 'wondering if Thula would still be fighting if she were alive' (360). Although the twenty-first-century generation has been co-opted into a consumerist lifestyle funded by oil extraction, we are told that 'the children of our children come to us and say, please, Yaya, please Big Papa, tell us a story' (360). This is the novel's final line, implying that the story they tell is of the grassroots, people's resistance movement and the murder of Malabo and Bongo at the hands of Pexton and the government; in other words, the tale that has been recounted to us as readers. In a similar move to Habila's novel, then, Mbue leaves the reader on a tone of hesitant hope that nevertheless remains cognizant of the sociopolitical challenges facing African nations involved in the oil industry.

Pesticides

Turning now from gas flaring to an examination of the toxification of the air due to the global proliferation of chemical pesticides, we can see how this type of toxification takes two interconnected forms at the levels of use and manufacture.[12] The use of pesticides in farming to achieve higher yields of crops has detrimental impacts on local ecologies, with residues 'found in soil and air, and in surface and ground water' (Kumar et al., 2013: 55), as well as damaging the health and socio-economic conditions of agricultural workers. The industrial manufacture of pesticides since the post-war Green Revolution has despoiled environments in the proximity of factories and has led to catastrophically lethal gas leaks, with the most well-known example being the Bhopal disaster of 1984.

In most literary criticism discussing the Bhopal disaster, there remains a tight focus on the event itself.[13] What is generally not mentioned is the fact that the pesticide plant in Bhopal was, as Govindan Parayil notes, 'an integral element of the Green Revolution's network' (1994: 25) that links post-independence India to the Cold War politics being pursued across Latin America and South Asia by the US, the Rockefeller Foundation, and the World Bank. The roots of Union Carbide's negligent cost-cutting at its Bhopal factory lie in the Green Revolution's focus on large-scale corporate forms of food production and the structural marginalization of small-scale farmers in India. This left many farmers in debt and unable to afford Union Carbide's chemical pesticides. The subsequent reduction in the company's profits led to the cost-cutting practices that caused the 1984 gas leak. This framing of the disaster attends to how the US government was leading the way in increasing the manufacture and use of chemical pesticides across the globe at a time when Rachel Carson's *Silent Spring* was warning America of the dangers of spreading 'chemicals of broad lethal powers' ([1962] 2002: 162) from the air to eradicate pests. It also emphasizes how the contamination of Bhopal's air is bound up with a history of Cold War geopolitics, which included American initiatives to use the Green Revolution as a means of opening up agricultural markets across the Global South.

In the sections that follow, we show how the dominant narrative that emerged following the disaster at Bhopal saw it as a consequence of India's inexperience with industrial technology and 'an aberration' in 'a large Third World nation's effort to get on to the road of modernization and economic growth' (Parayil, 1994: 24). The work of activists, artists, journalists, and scholars, however, has shown that the gas leak resulted from a culture of corporate negligence with regards to safety measures, training, and maintenance of the factory's infrastructure.[14] Literary responses to the Bhopal tragedy – notably Mohammad's 'Bhopal', Sinha's *Animal's People*, and Delahunt's *The Red Book* – have contributed to this counter-narrative. A shared aspect of these literary works is that they bear witness to the experiences of the victims of chemical gas leaks. Additionally, our analysis of these texts will explore the ways in which they differ in their scope: Mohammad and Delahunt concentrate on, and name, the Bhopal disaster, while Sinha's fictional setting of Khaufpur signals his attempt – described in an article for *The Guardian* – to represent the conditions of life in 'every place in which people have been poisoned and then abandoned' (2007b, n.p.).

Bhopal and the Green Revolution

The spread of pesticides across the globe can be traced back to the Green Revolution, which names a US- and World Bank-funded 'set of planned and targeted agricultural-intensification programs' (Parenti, 2011: 145) that took place across Latin America and South Asia during the post-war decades. As well as the marketing of chemical pesticides, the Green Revolution involved the use of 'high-yield-variety seeds, synthetic fertilizers, [...] and intensive, groundwater-dependent irrigation' (145). These programmes helped to prevent mass starvation in regions across the Global South that were experiencing booming urban populations and a decline in agricultural labour. Yet, they were also central to America's efforts to defeat the influence of Communism from the Soviet Union and China in 'non-aligned' countries at the outset of the Cold War, especially in India and Mexico.[15] As Patrick Kilby notes in his authoritative *The Green Revolution: Narratives of Politics, Technology and Gender*, the promotion of 'US know-how and technology' in Latin America and South Asia was part of 'a geo-political contest where the assertion of US interests was the main game, while poverty alleviation was secondary' (2019: 10).[16]

High-yielding variety (HYV) seeds, pesticides, fertilizers, and intensive irrigation were taken up in India over the 1960s and 70s in a bid to become self-sufficient in feeding a growing population, to 'free up labor that could be harnessed in cities as part of the new manufacturing sectors' (Parenti, 2011: 144) and, after a severe drought in 1965, to avoid 'an agricultural crisis' (Kilby, 2019: 30). 'The increase in HYV plantings', writes Kilby, 'together with good rains in 1967, resulted in a dramatic turnaround of India's agricultural fortunes' (32): over the course of 1966 to 1971, grain production increased from 63 million tonnes to 95 million tonnes. This food security in turn allowed then-Prime Minister Indira Gandhi more independence from American interference over domestic and foreign policy whilst enabling the market for pesticides in India to triple between 1956 and 1970 (Walker, 1990: 158).

While food supplies increased in the late 1960s, however, by the 1970s farmers discovered that pesticide use was stripping the soil of its nutrients as well as eliminating the natural enemies of pests, thus leading to a drop in output. In attempting to ensure a high crop yield, farmers found themselves in a vicious cycle as many increased their use of pesticides. This more frequent application poisoned local water sources, 'kill[ing] fish, water bugs, snails and aquatic plants, which are a part of the food web and play an important role in maintaining eco-balance' (Shetty, 2004: 5264).[17] With falling yields and profits, many small-scale farmers increasingly sought high-interest loans from banks and moneylenders.[18] When a drought hit India in 1977, rising levels of debt forced farmers to switch from pesticides being manufactured by the likes of Union Carbide to cheaper products being supplied by smaller firms (Varma and Varma, 2005: 41). This meant that, although Union Carbide's pesticide plant in Bhopal had been built in 1969 at the height of the turnaround in India's agricultural fortunes, by the beginning of the 1980s it was losing money. When a plan to dismantle and sell the factory failed, Union Carbide set up a Bhopal Task Force made up of US executives to manage the crisis; they immediately started to cut back on maintenance, training, and safety measures.

The Task Force's cost-cutting initiatives, according to Sinha's article 'Chemicals for War and Chemicals for Peace', included slashing the workforce by half, leaving just one operator to monitor the production of methyl isocyanate (MIC), 'a compound 500 times deadlier than hydrogen cyanide' (2014: 140).[19] Refrigeration of the MIC tanks was turned off in order to save $37 a day on Freon gas, even though the Mellon Institute had reported in 1963 and 1970 that when subjected to heat MIC breaks down into 'potentially lethal gaseous molecules that included hydrocyanide acid' (Mukherjee, 2011: 219). Inspections became infrequent and there was no new equipment provided for repairs. Safety training was cut from six months to two weeks, 'reducing it in effect to slogans, but the slogans were in English so the workers could not understand them' (Sinha, 2014: 140). Ignoring the workers' concerns, bosses covered up minor accidents, and in response to a growing number of small leaks, 'the alarm siren was turned off to avoid inconveniencing the neighbours' (140). At 11.30pm, December 2, 1984, a leak was detected, but the factory's warning signal was only set off at 1.30am the following morning and it was not until 2am that the public alarm was sounded, by which time 'people were already awakened by the irritation in the eyes and throat' (Varma and Varma, 2005: 41). The leak caused a 'dense cloud of heavier-than-air gas' to settle on the populated areas of the city 'showing no mercy to people, animals, and plants' (38). An estimated twenty thousand people were killed and almost two-hundred thousand people – a quarter of the city's population – were exposed to the poisoned air. By the end of December, almost half of the population had evacuated Bhopal and, in the years that followed, the toxicity of the gas meant that surviving victims experienced problems with their physical and mental health.[20]

The litany of decisions that led directly to the disaster, writes Sinha, 'were expressions of a Union Carbide culture of greed and double standards that one prosecuting attorney in a New York court would describe as a "reckless, depraved indifference to human life"' (2014: 141). The difficult fight for compensation and justice in the courts was ultimately confounded by a merger between Union Carbide and Dow Chemical, which provided both companies with a 'rationale for disclaiming responsibility for a disaster committed by a corporation that no longer exists' (Nixon, 2011: 63). Despite criminal and civil cases being filed in the US against Union Carbide and the then-CEO Warren Anderson, at the time of writing only Indian employees at the plant have faced convictions in Indian courts.[21] This outcome only fuels a Western chastisement of so-called 'developing' nations in their presumed inability to modernize. Indeed, although Indian newspapers reported the extensive cost-cutting measures that caused the chemical leak, Pablo Mukherjee notes that '[t]he American media [...] blamed the accident on India's failure to live with advanced technology', the very same technology that had already caused a rise in cancer rates and water pollution at Union Carbide's research institute in the Kanahwa Valley, West Virginia (2011: 218). In the following section we will see how literary texts provide a necessary space for confronting the lack of recognition for Bhopal victims in the courts, and the blaming of Indian employees at the factory.

The Bhopal Disaster in Writing by Delahunt, Mohammad, and Sinha

The framing story of *The Red Book* follows Françoise, an Australian photographer visiting India on the 20th anniversary of the Bhopal disaster; yet the tragedy remains largely in the background, glimpsed (via Françoise's focalization) in photographs and news stories, or by occasional insights from Naga, a Bhopal survivor and Buddhist monk whose sister experiences 'monthly pains' (Delahunt, 2008: 157) since the gas leak. From the outset of the novel Françoise explains that it was seeing a photograph in a newspaper of a deceased child in Bhopal that inspired her to travel to the disaster area as part of an international residency:

> I turned the page and the child's face looked up – like a pale moon buried in the earth – its opaque eyes open, an adult hand caressing its forehead. Sometimes you see an image which stops your breath, which calls out the terror and beauty and pain of the world. Sometimes you see an image which hints at your future, which sets you on your path.
>
> (4)

The path referred to is Françoise's journey to Bhopal, she says, 'to make my own photographs' (4). Thus, the narrative opens not only with the perspective of a Western outsider journeying into Bhopal but also with the privileging of a Western character's 'calling'. The picture of the child that Françoise sees is reinscribed in romanticized terms, no longer a real victim but a 'pale moon' whose death is de-contextualized as a cipher of a vaguely universal 'terror', 'beauty', and 'pain'.[22]

It is through Naga that we hear of the 'evil wind [...] full of the gas' that blew from the 'Carbide plant' over sleeping families in Bhopal (128). There are also allusions to the alarm sirens being 'switched off months before [the leak] by the Carbide' (156) and to the reliance of victims on moneylenders to afford medicines. In the novel's final moments, Naga is depicted meditating and imagining the death of Warren Anderson. As he is pictured having a heart attack in his garden in America, Anderson (who in fact died in a nursing home in 2014) is imagined by Naga as experiencing the suffocating effects of breathing poisoned gas, as well as a decade of 'wait[ing] in line to get medicine' and finds himself 'chained to a group of women with ruined eyesight and ruined wombs selling off bridal jewellery in exchange for medicine' (277). Following this vision, Naga's 'heart opens to Anderson' and he wishes that he may 'one day find peace' (278). Ultimately, however, Naga's narrative becomes secondary to the story of Françoise's relationship with Arkay, a Scottish man who has moved to India and taken up Buddhism to help him recover from alcoholism. Within this dominant story arc, Naga's primary role is to connect the two estranged Western characters when Françoise discovers that she is pregnant and Arkay is on his deathbed.

Mohammad's speaker in the poem 'Bhopal' not only makes the tragedy at Bhopal central to the poem but frames it as an event that has global – even cosmic – repercussions. The poem opens with the speaker recounting 'a day when the earth stood still, | The birds stopped mid-flight and the sun felt a chill' (2004: n.p.).[23] We discover that this scene of planetary mourning, whereby the wind is 'made tranquil' and the 'oceans even rose as her eyes did fill', has been caused by a 'day of human suffering of the likes unseen' on which '[i]nnocent souls' have been 'slain with the force of hurricane' (n.p.). The imagery, language, and regular rhyme scheme establish the poem's genre as a folk ballad, written to be performed by a speaker to large and diverse audiences who may not already be aware of the Bhopal tragedy. The ballad form enables Mohammad to frame the gas leak at Bhopal *not* as an accidental disaster, or as being caused by Indian factory workers, but as a battle between the powerful and powerless, one in which a 'beast' that 'was unleashed from the white-mans' venture' leaves '[t]housands of Indians maimed' and 'thousands dead' (n.p.). The folk imagery of the gas leak as a monstrous 'beast' capable of slaying and maiming innocent masses cuts through the legalistic manoeuvres that assist Union Carbide's evasion of responsibility, replacing it with a direct and accessible style of storytelling.

Whilst adopting a traditional form of poetic storytelling that draws on folk myths and is characterized by its accessibility, Mohammad's speaker also insists that the details of the Bhopal gas leak cannot be placed firmly in the past as an event of only historical concern: 'Now once upon a time ain't how this story goes | And the land of which we talk ain't as far as we're told | It's a recent event, not a story of old' (n.p.). In doing so, the poem contributes to a critique of what Rob Nixon calls the 'powerful strategies of distantiation' that enable corporations such as Union Carbide to avoid responsibility for 'the unfolding of slow violence across environmental time' (2011: 51). In the case of the Bhopal gas leak, Nixon notes that 'the slow emergence of morbidity', along with the 'legal procrastination' of Union Carbide, have provided 'prevaricative cover for the CEOs who wish to exploit time to defuse the claims of the afflicted' (51). In emphasizing the litany of cost-cutting measures that '[c]aused a poison cloud to be shot out and spread', and in stating that the '[a]ftermath' of the gas leak 'will remain till the day of reckoning' (2004: n.p.), Mohammad's speaker confronts this corporate prevarication, which leaves victims without compensation and which delays the clean-up of the Bhopal factory site.

Sinha's novel *Animal's People* is also structured around a battle between the powerless and the powerful, dramatizing the fight by a small group of activists for justice 20 years after a fatal gas leak at an American-owned pesticide plant in a small Indian city. When asked of their aims, the group's leader Zafar says that, '[i]nstead of breaking ground for new factories' they wish 'to grow grass and trees over the old ones, instead of inventing new poisons, to make medicines to heal the hurts done by those poisons, to remove them from the earth, water and air' (Sinha, 2007a: 237). This aim, which combines human and environmental rights, is met by the combined obfuscations of both the American company and Indian ministers to resist culpability. We also witness attempts by an American doctor, Ellie Barber, to establish a hospital in the city to treat victims of the gas leak. Since the American corporation that owned the factory first arrived with promises of a brighter future for the region's poorest, the activists and local residents have difficulty trusting another Westerner claiming that they wish to help them.

The protagonist-narrator of *Animal's People* is the disabled and orphaned Animal, who recites his life story into a tape recorder given to him by an Australian journalist, referred to by Animal as the 'Jarnalis' (3). When Animal is told that the 'jarnalis' will write his story so that '[t]housands will read it', he remarks not with the thrill of international recognition but with revulsion: 'I think of this awful idea. Your eyes full of eyes. Thousands staring at me through the holes in your head. Their curiosity feels like acid on my skin' (7). The narrative framing of Animal's story exposes what Nixon calls the 'discriminatory distribution of environmental visibility' (2011: 65), whereby environmental racism renders poverty and toxification as either invisible or worthy of attention only in the form of an exoticized spectacle. Heather Snell maintains that 'Animal points to the negative effects of [...] reading and interpretation that might translate him into an exotic object to be consumed' (2008: 1). Andrew Mahlstedt asserts that 'Animal and his people are "invisible" in the sense that, even when literally seen, they are only seen through the spectacle of "third-world poverty" that structures seeing' (2013: 59), while Brigette Rath reads Animal's first-person narration as exposing 'the pitfalls of disaster voyeurism [...] and the danger of a possible collusion by (even unwittingly) catering to these exploitative dynamics with his own story' (2013: 163).

Since Lucy Beresford's review of *Animal's People*, which commented on 'Sinha's flirtation with magic realism' (2007, n.p.), literary scholars have also concentrated on identifying the novel's generic tropes, reading it variously as a revitalization of realist and picaresque literature, or elsewhere as drawing on the aesthetics of crime fiction and ghost stories.[24] In response to Beresford, Mukherjee avers that *Animal's People* is not magic realism but 'realism fitted to express the horrors of a reality that threatens to escape the ordinary normative boundaries of style' (2011: 227). In this reading, Animal's poison-induced disability, along with his ability to communicate with the deformed fetus Kha-in-the-jar and the stray dog Jara, makes him 'the umbilical bond' that binds exploitation of the human and nonhuman worlds together, enabling a 'vision of collectivity [...] where personhood remains distinctive yet always relational' (227, 228). In a footnote in *Postcolonial Ecocriticism*, Graham Huggan and Helen Tiffin express concern with Mukherjee's interpretation and caution against any attempt to 'recuperate the figure of Animal in order to gesture towards more inclusive models of multispecies community and personhood' ([2010] 2015: 94 n13). Their insistence that Animal's disability is 'a *non*-metaphorical marker for a condition that is what it is', and not 'an alternative site for the reading of community engagement and social power' (94 n13), aligns more closely with Nixon's framing of Animal as the protagonist-narrator of an 'environmental picaresque' novel. Rather than seeing Animal as the bond that *transcends* the human, the dehumanized, and the nonhuman, Nixon argues that Sinha's narrator 'embodies a crushing neoliberal, transnational economic relationship and also marks him as a literal "lowlife", a social and anatomical outlier whose physical form externalizes the slow violence, the unhurried metastases coursing through the community' (2011: 56).

For Anthony Carrigan, Sinha not only draws on the traditions of picaresque literature but also incorporates private eye, noir, and spy genres. This 'hybrid detective subjectivity', Carrigan says, 'speaks to a need for reconfigured understandings of criminality that account for how the suffering referred to throughout the narrative is constituted in Union Carbide's own fusion of toxic capitalism and legal evasion' (2012: 163). More recently, Laura A. White has offered an interpretation of *Animal's People* as a ghost story in which the city is haunted by the 'residues of chemicals [that] impose effects across generations' (2020: 4). This reading, White maintains, also foregrounds the way in which Animal is 'haunted by the ideal of the able body that travels with him', and how 'the spirits of the dead' remain tethered to the factory site to 'demand redress' (4).

Existing literary criticism has thus provided productive close analysis of the complex ways in which, at the level of both content and form, *Animal's People* interrogates the environmental racism that led directly to the Bhopal gas leak. At the same time, however, these analyses have tended to be framed by a tight focus on the Bhopal tragedy and the presence of Union Carbide in India. Yet, where Delahunt's *The Red Book* and Mohammad's 'Bhopal' name the real-life site of the world's worst industrial disaster and the company that caused it, *Animal's People* is inspired by the disaster but pointedly avoids this overt correlation. Following the novel's publication, Sinha maintained that *Animal's People* 'is not "about" the Bhopal disaster [...], it is about people struggling to lead ordinary lives in the shadow of catastrophe' (2007b: n.p.). For this reason, Sinha sets the novel in the fictional Indian city of Khaufpur (which translates in Urdu as 'Terror Town') and the factory's owners are referred to only as the 'Kampani'. These textual choices underpin Sinha's insistence that the novel's setting 'is every place in which people have been poisoned and then abandoned' (n.p.). As such, *Animal's People* deviates from the approaches of *The Red Book* and 'Bhopal' in at least two notable ways: first, in Sinha's resistance to dramatizing a singular, real-life instance of lethal air toxification, and second, in its critique of a Western-centric human rights discourse.

Sinha resists an interpretation of the Bhopal tragedy as a standalone accident when Animal describes Khaufpur as the 'World capital of fucked lungs' (Sinha, 2007a: 230). In giving his hometown this appellation, Animal suggests that while the exposure to toxic air experienced by the city's inhabitants may be extreme, it is far from exceptional: Khaufpur is merely the capital amongst a host of cities across the globe contaminated by chemicals, smog, and the industrial extraction of oil that we examined earlier in the chapter. After all, it is not only the chemical leak that has despoiled Khaufpur's atmosphere; it is also a city beset by 'blacked out streets and killer traffic, [...] open sewers, garbage everywhere, poisoned wells, poisoned babies, [...] thousands of sick that no one seems to care about', especially not the 'corrupt politicians' or the 'doctors who don't do their jobs' (151). Moreover, in his final chilling assertion that '[a]ll things pass, but the poor remain. We are the people of the Apokalis. Tomorrow there will be more of us' (366), Animal gestures towards the proximity of the poor across the Global South to contaminated air and the infrastructure of chemical plants. In this way, the novel invites a consideration not only of Bhopal but of the global proliferation of the very same chemical pesticides that leaked from Union Carbide's failing factory in 1984. It is worth noting that, since the post-war introduction of Green Revolution initiatives in Mexico and India, chemical pesticide use has spread across Africa and the south and southeast regions of Asia. Focusing on Cambodia, Myanmar, Thailand, and Vietnam, for instance, a 2018 report by the Centre for Agriculture and Bioscience International (CABI) found that 'despite a significant increase in pesticide use, crop losses have not significantly decreased' (F. Williams et al., 2018, n.p.) due to the same problems that have faced Indian farmers, namely the stripping of nutrients in the soil and the eradication of the natural predators of pests. CABI also reports that in these countries '[p]esticides are [...] being over-used and used incorrectly, leading to human health and environmental concerns' (n.p.), including respiratory problems, allergies, and headaches. In response, CABI has promoted the use of non-chemical techniques, such as crop rotation and tillage practices.

In its critique of a Western-centric discourse of human rights, *Animal's People* does not only claim rights for the victims of chemical poisoning from the manufacture and use of pesticides, but challenges the very foundations upon which such rights are decided, foundations that have historically excluded those without a voice, and which continue to conceal the environmental degradation of postcolonial and Indigenous environments. This concern is established from the outset when Animal confronts the 'Jarnalis' – and, by extension, the book's readership – with the insistence that, on learning of the story of Khaufpur: 'You will bleat like the rest. You'll talk of *rights, law, justice*. Those words sound the same in my mouth as in yours but they don't mean the same' (Sinha, 2007a: 3, original emphasis). Animal goes on to establish a direct analogy between the chemical leak caused by corporate indifference to the lives of the Khaufpur community and the lofty but ultimately ineffectual language of human rights upheld by the governments of the Global North and the United Nations, asserting, '[o]n that night it was poison, now it's words that are choking us' (3). In such moments, Sinha foregrounds the disparity between the rhetoric of both universal human rights and economic development on the one hand and, on the other, the reality of life in the disenfranchised parts of the world where breathing means consuming poisoned air. The novel's dramatization of this disparity animates Paul Gilroy's critique of human rights and development discourse whereby disenfranchised populations across the globe are classified as 'already exist[ing] in a space of death, for which their characteristic lack of industry makes them responsible' (2004: 12). For Gilroy, this environmental racism marks certain populations with a 'lowly biopolitical status', categorizing them 'between animal and human' and thus unworthy of 'the same vital humanity enjoyed by their rulers, captors, conquerors, judges, executioners, and other racial betters' (12). In marked contrast to Delahunt's *The Red Book*, in which the character of Naga embodies a Buddhist-influenced hope that Union Carbide's CEO will regain his humanity after undergoing a transformative sense of remorse on his deathbed, Animal presents the category of the human as always contingent when it comes to a discussion of rights. Animal's ownership of his lowly biopolitical status and his insistence that he 'long ago gave up trying to be human' (Sinha, 2007a: 186) thus satirizes the forms of environmental racism that see both the natural world, and the lives of the poor, as disposable.

Conclusion

Reading the depiction of a range of forms of air pollution across prose and poetry set in Africa and South Asia assists with an interrogation of 'eco-apartheids' that are structured by class and race. In Gaard's examination of air pollution across China, India, and the US, for instance, she maintains that '[e]cological, economic, and affective disconnection' between the privileged and the poor 'are integral to the functioning of smog cultures' (2020: 19). Similarly, Neel Ahuja has discussed how the 'risks of toxicity' in the US 'emerged out of historical forms of segregation and were geographically concentrated in ways that unequally affect Black and poor communities' (2021: 62).[25] Thus, whilst the texts we have examined in this chapter are concerned specifically with the geographical contexts of Africa and India, a critical focus on depictions of 'eco-apartheids' in literature contributes to debates about the locally specific ways in which forms of socio-economic separation and segregation are intrinsic to air polluted cultures across the globe.

Notes

1 See 'WHO's Science in 5: Air pollution, a public health emergency': https://www.youtube.com/watch?v=8zktuV75u4U [accessed April 4, 2023].
2 Neira and Ramanathan argue that 'placing a price on polluting fuels in line with their health impacts through air pollution would result in a reduction of more than 50 percent of premature global air pollution deaths, a 20 percent reduction in greenhouse gas emissions, and the generation of some US$3000 billion in tax revenues every year – more than 50 percent of current global health spending by governments' (2020: 99).
3 See also Cohen (2019) and Baigrie (2019).
4 In 2005, the Nigerian environmental activist and representative of the Iwherekan community, Jonah Gbemre, sued Shell for the use of gas flaring, maintaining that the practice 'violates the right to life and human dignity guaranteed by the Nigerian Constitution and the African Charter'. Reporting on the court case, ActionAid noted that '[t]he Benin Judicial Division of the Federal Court of Nigeria ruled in his favour, but it was never upheld' (see 'How Shell is devastating the Niger Delta', ActionAid, November 27, 2020, https://actionaid.org/stories/2020/how-shell-devastating-niger-delta [accessed May 27, 2023]).
5 Nigerian legislation from the 1960s and 70s recognized that natural gas obtained from oil extraction could be used as a possible energy source and the Associated Gas Re-injection Act of 1979 made flaring illegal. Yet, this law allowed the country's 'minister to authorize companies to flare gas that cannot be re-injected or utilized' (Ejiogu, 2013: 988) at the cost of a relatively small fee. Given the country's reliance on oil revenues, and the additional income that a flaring fee generates for the government, gas flaring became standard practice. The subsequent treatment of so-called 'associated gases' as waste is due to the fact that oil extraction infrastructure was built in Nigeria when 'gas was not a popular energy source as it was more difficult to produce and transport than crude oil' (Eweje, 2006: 39). With more of a global market for gas energy, Shell has sought more recently to phase out gas flaring, having recognized that it 'wastes a valuable resource and is environmentally damaging' (39). Conservative World Bank estimates have suggested that 'gas flared in Africa [...] could produce 200 Terawatt hours (TWh), which is about 50 percent of the current power consumption of the African continent, and more than twice the level of power consumption in sub-Saharan Africa (excluding the Republic of South Africa), (Ejiogu, 2013: 984).

6 See 'Seven Countries Account for Two Thirds of Global Gas Flaring', The World Bank, April 26, 2021: https://www.worldbank.org/en/news/press-release/2021/04/28/seven-countries-account-for-two-thirds-of-global-gas-flaring [accessed May 30, 2023].
7 In his assessment of urbanization and waste management across sub-Saharan African cities, Jonathan Silver (2019) also demonstrates how Fanon's insistence on the spatialized nature of colonial racism assists with understanding air pollution across the Global South as a form of socio-ecological violence.
8 For detailed analysis of the representation of midwifery in the novel, see Barnsley (2022).
9 The study found a 'low prevalence of diagnosed asthma [...] (0.9%), despite a relatively high prevalence of self-reported symptoms such as wheeze (5.4%)', which 'may indicate undiagnosed asthma due to limited access to health services in this low socioeconomic status area' (1418).
10 See Babatunde (2017).
11 In part, Munir has found, local chiefs mobilized women to bolster the number of protesters, to help avoid police violence, to bring oil companies back into negotiation, and, somewhat counter-intuitively, to help assert their own authority. Effectively, women were called on to protest in a manner that benefitted male leaders 'no matter the outcome, either in the form of a reward from the [oil] company for ending the protest or in the form of control over communal compensation from the company if the women [were to] succeed' (2021: 89, 85). This is not, Munir says, 'to minimize female contributions to resistance practices in Nigeria, contributions which call for celebration in other contexts' (90). Indeed, she acknowledges that some of the 2002–2012 protests were 'able to shut down oil operations, and thus cost oil companies profit' whilst also proving to be more effective than previous campaigns 'in garnering both domestic and international media attention to their all-female actions' (83). Attending to the complexities of the protests, however, offers a better understanding of the durability of class, race, and gender relations in contemporary resistance struggles. It recognizes the way in which Indigenous Nigerian women are often marginalized by the oil industry both economically and 'in resistance efforts as well' (91), a dimension of the relationship between women's rights and climate justice that the depiction of the all-female protest in *Tiny Sunbirds* does not attend to.
12 In referring to chemical pesticides, this term, as Sachin Kumar et al. (2013) note, includes insecticides, fungicides, herbicides, rodenticides, molluscicides, nematicides, and plant growth regulators.
13 Rob Nixon is the notable exception. His comparison between the chemical and nuclear leaks at Bhopal and Chernobyl respectively demonstrates how both instances of catastrophic contamination reveal how 'slow violence' is managed by the powerful by 'foot-dragging, equivocation, and denial' (2011: 49).
14 This stance was also reinforced by the 'Reframing Disaster' project established by Anthony Carrigan and Clare Barker at the University of Leeds. See https://www.bhopal.org/industrial-hazards/reframing-disaster-project-held-in-leeds/ and https://theconversation.com/bhopal-how-activists-and-artists-kept-this-ongoing-disaster-in-the-public-eye-34998 [accessed May 30, 2023].
15 For a comparative discussion of the impact of the Green Revolution across India, Pakistan, Mexico, China, and the US, see Kumar et al. (2017).
16 For more on the impact of the Green Revolution on Indian agriculture, see Shiva ([1989] 2016).
17 Additionally, pesticide use can kill birds through atmospheric exposure and the ingestion of treated seeds, and can contaminate livestock fodder, thus exposing humans to pesticide poisoning through their consumption of meat and dairy products. According to Sachin Kumar et al., '[m]ild to moderate pesticide poisoning mimics intrinsic asthma, bronchitis, and gastroenteritis', and exposure to

chemical toxicity has also been linked to such health issues as reproductive problems, birth defects, cancer, depression, and memory disorders with a 'disproportionate burden' being 'shouldered by the people of developing countries and by high risk groups in each country' (2013: 53). Indian farmers and agricultural labourers with low levels of education have been seen as especially vulnerable to the inhalation of pesticides because too often 'they cannot identify the warning symbols on the label' (Shetty, 2004: 5265). Critics of the state-sponsored proliferation of pesticide use in India have thus called for a complementary focus on the accessibility of education and literacy programmes for workers in the agricultural sector. Shetty recommends that, 'Government and non-government organisations need to promote programmes on education of farmers about basic pesticide use, so that misuse of these chemicals could be prevented to a greater extent' (2004: 5266). Similarly, Wasim Aktar, Dwaipayan Sengupta, and Ashim Chowdhury advise that, 'There is [...] every reason to develop health education packages based on knowledge, aptitude and practices and to disseminate them within the community in order to minimise human exposure to pesticides' (2009: 9).

18 This debt crisis has led to hundreds of thousands of suicides, most of which have been caused by the ingestion of the very pesticides that have been damaging the health and financial circumstances of farmers in India for decades. Such stories of suicidal poisoning, according to Ajay Dandekar, 'are legion and collectively make up the narrative of a tragedy unfolding on an unprecedented scale across the landscape, from the dryland farming areas of the peninsula to the perennial wet fields of Punjab' (2016: 49). A number of Indian writers have sought to raise awareness of both the damaging proliferation of pesticides in India and the epidemic of farmer suicides by pesticide poisoning. These include Mahasweta Devi's 1990 short story 'Dhowli', Ambikasutan Mangad's Malayalam-language novel *Enmakaje* (2009; translated in English and published in 2017 as *Swarga*), and Neel Mukherjee's 2014 novel *The Lives of Others*. In her assessment of the legacy of India's agricultural reforms in *Capitalism: A Ghost Story*, Arundhati Roy asserts that the country's three hundred million-strong middle class must 'live side-by-side with spirits of the netherworld, the poltergeists of dead rivers, dry wells, bald mountains, and denuded forests; the ghosts of 250,000 debt-ridden farmers who have killed themselves, and of the 800 million who have been impoverished and dispossessed to make way for us' ([2014] 2015: 8).

19 Even prior to the factory's financial losses, US engineers had cut costs by choosing to store the MIC in large storage tanks, as opposed to much safer, smaller containers. 'At the time of the disaster', Sinha writes, 'the tanks held 67 tons, 13,400% more than the European safety limit' (140). In *Five Past Midnight in Bhopal*, Dominic Lapierre and Javier Moro report that this decision was likened by European engineers to 'putting an atom bomb in the middle of [the] factory that could explode at any time' (2002: 98).

20 A dramatization of the disaster is provided in the film *Bhopal: A Prayer for Rain* (2014), starring Martin Sheen as Union Carbide's CEO, Warren Anderson.

21 It has been left to survivors of the Bhopal gas leak to continue to campaign for Dow Chemical to take responsibility for the clean-up of the disaster site, with a group led by Rashida Bee and Champa Devi Shukla being awarded the Goldman Environmental Prize in 2004 (Varma and Varma, 2005: 43).

22 Delahunt's descriptions of Françoise's journey also recirculate stereotypical tropes of Indian exoticism. In visiting Delhi for the first time, Françoise is 'pulled under by the press of colour and sound' (5). When she returns to Delhi at the novel's closing scenes, she states that she 'felt comfortable' because '[t]he colony had absorbed me', and she signals her presumed 'acceptance' by India through reference to an 'old paan seller [who] would wave to me from outside the gates [of a park] and I'd wave back' (282).

23 The poem was commissioned by BBC Radio 4 and won an Amnesty International Media Award (see 'Avaes Mohammad', https://commapress.co.uk/authors/avaes-mohammad/ [accessed May 27, 2023]). All references to the poem are taken from the only published version that is available to date via *Critical Muslim* magazine's website: https://www.criticalmuslim.io/bhopal/.
24 The novel is arguably framed by a subtle resistance to the marketability of Indian literature as 'magic realist' following the international renown of Salman Rushdie. That *Animal's People* is told from the perspective of a young man whose childhood development is intrinsically linked to a traumatic event that occurred around midnight invites a comparison to Rushdie's *Midnight's Children* (1981): Sinha's narrator 'was born a few days before that night, which no one in Khaufpur wants to remember but no one can forget' (2007a: 1), while Rushdie's narrator Saleem Sinai was born at the moment of Partition between India and Pakistan. A marked divergence between *Midnight's Children* and *Animal's People* is underscored, however, at the close of 'Tape One' when Animal addresses the listener/reader stating that, 'I'm not clever like you. I can't make fancy rissoles of each word. Blue kingfishers won't suddenly fly out of my mouth. If you want my story, you'll have to put up with how I tell it' (2). This assertion sees Animal take agency over the delivery of his version of events in a manner that appears to signal to the reader that *Animal's People* will not conform to the familiar magic realist aesthetics that might be expected from Indian literature following Rushdie's success.
25 For an account of the prevalence of smog in China, see *Smog Is Coming* by Li Chunyuan, who is the deputy head of the environmental protection bureau in the Hebei city of Langfang. The novel will not be examined here due to the fact that, at the time of writing, it is not available in translation. For an account of smog in India, see *The Great Smog of India* by Siddharth Singh.

Bibliography

Ahuja, Neel. 2021. *Planetary Specters: Race, Migration, and Climate Change in the Twenty-First Century*. Chapel Hill: University of North Carolina Press.

Babatunde, Abosede Omowumi. 2017. "Environmental Insecurity and Poverty in the Niger Delta: A Case of Ilaje." *African Conflict and Peacebuilding Review* 7, no. 2 (Fall): 36–59.

Baigrie, Bruce. 2019. "Climate Change and Capital Together Create Eco-Apartheid." *New Agenda: South African Journal of Social and Economic Policy* 75 (February): online.

Barnsley, Veronica. 2022. "Midwifery Narratives and Development Discourses." *Journal of African Cultural Studies* 34, no. 3: 278–293.

Beresford, Lucy. 2007. "Village of the Damned." *Star Weekend Magazine* 6, no. 37 (September). https://archive.thedailystar.net/magazine/2007/09/03/bookr.htm [accessed 2023].

Carrigan, Anthony. 2012. "'Justice is on our side'? Animal's People, generic hybridity, and eco-crime." *Journal of Commonwealth Literature* 47, no. 2: 159–174.

Carson, Rachel. [1962] 2002. *Silent Spring*. New York: Houghton Mifflin Co.

Checker, Melissa. 2008. "Eco-Apartheid and Global Greenwaves: African Diasporic Environmental Justice Movements." *Souls* 10, no. 4: 390–408. doi:10.1080/10999940802523968.

Cohen, Daniel Aldana. 2019. "Stop Eco-Apartheid: The Left's Challenge in Bolsonaro's Brazil." *Dissent* 66, no. 1: 23–31.

Dandekar, Ajay. 2016. "India's Agriculture and Farmer Suicides: An Anatomy of a Crisis." *India International Centre Quarterly* 43, no. 2 (Autumn): 48–55.

Delahunt, Meaghan. 2008. *The Red Book*. London: Granta.

Egya, Sule Emmanuel. 2018. "Sexualized body, exploited environment: A feminist ecocritical reading of Kaine Agary's *Yellow-Yellow* and Christie Watson's *Tiny Sunbirds Far Away*." *Journal of the African Literature Association* 12, no. 2: 116–128. doi:10.1080/21674736.2018.1503928.

Ejiogu, Amanze R. 2013. "Gas flaring in Nigeria: Costs and policy." *Energy & Environment* 24, no. 6: 983–998.

Eweje, Gabriel. 2006. "Environmental Costs and Responsibilities Resulting from Oil Exploitation in Developing Countries: The Case of the Niger Delta of Nigeria." *Journal of Business Ethics* 69, no. 1 (November): 27–56.

Fanon, Frantz. [1961] 2001. *The Wretched of the Earth*. Translation by Constance Farrington. London: Penguin.

Fuller, Gary, et al. 2023. *"Impacts of air pollution across the life course – evidence highlight note."* Imperial College London Projects: Environmental Research Group. https://erg.ic.ac.uk/research/home/index.html [accessed 2023].

Gaard, Greta. 2020. "(Un)storied air, breath and embodiment." *ISLE: Interdisciplinary Studies in Literature and Environment* 138: 1–28.

Gilroy, Paul. 2005. *After Empire: Multiculturalism or Convivial Culture?* London: Routledge.

Habila, Helon. 2011. *Oil on Water*. London: Penguin.

Huggan, Graham, and Helen Tiffin. [2010] 2015. *Postcolonial Ecocriticism: Literature: Animals, Environment*. London: Routledge.

Hugo, Estie. 2021. "A 'violence just below the skin': Atmospheric terror and racial ecologies in Ben Okri's 'In the City of Red Dust'." *ISLE: Interdisciplinary Studies in Literature and Environment* 29, no. 2: 270–283.

Kilby, Patrick. 2019. *The Green Revolution: Narratives of Politics, Technology and Gender*. Abingdon: Routledge.

Kumar, Prakesh, et al. 2017. "New Narratives of the Green Revolution." *Agricultural History* 91, no. 3 (Summer): 397–422.

Kumar, Sachin, et al. 2013. "Use of Pesticides in Agriculture and Livestock Animals and its Impact on Environment of India." *Asian Journal of Environmental Science* 8, no. 1: 51–57.

Lewis, Simon L., and Mark A. Maslin. 2018. *The Human Planet: How We Created the Anthropocene*. London: Pelican Books.

Mahlstedt, Andrew. 2013. "Animal's Eyes: Spectacular Invisibility and the Terms of Recognition in Indra Sinha's *Animal's People*." *Mosaic: An Interdisciplinary Critical Journal* 46, no. 3, special issue: Blindness (September): 59–74.

Mbue, Imbolo. [2021] 2022. *How Beautiful We Were*. Edinburgh: Canongate.

Munir, Laine. 2021. "Gender Roles in Nigeria's Non-Violent Oil Resistance Movement." *Canadian Journal of African Studies* 55, no. 1: 79–97. doi:10.1080/00083968.2020.1718512.

Mohammad, Avaes. 2004. "Bhopal." *Critical Muslim*. https://www.criticalmuslim.io/bhopal [accessed 2023].

Mukherjee, Pablo. 2011. "'Tomorrow There Will be More of Us': Toxic Postcoloniality in *Animal's People*." In *Postcolonial Ecologies: Literatures of the Environment*, edited by Elizabeth DeLoughrey and George B. Handley, 216–231. Oxford: Oxford University Press.

Mustapha, B. Adetoun, et al. 2011. "Traffic Air Pollution and Other Risk Factors for Respiratory Illness in Schoolchildren in the Niger-Delta Region of Nigeria." *Environmental Health Perspectives* 119, no. 10 (October): 1478–1482.

Neira, Maria, and Veerabhadran Ramanathan. 2020. "Climate Change, Air Pollution, and the Environment: The Health Argument." In *Health of People, Health of Planet and Our Responsibility: Climate Change, Air Pollution and Health*, edited by W. K. Al-Delaimy, V. Ramanathan, and M. Sánchez Sorondo, 92–103. SpringerOpen.

Nixon, Rob. 2011. *Slow Violence and the Environmentalism of the Poor*. Cambridge, MA: Harvard University Press.

Oak Taylor, Jesse. 2016. *The Sky of Our Manufacture: The London Fog in British Literature from Dickens to Woolf*. London: University of Virginia Press.

Parayil, Govindan. 1994. "The 'Revealing' and 'Concealing' of Technology." *Southeast Asian Journal of Social Science* 26, no. 1: 17–28.

Parenti, Christian. 2011. *Tropic of Chaos: Climate Change and the New Geography of Violence*. New York: Nation Books.

Rath, Brigette. 2013. "'His words only?' Indra Sinha's Pseudotranslation *Animal's People* as Hallucinations of a Subaltern Voice." *AAA: Arbeiten aus Anglistik und Amerikanistik* 38, no. 2: 161–183.

Roy, Arundhati. [2014] 2015. *Capitalism: A Ghost Story*. London: Verso.

Shetty, P.K. 2004. "Socio-Ecological Implications of Pesticide Use in India." *Economic and Political Weekly* 39, no. 49 (December): 5261–5267.

Shiva, Vandana. 2013. "From Eco-Apartheid to Earth Democracy." *Next Nature* (May 26). https://www.nextnature.net/story/2013/from-eco-apartheid-to-earth-democracy [accessed April 21, 2023].

Shiva, Vandana. [1989] 2016. *The Violence of the Green Revolution: Third World Agriculture, Ecology and Politics*. Lexington, Kentucky: University Press of Kentucky.

Silver, Jonathan. 2019. "Suffocating Cities: Climate Change as Socio-Ecological Violence." In *Urban Political Ecology in the Anthro-Obscene: Interruptions and Possibilities*, edited by Henrik Ernstson and Erik Swyngedouw, 129–147. Abingdon: Routledge.

Sinha, Indra. 2007a. *Animal's People*. London: Simon & Schuster.

Sinha, Indra. 2007b. "Bhopal: A Novel Quest for Justice." *The Guardian*, October 10. https://www.theguardian.com/world/2007/oct/10/india-bhopal [accessed April 25, 2023].

Sinha, Indra. 2014. "Chemicals for War and Chemicals for Peace: Poison Gas in Bhopal, India, and Halabja, Kurdistan, Iraq." *Social Justice* 41, no. ½, special issue: Bhopal and After: The Chemical Industry as Toxic Capitalism: 125–145.

Varma, Daya R., and Roli Varma. 2005. "The Bhopal Disaster of 1984." *Bulletin of Science, Technology & Society* 25, no. 1 (February): 37–45. doi:10.1177/0270467604273822.

Walker, Gordon. 1990. "Bhopal: Five Years On." *Geography* 75, no. 2 (April): 158–160.

Wallace-Wells, David. 2019. *The Uninhabitable Earth: A Story of the Future*. London: Penguin.

Watson, Christie. 2011. *Tiny Sunbirds Far Away*. London: Quercus.

White, Laura A. 2020. *Ecospectrality: Haunting and Environmental Justice in Contemporary Anglophone Novels*. London: Bloomsbury.

Williams, F., et al. 2018. "*Plant clinics in Asia: reducing the use and risks of pesticides*." CABI Study Brief 27.

4 Life

Current forecasts predict that around one million species of animal and plant life are threatened with extinction across the globe, a rate only seen five times in the earth's history, with the most recent being the mass dinosaur extinctions of the Cretaceous period 66 million years ago. In her ground-breaking study, *The Sixth Extinction* (2014), Elizabeth Kolbert states that, in ordinary geological epochs, it is expected that a single species will disappear roughly every seven hundred years. She notes that today, the highest global extinction rate is that of amphibians, which is currently around forty-five thousand times higher than what is expected, with other forms of life following suit. 'It is estimated', writes Kolbert, 'that one-third of all reef-building corals, a third of all freshwater mollusks, a third of sharks and rays, a quarter of all mammals, a fifth of all reptiles, and a sixth of all birds are headed toward oblivion' (2014: 17–18). According to the U.N.'s 2019 Global Assessment Report on Biodiversity and Ecosystem Services, the top three drivers of this rate of biodiversity loss are habitat eradication, exploitation (such as hunting and fishing), and climate change.[1] A global 'sixth extinction' is thus being caused by the treatment of nonhuman life as either a resource to be exploited for profit, or else an obstruction to be exterminated.

Environmental scientists have warned that there is an urgent need to recognize species loss 'not only as a conspicuous consequence of human impacts on the planet but also a primary driver of global environmental change in its own right' (Dirzo et al., 2014: 401). This extends our discussion in previous chapters of the ways in which global literatures generate awareness of how the despoiling of the land, water, and air is both a consequence and cause of climate catastrophe. We know, for instance, how forests, oceans, and icescapes are important carbon sinks that draw down and store harmful CO_2 emissions from the air. Deforestation, ocean acidification, ice melt, and air pollution thus collectively exacerbate global warming and contribute to potentially irreversible global 'feedback loops'. Species loss is no different. Where forests and oceans absorb more carbon than they release, species loss, according to Rodolfo Dirzo et al., 'clearly threatens to fundamentally alter basic ecological functions and is contributing to push us toward global-scale "tipping points" from which we may not be able to return' (405). It is for this reason that Dirzo et al. advocate for the term 'defaunation' rather than the more elegiac 'species loss': a language of defaunation, they say, describes the endangerment and extinction of biological life as a systemic problem in 'the same sense as deforestation, a term that is now readily recognised and influential in focusing scientific and general public attention on biodiversity issues' (401). A global perspective on species extinction that frames it alongside deforestation, as well as ocean acidification, ice melt, and air pollution, in turn helps us to draw on solutions to the global climate emergency: if all four can be identified as both consequences and causes of climate catastrophe, then a concerted commitment to restoring and revitalizing forests, oceans, icescapes, the air, and nonhuman life would assist in preventing global ecological collapse.

The burgeoning twenty-first century awareness of mass extinction brings to light the much longer history of global species depletion following European colonial expansion. Indeed, the paradigmatic symbol of extinction, the dodo, was one of the first nonhuman victims of this: native to Mauritius, the dodo was hunted by Portuguese sailors as a food source and extirpated by 1681. Other lesser-known examples include, but are by no means limited to, the subspecies of North African Barbary and South African Cape lions, last known to have been hunted in the wild in 1858 and 1942 respectively; the quagga, a subspecies of the South African plains zebra that was hunted as a pest and declared extinct in 1900; the passenger pigeon of North America, which was declared extinct in 1914 after its habitat was deforested and it was over-hunted as a cheap source of food; the sea mink, hunted in North America by fur traders and declared extinct in 1920; and the Tasmanian tiger (or thylacine), which was seen as a threat to the livestock of European settlers and officially declared extinct in 1986. The North American and European whaling industries came close to extinguishing fin, sperm, and right whales until the discovery of petroleum and the invention of plastics replaced spermaceti and whalebone in the production of candles and other commodities, thus curtailing over-hunting. Similarly, the rapacious, centuries-long trade in ivory has led to the steep decline of African savannah and forest elephant populations.

The history of species endangerment and extinction also reveals how defaunation coincided in many regions with the spread of European colonialism and the ensuing genocides of Indigenous societies. The combined ecocides and genocides that followed in the wake of colonial expansion since the sixteenth century were legitimized by the belief in a European epistemological dominance when it came to the relationship between humans and the environment. This meant that Indigenous forms of environmental knowledge, based on stewardship of the earth and kinship with other lifeforms and environmental forces, have been derided as vanishing, anti-modern superstitions in relation to Western epistemologies, and European settler colonialism has historically worked to exterminate Indigenous cosmologies through both genocide and forms of what Gayatri Spivak has termed 'epistemic violence' ([1988] 1994). As Graham Huggan and Helen Tiffin write specifically in relation to the so-called 'white Dominions': '[t]he triumph of Anglo-European settlers over North American (and subsequently South African and Australian) indigenous populations was effected over [...] centuries through environmental – and hence cultural – derangement on a vast scale' (2015: 11). This history of human and ecological destruction was premised, they say, on the assumed '*ontological* and *epistemological* differences between European and Indian ideas of human and animal being-in-the-world' whereby 'respect for animals and nature' was 'righteously scorned' (11, original emphasis). The Potawatomi botanist Robin Wall Kimmerer notes, for instance, how the spread of the English language is central to an anthropocentric worldview that is antithetical to Indigenous knowledge given that, in English, 'the only way to be animate, to be worthy of respect and moral concern, is to be a human' ([2013] 2020: 57). In response to this, Kimmerer advocates for 'a grammar of animacy' that promotes 'a democracy of species, not a tyranny of one – with moral responsibility to [for example] water and wolves, and with a legal system that recognises the standing of other species' (57–58).

With the increased awareness about the sixth extinction, alongside the wider climate-related catastrophes facing the planet today, non-Natives are belatedly comprehending Indigenous lessons of human–animal kinship. Doing so, however, must also involve an attentiveness to the dehumanization, dispossession, and decimation of Indigenous populations, and the durability of settler colonial and capitalist–imperial relations across the globe. These structural forces have long been the focus of Indigenous activism, which is overtly and necessarily anti-capitalist and anti-colonial. 'Indigenous ways of relating to human and other-than-human life', writes the activist Nick Estes (Lower Brule Sioux) in *Our History is the Future*, 'exist in opposition to capitalism, which transforms both humans and non-humans into labor and commodities to be bought and sold' (2019: 16). They also 'exist in opposition to capitalism's twin, settler colonialism, which calls for the annihilation of Indigenous peoples and their other-than-human kin' (16), which includes the land, air, and water alongside flora and fauna. This stance underpins the high-profile Indigenous resistance movements in North America against, for instance, the Dakota Access Pipeline and the campaigns led and supported by the Idle No More movement.[2]

In examining literature that attends to the systemic forces that have decimated human and nonhuman life, we draw on Ursula K. Heise's assertion that '[b]iodiversity discourses revolve at bottom around [...] cultural values and narratives, which are crucial to take into account in any consideration of the future of conservation' (2016: 23). It is for this reason that Heise maintains that cultural responses to species extinction 'allow their readers or viewers to reflect on turning points of cultural history as the loss of a particular species comes to stand in for the broader perception that human relationships to the natural world have changed for the worse' (48). We will also combine the reading practices rooted in postcolonial and Indigenous studies already developed over the course of this book with an animal studies framework. This combination of methodologies follows Philip Armstrong's call for an 'alliance' between postcolonialism and animal studies due the fact that a 'common antagonist can be recognized immediately in the continued supremacy of that notion of the human that centers upon a rational individual self or ego' (2002: 414). The anthropocentricism so central to the exploitation of the environment, Armstrong notes, 'was fundamental to the practice of European Enlightenment colonialism as a "civilizing" mission, involving the pacification (and passivication) of both savage cultures and savage nature' (414).

Since Armstrong's provocation, scholars in postcolonial, Indigenous, and animal studies have emphasized the confluent forms of genocide and ecocide caused by colonialism, exemplified by Huggan and Tiffin's insistence in *Postcolonial Ecocriticism* that we must attend to the ways in which 'human societies have constructed themselves in hierarchal relation to other societies, *both* human *and* non-human' ([2010] 2015: 22, original emphasis). An awareness of the sixth extinction underpins the research of the interdisciplinary Extinction Studies Working Group led by Thom van Dooren, Deborah Bird Rose, and Matthew Chrulew. In their edited collection *Extinction Studies: Stories of Time, Death, and Generations*, the group state their intention to 'make use of the detailed observations and understandings of other knowledgeable peoples: from hunters and farmers, to artists, Indigenous peoples, wildlife carers, and many others' (2017: 4). Doing so, they say, 'is part of the critical work of decolonizing Western boundaries around knowledge and expertise' (4). Susan McHugh's *Love in a Time of Slaughters* also sees Indigenous storytelling as providing 'ancient and highly localized knowledges of being in the world', offering in the process urgent insights into the ways in which 'processes of domination become interwoven' and 'advancing conversations about the difficult realities of massive deaths of humans alongside other species' (2019: 2, 7). In the Introduction to their collection *Postcolonial Animalities*, Suvadip Sinha and Amit R. Baishya assert that,

> [i]n conditions of colonization and racialization, the evocation of the grammar of animality should not be viewed only as the production of bare animalized life, *as if* the image of the 'human' preexists with the reduction to animality being a 'fall' from it.
>
> (2020: 5, original emphasis)

Rather, from the perspective of the colonized, 'the human is never present as an ontological given' but must instead be 'struggled for' (5). It is for this reason, they argue, that it is necessary to explore the 'entanglements of race and species in colonial and neocolonial frameworks without [...] privileg[ing] one category over another' (13).

In the following sections we will expand on this existing scholarship to explore how the depletion of fauna is bound up with the dehumanization of colonized peoples *and* the categorization of nonhuman species as either repositories of valuable resources, game animals to be hunted as trophies, or pests to be exterminated. Focusing firstly on the mass killing and disassembly of nonhuman life as integral to the production of commodities, we will examine depictions in novels and poems of the ivory, whaling, and food industries. The ivory trade, as Keith Somerville notes, has 'not one but many histories' and is 'a highly complex and constantly shifting enterprise' where a 'mix of corruption, crime and conflict varies across time and across range states' (2016: 2–3). As it emerged out of the hunting of elephants across Africa, we will examine Joseph Conrad's *Heart of Darkness* (1899), Dan Wylie's 'Where in the waste is the wisdom?' (2013), and Inua Ellams's 'Fuck/ Empire' (2020), which are set in Central, Southern, and West Africa respectively. A comparative analysis of these texts allows for a discussion of elephants as a species that is seen as either a source of valuable ivory or a paradigmatic example of charismatic megafauna that is central to eco-tourism and conservationism. An awareness of this duality leads us to an examination of the depiction of whales as a comparable species that has been both commodified and spectacularized. Using Herman Melville's *Moby Dick or, The Whale* (1851), Witi Ihimaera's *The Whale Rider* (1987), and Keri Hulme's 'One Whale, Singing' (1986), we explore the significance of whales to the burgeoning of a global, industrialized trade in commodities reliant on ecocide and to a Māori environmental ethics in Aotearoa New Zealand.

Texts focusing on the ivory and whaling industries set up an engagement with issues of animal rights and arguments for the bestowal of personhood to both elephants and whales. Such debates in turn, however, disregard the treatment of nonhuman animals in the food industry, an issue we will explore through an analysis of J.M. Coetzee's *Elizabeth Costello* (2003), Gerald Vizenor's *Griever: An American Monkey King in China* (1987), and Thomas King's *Truth and Bright Water* (1999). In Coetzee's novel, an analogy is established between the mass killing of animals in abattoirs or processing facilities and the Holocaust, while Vizenor draws a comparison between the caging and killing of chickens and the persecution of Chinese people under Communist totalitarianism. The presence of bison in King's novel, by comparison, signals how the establishment of an industrial network of food production and consumption in North America was predicated upon the extirpation of the species by European settler colonists and the corresponding decimation and displacement of Native American societies.

King's depiction of bison also alludes to the settler colonial pastime of hunting animals for sport, which became an especially popular leisure activity in Kenya (formerly British East Africa). We will explore the treatment of nonhuman life as game through a discussion of H. Rider Haggard's *She* (1886), Karen Blixen's *Out of Africa* (1937), and Yomi Ṣode's poem 'Untitled' (2019). These texts show how colonial-era game hunting is intrinsically linked to the birth and popularity of natural history in Europe. In addition, a core thread running through the discussion of the mass killing of biological life for commodities or for sport is the story of the international conservation movement. We will discuss how conservationism has its roots in the nineteenth-century ivory trade, trophy hunting business, and natural history institutions. Today, conservationism is seeing new initiatives emerge under the banners of rewilding and de-extinction science, both of which seek to prevent the global sixth extinction through the revival of wildlife: the former with a focus on ecosystems; the latter with a focus on individual species. Turning to the context of defaunation and revival in Australia in Julia Leigh's *The Hunter* (1999) alongside the South African setting of Henrietta Rose-Innes's *Green Lion* (2015), we will conclude by examining how literature can interrogate the ethical questions that arise from scientific attempts to bring extinct animals back from the dead.

Commodification

In examining texts that depict the ivory, whaling, and food industries, we follow Robert P. Marzec's assertion that turning animal life into a 'resource' for the production of commodities involves 'reterritorializing an ecosystem for the purposes of capitalist production and development' (2019: 75). Across the ivory trade, the whaling industry, and the food industry, animal bodies are transformed into resources that, in Marzec's words, are 'not understood to be "within" nature' but are seen as 'a "discovered" element entrapped by nature' (75). Importantly, Marzec's formulation extends beyond fauna to include 'the reduction of indigenous diversity to a single "resource" [that] constitutes an obvious erasure of that diversity, and the transformation of human inhabitants themselves into a raw labor resource' (75). Thus, in examining cultural depictions of the ivory, whaling, and food industries, it is possible to further investigate the corresponding structural dependency of colonized and Indigenous peoples on capitalist–imperial modes of resource extraction.

Ivory

In line with Marzec's definition of 'resources' being regarded as 'entrapped by nature', the South African critic and poet Dan Wylie notes that, '[o]nce, elephants were regarded as little more than mobile repositories of ivory encased in redundant flesh' (2006: 30). This is especially true in relation to the historic treatment of elephants in Africa.[3] As Edward I. Steinhart explains in his authoritative account of colonial hunting in Kenya, up to two thousand years ago, 'elephant ivory [...] was being exported from the coastal regions of East Africa to Asia and the Mediterranean', while the 'undersea archaeological find of ivory among the cargo of Egyptian vessels plying the eastern Mediterranean' (2006: 18) suggests the possibility of elephant hunting fourteen centuries earlier. In his ground-breaking study *The Empire of Nature*, John M. MacKenzie affirms this, maintaining that '[s]ince the Middle Ages a complex network of African hunters and traders, Muslim middlemen and shippers, and Indian capitalists had supplied the Asian and later the European [ivory] markets' (1988: 148). In the seventeenth and eighteenth centuries, the trade in ivory had reached Europe, where it was used for the creation of artefacts ranging from the sacred to the mundane, including crucifixes, statues, tankards, and combs, and was imported predominantly from West Africa, giving Côte d'Ivoire its name (Feinberg and Johnson 1982: 450).

By the nineteenth century, the hunting of elephants became a popular pastime and a source of income for colonialists and settlers across Southern, East, and Central Africa, as well as for African communities who oversaw local trade routes (Somerville, 2016: 12). The 'white Dominion' of Southern Africa was favoured by sport-hunters who, according to Angela Thompsell, wished to 'offset the cost of a trip by selling some of their ivory, horns and specimens' (2015: 30), leading to the decimation of elephant numbers in the region. This ecocide across Southern Africa, along with the increased demand for ivory in Europe and America for such varied commodities as pianos, billiard balls, and cutlery, meant that by the end of the nineteenth century East and Central Africa had become the new frontiers in the mass slaughter of elephants (MacKenzie, 1988: 148; Steinhart, 2006: 70). Following the 'Scramble for Africa' in the 1880s, and the subsequent colonization of East Africa by the British East Africa Company, hunting for ivory in what is now Kenya became vital in bankrolling Britain's imperial mission. Indeed, profits from ivory exports 'often represented as much as half of the government's tax revenues annually and amounted to as much as 75 per cent of the East African Protectorate revenues in 1902' (Steinhart, 2006: 150–51). In Central Africa, King Leopold II of Belgium penetrated what was then the Congo Free State, fuelled by a desire to join the other European imperial powers in the extraction of lucrative ivory along with rubber and minerals.

The high value of ivory and the corresponding decimation of elephant populations led, at the turn of the century, to contradictory attempts by the British East Africa Company to establish 'a game department as an instrument for saving the elephants' whilst also seeking to continue drawing on 'the extraordinary value of ivory to colonial revenues' (Steinhart, 2006: 150, 151). The conflict between these two positions continued through to the interwar years when the conservation ethos was spurred on due to 'the perennial problem of ivory smuggling from Kenya to Italian territory in East Africa' (175): ultimately, game reserves could be used both to protect elephant populations and to stymie the loss of valuable ivory to Britain's imperial rival. 'The end of the era' of legal elephant hunting, says Steinhart, came in the 1930s, when the outbreak of the Second World War led to 'the steep drop in ivory prices below 10 shillings a pound' (77). At the same time, as Wylie writes, the remaining elephants native to the Eastern Cape in South

Africa had been 'systematically shot out in order to protect the emerging fruit-farmers of the nearby Sundays River valley', meaning that the number of elephants had decreased to 'a tiny remnant [of just 16] hiding out in the impenetrable thickets of the Addo bush' (2006: 29). The response to this shocking reality also spurred conservation efforts in the region and led to the creation of the Addo Elephant National Park in 1931, which is now home to over 600 elephants (as well as a range of other fauna including lions, buffalo, leopard, antelope, and the rare flightless dung beetle).[4] In 1989, the Convention on International Trade in Endangered Species (CITES) declared a ban on ivory trading. Yet, despite such efforts, at the time of writing, the IUCN Red List classifies the African savannah elephant as 'endangered' and the African forest elephant as 'critically endangered', largely as a consequence of the ivory trade continuing illegally.

A reading of Conrad's novella *Heart of Darkness* can provide important insights into the ivory trade and the near extinction of elephants during the height of European colonialism in Africa in the late-nineteenth century. As Jesse Oak Taylor asks of Marlow's account of the Belgian presence in the Congo interior: 'What is the "fantastic invasion" for which the wilderness wreaks its "terrible revenge" if not the unsustainable extraction of ivory for profit?' (2019: 24). Indeed, it is word of Kurtz's 'unsound method' (Conrad, [1899] 2007: 77) of acquiring ivory that leads to the Company employing Marlow as captain of the steamer that will carry them to Kurtz's compound. Yet, it has also been recognized that elephants themselves do not appear in the text, and ivory is often referred to as 'fossil', a term that refers to tusks that have been extracted and buried. For Jennifer Wenzel, '*Heart of Darkness* [...] tallies the costs of the ivory trade in terms that [...] broach the metaphysical but has not a word to say about elephants' (2011: 575). Similarly, Huggan and Tiffin align Chinua Achebe's critique of the absence of African subjectivity in *Heart of Darkness* with the 'conspicuous' (2015: 162) absence of elephants. Such an alignment, they argue, enables an awareness of the ways in which 'speciesism underpins racism, [...] as even the traditional linkage of ivory and slavery implicitly suggests' (165, 166).

Elsewhere, critics have read the absence of elephants in *Heart of Darkness* not as a conspicuous omission but as a purposeful comment on the fact that, at the time Conrad was writing, the rapacious commodification of elephant tusks by European colonial powers had pushed elephants to the edge of extinction. Ryan Francis Murphy asserts that, although 'the elephant is missing' (2013: 2) in *Heart of Darkness*, the sole use of the word 'elephant' occurs when Marlow surmises that the ivory adorning Kurtz's mistress 'must have had the value of several elephant tusks' (Conrad, [1899] 2007: 76). In acknowledging this fact, Murphy maintains that this sole reference to elephants as a source of 'value' is part of

> Conrad's greater analogy of detachment: Marlow is detached from the ivory trade as ivory is detached from the elephant as the word elephant

is detached from the beast it signifies. In this way, Conrad is able to control his calculated omission, commenting on the deplorable mammalian holocaust without diminishing the human thrust of his narrative critique; he acknowledges and deletes in a single move.

(2013: 12)

Murphy's reading of a 'calculated', as opposed to conspicuous, omission influences Oak Taylor's assertion that '[t]he absence of elephants from *Heart of Darkness* is [...] not an oversight but a formal incorporation of the threat of extinction hovering over the species' (2019: 38). Oak Taylor points out that the scenes that take place in Europe, and which bookend Marlow's tale, work to emphasize the detachment of bourgeois, European society from the brutal 'logic of extractivist capitalism' (38) taking place in the colonies. 'It is no accident', he writes, 'that it is the accountant who toys with a set of (ivory) dominoes – referred to as "bones" – on board the *Nellie*' (39). The implied presence here of the commodified and reterritorialized elephant tusk is counterpointed at the novella's close: when Marlow meets Kurtz's Intended in Brussels she is 'surrounded by objects whose origins lie in imperial conquest – [the] mahogany door, the keys of the piano [...] – but which exist for her only as commodities divorced from the ecological and social processes of their production' (38–39). It is notable too that the piano keys combine two forms of biotic resource extraction: the ivory on the piano sits alongside ebony keys, which were mass produced by deforesting ebony trees across the colonized regions of Mauritius, Sri Lanka, Indonesia, and West Africa.

Where Conrad's 'analogy of detachment' can be read as operating through allusions to the presence of reterritorialized ivory commodities but without any direct reference to elephants, the detachment between humans and elephants is confronted in Wylie's poem 'Where in the waste is the wisdom?', published in the 2013 collection *Slow Fires*. The poem's staging of this detachment, which has led to the 'systematic destruction of elephants', operates through the reversal of the dominant human gaze: 'What do you see in my amber eye', the elephant speaker asks, 'as I watch you | across the aeons, the water between us contemplative?' (Wylie, 2013: 42). This opening question establishes a tone of tentative confrontation in the meeting between human and elephant, leaving the reader disarmed by the inquisitive voice of a supposedly voiceless, passive, and objectified animal. The focus on the animal's eye, moreover, signals that this is a confrontation not with all humans but with hunters and tourists, two specific groups whose interaction with elephants is enabled by their race and class positions. These middle-to-upper-class, predominantly white sport-hunters and safari-goers, the speaker says, 'gape and shoot, or shoot and then gape, or just gape' (42). The use of the word 'shoot' in this instance carries the double meaning of capturing elephants with both a camera and a gun, thus alluding to the intertwined trajectories of colonial hunting practices and game reserve safaris.

Answering its own question of what humans 'see' when they look at an elephant, the speaker affirms that it is not, in fact, seen at all, but rather transformed into an anatomy of symbols: 'I shake my continental ears: a sigh goes up, *Ahh, Power!* | I trumpet mud across my back: *Wisdom!* Is the sigh' (42, original emphasis). Here, the 'contemplative' physical distance across the water of the poem's setting becomes an interpretive distance between the mundanity of the elephant's movements and the awed allegorizing of its physicality. Acknowledging the versatility of the elephant's symbolic currency, the speaker goes on to ask of the reader: 'Have I become no more than a projection of sorrows, | a landscape of wrinkles, a cipher of largesse?' (42). The versatility of ivory being used for commodities ranging from dominoes to piano keys is replaced here by a symbolic versatility. In his article 'Why Write a Poem About Elephants?', Wylie asserts that the elephant's symbolic dynamism ranges from 'the mass, the power, the mystery of "Africa" as conceived by white colonials' through to their role as 'a flagship species for all conservation, a quasi-human, psychologically sensitive social being, the welfare of which raises human emotional temperatures to the highest pitch' (2006: 41, 30).

In the second stanza of 'Where in the waste is the wisdom?' the tone shifts from the 'contemplative' to the critical when the elephant speaker turns to inspect the human reader. In doing so, this now vocal, questioning animal, able to transcend human temporalities, reduces the history of modern human progress to 'brief centuries of your communal idiocies' and 'tedious decrees and fiefdoms of tin' (Wylie, 2013: 42). From this nonhuman perspective, the history of humanity is not one of universal uplift but one of 'mad rapacities' (42), the language here echoing Marlow's account of the ivory trade in *Heart of Darkness* as being imbued with a 'taint of imbecile rapacity' (Conrad, [1899] 2007: 27). Just as Marlow compares this 'taint' to 'a whiff from some corpse' (27), for the elephant speaker of Wylie's poem the rapacity of human history has driven elephants to 'the point of extinction' (2013: 42). When the gaze of the predatory hunter and exoticizing tourist is reversed, the elephant speaker finds an animal 'without carapace or claws, without strength or speed' (42). In this bluntly biological, taxonomic evaluation, the human animal is categorized as inferior to other lifeforms, marked not by its assumed civilizational advancements but by *negation*, namely the negation of physical features evolutionarily designed for survival against predation. This negation then extends to more existential and cultural forms of inferiority: 'Behind the laughter', the speaker sees 'weak self-loathing', and 'behind the whispered awe, your terrible rootlessness' (42). By the final stanza, the elephant speaker addresses the pleas for human redemption based on innovations in the use of tools ('the invention of the stylus or the wheel') and cultural advancements ('your sanctifying songs, your remorseful poems'), only to dismiss them (42). Dispensing fully with the initial tone of inquisitive contemplation, the speaker – having assessed the assumed exceptionalism of its human subject – concludes, 'I despise; I accuse. | I see nothing to detain me here' (42). In this final pronouncement, the 'here' remains ambiguous, alluding to the fictional space of the poem's setting and the literary space of the poem itself. In this way, Wylie can be read as imagining the elephant abandoning its role as speaker, suggesting a self-reflexively ironic tone in which the poet is aware of the limitations of the poetic form – and by extension the English language – to ventriloquize the lives of elephants.

So far, we have discussed the killing of elephants for ivory by European colonists across East, Central, and Southern Africa. In West Africa, as Thompsell notes, 'European companies competed for control over the lucrative trade' but 'the actual hunting was largely left in the hands of African hunters' (2015: 26). Alongside the trading of ivory for a variety of commodities, elephant tusks in West Africa were also turned into souvenirs and ceremonial artefacts. According to Wenzel, carved tusks from the Kingdom of Loango 'were commissioned by and produced for European traders, as souvenirs of their African sojourns. The tusks served as mnemonic devices that could supplement the tales with which returned traders would regale family and friends' (2011: 577). The reliefs carved onto the tusks would show

> images of human and animal figures, in which the violence of the African/European trade in palm wine and palm oil, rubber, ivory, and slaves is on full view. [...] Elephants, elephant hunts, and human porters bearing ivory tusks are depicted in these narratives, in which the commodity tells its story, inscribed on its very body.
>
> (575)

For Edo communities in Benin, on the other hand, 'carved elephant tusks serve as spiritual points of contact, and are placed in elaborate shrines dedicated to the Oba's royal predecessors' (Winston Blackmun, 1997: 149). Prior to the British invasion of Benin in 1897, the ivory trade was maintained by the royal lineage of Obas and 'any hunter who killed an elephant forfeited one of its tusks to the Oba, who had the option of buying the other' (150). Ivory was also offered as a 'tribute to the Kingdom of Benin by neighbouring states as far away as Idah near the Niger-Benue confluence, and Lagos on the coast' (150). When Benin City was invaded by British soldiers, and the Oba Ovonramwen Nogbaisi was exiled, '[t]he British confiscated all of the objects [...] that they associated with divine kingship, and sent them back to London to be sold' (149). This led to around 135 carved tusks being scattered across museum collections or sold to private owners.

In his poem 'Fuck/Empire', written and performed as 'Tusk' for the 2019 Manchester Literature Festival and published in his 2020 collection *The Actual*, the Nigerian poet Inua Ellams (whose father is Edo) writes of a carved tusk that was looted by the British in the punitive expedition of 1897 and which, at the time of writing, is being held in Manchester Museum pending repatriation.[5] In his account of how the tusk was 'smuggled [...] across the ocean' after 'Benin City burned' and 'whole families died clinging to each other | their hands clawing the smoke for air', Ellams depicts the elephants taking revenge on the British Empire, playing on the popular conception that 'they do not forget' (2020: 77, 78). Adopting a similar strategy to Wylie, Ellams offers the elephants' perspective as they become aware of the ways in which 'their very bones' have been used by humans 'to trade | to display | in Monday meeting rooms | to bury in cellars | to hide in sheds | to leave in toy chests | to poke and prod like curiosities' (78). This awareness generates an understanding of how they have been 'dissected | mishandled | misrepresented | mislabelled | misused | misremembered and forgotten' (78). The list – and the repetitive use of the prefix 'mis' – expands upon the reading of *Heart of Darkness* above to emphasize how the exploitation of elephant bodies for commodities *and* natural history displays has historically worked to detach ivory-based products and museum specimens from the material reality of elephant existence. In response to their objectification and exploitation, Ellams imagines the spirits of dead elephants awakening and reasserting themselves: 'like clouds of conscience | like continents of questions', the spirits 'swarmed into the spaces where men bury answers | and began to push them out' (78). This image contains a double meaning, suggesting both that the buried 'answers' – a reference to the realities of colonial violence inflicted on Benin City – are being pushed to the surface *and* the anthropocentric dominance of hunters, colonists, and naturalists is being replaced by the elephants' presence.

In Ellams's description of elephants as 'the whales of their world | custodians of its land | forefathers of forefathers', the comparison signals how elephants and whales are two of the most prominent and charismatic symbols of the precarity of the natural world when faced with the exploitative interests of resource extraction. They also sit at the heart of the trajectory from hunting to conservation and eco-tourism. It is for this reason that the history of human interactions with whales offers a means of further examining the connections between resource extraction, colonialism, species extinction, and animal conservation.

Whaling

Where elephants offer only their tusks when it comes to animal resource extraction, the physiognomy of whales lends an incredible level of versatility: virtually every part of the hunted whale's body, from the blubber and bones to the organs and digestive system, have been used as resources. For members of the Alaskan Native nation that we discussed in the 'Water' chapter, whaling, as Rachel Nutaaq Ayałhuq Naŋinaaq Edwardson maintains, has historically been the source of 'materials to build our houses and make the tools we needed to survive in our environment' (2020: 98). It is a practice, she says, that provides Inuit communities with 'physical, cultural and spiritual sustenance' and is 'the safety net of our whole community, our whole way of life', but it could not continue without 'a holistic (or multi-disciplinary) and longterm (or sustainable) relationship with the environment, animals and the people' (98). The globalized whaling industry that peaked in the mid-nineteenth century, by contrast, coincided with the proliferation of new industrialized processes that shifted food and commodity production away from agricultural practices and towards the assembly line. It is this industrial form of whaling that provides the setting for *Moby Dick or, The Whale*, Melville's account of life on the *Pequod* that set sail from Massachusetts. For Armstrong, *Moby Dick* represents 'a period in which industrialization was energetically at work, producing – along with urbanization, alteration in the economic status of women, redefinition of labour structures and environmental degradation – a radically new relationship between humans and other animals' (2008: 100). The whaling ship became, in effect, a mobile, sea-faring factory dedicated to the capture and disassembly of whales for the production of a wide range of commodities to be sold on the global marketplace.

Melville's narrator Ishmael acknowledges this fact, saying that sperm whales were regarded as 'the most valuable in commerce' ([1851] 2003: 149) since the spermaceti found in the cavities of their skulls provided the wax for 'almost all the tapers, lamps, and candles that burn around the globe' (119). This discovery made the candle one of the most lucrative commodities linked to the hunting of whales, replacing the use of tallow which, prior to the late eighteenth and nineteenth centuries, was supplied by the melted fat of sheep (Shannon, 2011: 311). Whalebone, the material that bedecks the *Pequod* and out of which Ahab's prosthetic leg is made to replace the one 'taken' by Moby Dick, was also used in a wide range of consumer items, such as women's dresses, men's shirts, umbrellas, and backscratchers. The highly prized, 'soft, waxy' ambergris that is retrieved from a sperm whale's intestines has been used in 'perfumery, in pastiles, precious candles, hair-powders, and pomatum' (Melville, [1851] 2003: 447). In Turkey, Ishmael notes, ambergris had been central to cooking, while '[s]ome wine merchants drop a few grains in claret, to flavor it' (447). It is this versatile use of the whale's carcass that leads Ishmael to draw a comparison with 'that famous elephant, with jewelled tusks, and redolent with myrrh' (449).

At the same time, whales can be situated in an ambivalent position in debates about environmental degradation and species extinction. This is because the global over-hunting of whales may have continued apace well into the twentieth and twenty-first centuries if not for the discovery of petroleum and the subsequent invention of both plastics and paraffin wax. The availability of petroleum, as Nancy Shoemaker has shown, 'made the American need for whale oil and whalebone obsolete and meant that, when an environmental conscience intent on saving whales emerged in the 1970s, Americans could embrace this particular cause without suffering any loss' (2005: 272). In this way, it is the discovery of the very fossil fuels that are warming the planet that helped elevate the conservation of whales to global levels.

The status of whales as 'endangered charismatic megafauna' has informed what Jonathan Steinwand identifies as a 'cetacean turn in environmentalist iconography and postcolonial literature' whereby '[w]hales and dolphins became symbols for environmentalist pleas to save the world's ocean ecosystems' from 'pollution, extraction, and catastrophe' (2011: 183, 182). This 'turn' can be recognized in Ihimaera's *The Whale Rider*, alongside Linda Hogan's *People of the Whale* (2008), Zakes Mda's *The Whale Caller* (2005), and Amitav Ghosh's *The Hungry Tide* (2004). For Steinwand, in Ihimaera's and Hogan's novels (set in Aotearoa New Zealand and North America respectively) cetaceans symbolize a connection to an Indigenous ancestral past, whereas in Mda's and Ghosh's novels (set in South Africa and India respectively), cetaceans are depicted as 'companion species' (2011: 185). In both instances, the texts depict 'nonhuman others in ways that risk but ironically resist domesticating and romanticizing the other by focusing attention on the lives, the knowledge, the arts, the values, and the beliefs of the people who dwell among these species' (185). In what follows, we will concentrate on the context of Aotearoa New Zealand as a region that has been shaped by the presence of whales (perhaps more so than North America, South Africa, and India). As Ryan Tucker Jones and Angela Wanhalla maintain, '[w]haling has long enjoyed a central place in narratives of Pacific history. Long before Europeans came to that ocean, many Pacific peoples traced their ancestries and in some cases built their societies on the backs of whales', with the cetaceans featuring 'in accounts of voyaging traditions, often as protectors, and their significance remembered in songs and carvings' (2019: 5). When the globalized whaling industry emerged in the nineteenth century, they say, 'many colonial histories around the [Pacific] ocean turned on how, when, and by whom whales were killed and their products distributed', meaning that it is necessary to recognize 'the coercive role whaling often played in Pacific colonialism' (6). Turning to the centrality of whales both for Māori culture and the history of European settler colonialism in Aotearoa New Zealand, we will offer close readings of *The Whale Rider* and an additional lesser-known text, Keri Hulme's short story 'One Whale, Singing', which shares Ihimaera's confrontation with an anthropocentric Western rationalism, but without a specific emphasis on Māori customs.

In *The Whale Rider*, Ihimaera presents an Indigenous, Māori cosmology as offering a sustainable and ecocentric alternative to the treatment of whale bodies as repositories of resources to be extracted. The narrative is set in the region of Gisborne, Aotearoa New Zealand, during a period of crisis due to a fracture in the relationship between humans and the environment. This fracture is articulated specifically in terms of the traditional Māori conviction that humans must 'live in harmony' with the sea god Tangaroa, which requires blessing 'every new net and new line to Tangaroa', placing 'talismanic shrines' in fishing areas, and preventing overfishing (Ihimaera, [1987] 2005: 38). In recounting this 'pact with Tangaroa', however, the Māori chief Koro Apirana notes solemnly that 'in these days of commercialism it is not always easy to resist temptation', imploring his tribe's youth to '*Listen how empty our sea has become*' (39, original emphasis). The rapacious commodification of animal life, in contrast to a sustainable relationship that is underpinned by Māori customs, is dramatized when two hundred whales become stranded on the beach at Gisborne and a scene of 'human butchery' (80) ensues whereby the animals are regarded as nothing more than vessels for the extraction of bone and blubber. When a group of men use a chainsaw to cut through the jaw of a living whale, 'laughing as they wrench the jaw from the butchered whale', the scene becomes one of '[b]lood, laughing, pain, victory, blood' (80).

This violent form of resource extraction is countered in the novel by an evocation of the ecological importance of Māori belief systems. Koro Apirana voices a critique of the way in which such Indigenous cosmologies have been dismissed as 'irrational' (94) since 'man assumed a cloak of arrogance and set himself up above the Gods', thus driving a 'wedge through the original oneness of the world' and dividing the 'natural and supernatural', the 'present and the past', the 'scientific and the fantastic' (93). When a whale beaches itself in Koro's village, he sees it as a calling to repair the broken unity of the world: 'If we are able to return it to the sea', he instructs his tribal community, 'then that will be proof that the oneness is still with us. [...] If it lives, we live. If it dies, we die' (94). In this way, Steinwand notes, Ihimaera 'calls attention to a long tradition' across cultures indigenous to the Pacific 'of a nonanthropocentric environmental ethic in which there is no great divide between animal and human' (2011: 186).

An insistence on the unity of the earth, the water, the air, and all biological life is established in the novel's Prologue, in which we are given an account of the cosmological origin story of the Māori ancestor Paikea. Prior to the arrival of human life,

> The mountains were like a stairway to heaven, and the lush green rainforest was a rippling cloak of many colours. The sky was iridescent, swirling with the patterns of wind and clouds; sometimes it reflected the prisms of rainbow or southern aurora. The sea was ever-changing and seamless to the sky.
>
> (Ihimaera, [1987] 2005: 2)

Throughout this world of natural abundance teemed nonhuman life. On land, the narrator describes the presence of tuataras (a reptile species once extinct on the mainland of Aotearoa New Zealand but since reintroduced) and Moas (a now-extinct flightless bird), alongside the kiwi and weka birds, the sounds of which mingled with 'the chatter of tree bark, chatter of cicada and murmur of fish-laden streams' (2). At sea could be found stingray and fish that 'swam in brilliant shoals [...] herded by shark or mango ururoa' (2).

Rather than depicting this human-free world as purely paradisiacal, the land and sea are described as feeling 'a great emptiness, a yearning [...] [w]aiting for the blessing to come' (2, 3). It is with the appearance of canoes on the horizon that the earth and the sea 'began to feel the sharp pangs of need, for an end to the yearning' (3). The first human to arrive – known as Kahutia Te Rangi – appears on the back of a whale that has 'a swirling tattoo imprinted on the forehead' (4), a reference to the koru, a Māori symbol of cyclical time and rebirth. Celebrating the arrival of the whale rider, '[t]he song in the sea drenched the air with ageless music and land and sea opened themselves to him, the gift long waited for: tangata, man' (4). In this retelling of the Māori origin story, the settlement in Aotearoa New Zealand of people indigenous to Polynesia does not spell the beginning of environmental catastrophe but sees humans possessing 'the power of *interlock*' (31, original emphasis) and able to contribute to an ecosystem to which they belong in a reciprocal relationship. As such, the novel's origin story refuses the Anthropocene narrative of ecological destruction being created by an undifferentiated humanity, envisioning instead a possible kinship between humans, flora, and fauna. At the same time, it offers an alternative to the Christian origin story, relayed in the Book of Genesis, of a God-given dominance of humans over the nonhuman world.

The privileging of a traditional Māori cosmology that understands kinship between humans and/as nature in *The Whale Rider* also brings with it a message of modernization. Koro is insistent that only a male member of the tribe can save the beached whale and repair the world's oneness. The novel's primary narrative, however, follows Koro's adolescent granddaughter Kahu. Named after the original whale rider, Kahutia Te Rangi, the young Kahu discovers that she is able to communicate with whales. Rather than being celebrated, this gift leads to a confrontation with Koro, whose conservative and patriarchal interpretation of Māori customs prevents him from accepting that the whale rider could return to his community in female form. As such, as Steinwand maintains, in its attempt 'to repair the separation between human and animal, between land and sea, between modern and mythic perspectives', *The Whale Rider* demonstrates that 'such reconciliation requires not merely respect and humility but also innovation and open-mindedness' (2011: 186). Or, as Hubert Zapf puts it in his reading of the novel, '[o]nly by their continuing self-renewal can traditional forms of culture-nature symbiosis be maintained' (2017: 202).

Kahu's role as a symbol of innovation and self-renewal concerning a Māori environmental ethics is emphasized by the imagery of the umbilical cord. In his denunciation of the disunity of the world, Koro insists that there exists a 'birth cord joining past and present, reality and fantasy' (94). Koro's figurative evocation of the birth cord is made literal by Kahu's narrative arc, which begins when her grandmother, Nanni Flowers, buries her umbilical cord in front of the community's statue of Kahutia Te Rangi. This is the same site at which, in the tribe's foundation myth, Kahutia Te Rangi planted a spear upon his arrival to the island stating, 'Let this be the one to flower when the people are troubled and it is most needed' (5). Similarly, the novel's form, which is structured around the passing of the four seasons beginning with Spring, makes the circularity of nature-time and the renewal of life central to the text in opposition to a Euro-centric, capitalist conception of time as linear. This circularity is paired with the text's formal juxtaposition of human and whale stories, in which Koro Apirana's patriarchal vision of the tribe's future is comparable to the male leadership of the whale pod that inadvertently leads them into danger. In both cases, reductive gender stereotypes that are legitimized by a recourse to traditional ways of living are revealed to be antithetical to future survival.

A formal structure that combines the narratives of humans and whales, alongside an exploration of human gender relations, is evident also in Hulme's short story 'One Whale, Singing', taken from the 1986 collection *Te Kaihau: The Windeater*. The story, as Ben Holgate notes, 'parallels *The Whale Rider* in according whales with consciousness, intelligence, memory and communication' (2019: 113). Hulme achieves this in her use of both form and characterization, which allow two juxtapositions to be staged above and below the water with an unnamed pregnant female poet acting as the bridge between the two. The first juxtaposition places the narratives of expectant motherhood provided by the woman on the boat and the whale underwater in dialogue with each other; the second stages the opposing perspectives on whales voiced by the woman and her male partner. At the heart of the story is an interrogation of communication within and between species. The juxtaposition of the woman's perspective with that of the whale envisions the fleeting and tentative possibility of kinship and inter-species communication between the two pregnant females. By contrast, the discussion that unfolds on the boat stages a conflict between two members of the same species whose 'arguments follow well-worn tracks and go in circles' (Hulme, [1986] 1988: 64): the husband, a scientist who is practising a lecture on the lack of intelligence in animals, repeatedly dismisses the non-anthropocentric views of his partner, who considers the possibility that 'we may be at the bottom of the pile, not the top. It may be that other creatures are aware of their place and purpose in the world, have no need to delve and paw a meaning out' (67).

The husband represents the same form of arrogant rationalism derided by Koro Apirana in *The Whale Rider*, as is evident in his pronouncements that: 'We can conclusively demonstrate that to man alone belong true intelligence and self-knowledge' and 'Man alone as a species, makes significant artefacts, and transmits knowledge in permanent and durable form' (62). While the activity of whaling is not referred to, it is this anthropocentric, Cartesian understanding of nonhuman animals as automata that underpins the treatment of whales as mere repositories of resources to be extracted and commodified. Counter to her partner's perspective, the woman thinks to herself: 'Man indeed! How arrogant! How ignorant! Woman would be as correct, but I'll settle for humanity. And it strikes me that the quality humanity stands in need of most is true intelligence and self-knowledge' (62). In considering the ways in which humanity transmits knowledge through material artefacts, the woman frames this ability not as a marker of superiority but as a consequence of the fact that humans 'have such pathetic bodies, and no especial ecological niche', meaning that humans are in need of 'a wasteland of drear ungainly hovels to shelter our vulnerable hides' (63).

Importantly, for the most part, the woman's opinions are not spoken out loud to her husband but shared with the reader via an internal monologue, demonstrating the absence of genuine communication with her partner. When she does voice an observation, such as the view that '[d]olphins and whales are still largely unknown entities', it is 'murmured, more to herself than to him' (65). Emphasizing the gulf between the two, the man responds in a dismissive and patronizing manner: 'Nonsense, my sweet. They've been thoroughly studied and dissected for centuries. [...] Rather dumb animals, all told' (65). The man's insistence that nonhuman animals can be categorized as inferior based on dissection and human observation alone is ironized by the story's inclusion of the whale's '[d]eep' connection to its unborn calf: with a 'crooning tenderness' the whale feeds her calf 'love and music' and transmits 'dark pictures' based on her memories of an 'oil-bedraggled albatross' and an escape from the killer whales who ended the life of 'the other female who had accompanied her south' (64). Without the need for material artefacts, then, the whale is shown to possess an ability to pass on to its calf an instinct for survival against both man-made and natural risks to its life.

The contrast between the man's investment in scientific observation and the whale's power to transmit pictures to its unborn infant establishes the imagery of sight and blindness, which becomes increasingly central as the story reaches its dramatic conclusion. For instance, when the woman is confronted with her husband's anthropocentric arrogance, she speculates to herself that, '[o]ther species may somehow be equipped to know fully and consciously what truth is, whereas we humans must struggle, must struggle blindly to the end' (67). At the very moment when the woman fully acknowledges the lack of genuine communication between her and her partner, exclaiming to herself how '[h]e won't see, he won't see, he won't see anything' (69), she feels 'uncomfortably aware of her protuberant belly, and begins to croon a song of comfort to herself' (69). It is an action that replicates the 'crooning tenderness' (64) that defines the whale's relationship with her own unborn infant, foreshadowing the story's final scene of inter-species communication.

The two narratives taking place on the boat and underwater collide at the story's close when the whale, 'full of her dreams and her song', swims to the water's surface only to be 'shocked by the unexpected fouling' (70) of the couple's boat. In this moment, the boat is smashed and sinks and the woman loses her husband, but she discovers what Holgate refers to as an 'intimate physical proximity' with the whale that stages a 'reconciliation between human and non-human' (2019: 113). The whale emits a 'long moaning call [...] that reverberates through [the woman]', who is 'physically swept, shaken by an intensity of feeling, as though the whale has sensed her being and predicament, and has offered all it can, a sorrowing compassion' (Hulme,

[1986] 1988: 70). The whale departs, having shown the woman in this encounter more kindness and understanding than her husband. The connection, however, is only fleeting and the woman is left 'alone in the dark' (70), thus making literal the blind struggle that she sees as humanity's fate. Although she is now stranded at sea, the woman experiences a merging of the movement of her unborn child with the rhythms of the sea: 'In her womb the child kicked. Buoyed by the sea, she feels the movement as something gentle and familiar, dear to her for the first time' (70). Rather than being a space of danger, she 'begins to laugh' at the discovery that the sea is 'warm and confiding, and it is a long long way to shore' (71). As such, the story's conclusion is ambivalent and open-ended: there is the possibility that the woman is shown to have found a sense of belonging at sea, with John Bryson suggesting that she 'may become a whale after the story's end' (Hulme and Bryson, 1994: 131).

In both *The Whale Rider* and 'One Whale, Singing', whale song is presented as evidence of the complex nature of cetacean culture that contrasts starkly with the view of whales as repositories of blubber and bone. According to Graham Huggan in *Colonialism, Culture, Whales*, it is the 'sophistication of whale song' that

> has been used by scientists to support the increasingly accepted view that whales have culture, and to open up fresh debates on the moral standing of cetaceans, which many now see as being entitled to the personhood that humans tend to reserve for themselves.
>
> (2018: 95–96)

Similarly, in response to their near extinction at the hands of industrial-level forms of ecocide, and the wider appreciation of the complexities of their social lives, elephants have become central to debates about whether nonhuman animals can be afforded personhood, with all of the rights that such a status bestows.[6] This insistence may well be beneficial in advocating for the rights of a select group of high-profile species (deemed to be 'charismatic megafauna') but, as Cary Wolfe maintains in *Animal Rites*, the extension of rights to nonhuman animals 'who are (symptomatically) "most like us" only ends up reinforcing the very humanism that seems to be the problem in the first place' (2003: 192). In other words, rather than contributing to a truly ecocentric perspective on nonhuman life, debates about the potential personhood of nonhuman animals can have the effect of expanding and thus upholding anthropocentrism. In so doing, the expansion of personhood neglects an examination of the treatment of nonhuman life as a source of food.

Food

The previous focus on the ivory and whaling industries demonstrates how explorations of human forms of domination over nonhuman life, and the literatures that best dramatize these relations, are dominated by charismatic megafauna. Yet, human exploitation of animals as resources has also led to the production and proliferation of some of the world's most common animals that rarely make an appearance in literature: namely, those that are almost ubiquitous as a presence in the domestic and diurnal realm of meat-eating households. Tuning to these animals in this final section involves a more nuanced formulation of Marzec's definition of resources that are thought of as being 'entrapped by nature' (2019: 75), as animals that provide meat are, in many cases, developed on industrial scales as opposed to being extracted from the natural world. The factory-farmed chicken, for instance, as Raj Patel and Jason W. Moore note, is the product of biopiracy practices that produced an animal that 'can barely walk, reaches maturity in weeks, has an oversize breast, and is reared and slaughtered in geologically significant quantities (more than sixty billion birds a year)' (2018: 3–4).[7] The centrality of the chicken to everyday, modern life, and the fact that its fossilized bones will act as a significant geological marker of intercontinental networks of food production, mean that, for Patel and Moore, '[t]he most iconic symbol of the modern era isn't the automobile or the smartphone but the Chicken McNugget' (5).

This provocation aligns with Nicole Shukin's examination in *Animal Capital* (2009) of the role of abattoirs in the trajectory of capitalist modernity. Traditionally, the modern world of mechanized labour and culture is thought to have been ushered in by Henry Ford's invention of the assembly line for producing automobiles, the first of which opened at Highland Park in Chicago in 1910. This origin story is reinforced by Aldous Huxley's dystopian depiction of the Fordist technologies determining human life, along with the car manufacturer's deification, in *Brave New World* (1932). Yet, as Shukin reveals, it was the abattoirs of Chicago, which had been in operation since the mid-nineteenth century and offered tours to spectators, that directly influenced Ford's invention of the assembly line. 'The auto assembly line', writes Shukin, 'so often taken as paradigmatic of capitalist modernity, is [...] mimetically premised on the ulterior logistics of animal disassembly that it technologically replicates and advantageously forgets in a telling moment of historical amnesia' (2009: 87). This insight reveals that the organization of atomized and alienated labour relations that characterizes capitalist economic development, and for which Fordism is a synecdoche, emerged out of the domestication and systematic slaughter of nonhuman animals as a source of food.

The industry of mass animal slaughter is addressed by Coetzee in *The Lives of Animals*, which also forms the central two 'Lessons' of *Elizabeth Costello*. Coetzee's fictional Australian writer Costello uses an invited talk at an American university to point not to the historical connection between abattoirs and assembly lines but to the other twentieth-century legacy of the Chicago stockyards: it was from this industry, Costello says, 'that the Nazis learned how to process bodies' ([2003] 2004: 97). An analogy between abattoirs and the gas chambers of the Third Reich thus forms the central rhetorical assertion of Costello's lecture, in which she confronts her audience with 'what is being done to animals at this moment in production facilities [...], in abattoirs, in trawlers, in laboratories, all over the world' (63). This analogy is founded on both the scale of mechanized murder for which abattoirs, trawlers, and laboratories are built and the 'willed ignorance' (64) of the general population who may not actively participate but who turn a blind eye. To these 'places of slaughter', Costello says, 'we close our hearts. Each day a fresh holocaust, yet, as far as I can see, our moral being is untouched. We do not feel tainted' (80). In her criticism of factory farming, Costello rejects the distinction – which has its roots in the thinking of René Descartes – between animals as mere automata and humans as rational, thinking, and feeling beings. For Costello (as her daughter-in-law Norma summarizes), 'animals have their own accounts in accordance with the structure of their own minds, to which we don't have access because we don't share a language with them' (91). As such, the appeal to end animal slaughter is not based on conceptions of personhood, as is the case with elephants and whales, but on the inherent unknowability of animal lives.

Coetzee's central analogy, and the construction of Costello as a mouthpiece for the author, has seen *The Lives of Animals* being read by Robert McKay as 'the most profound attempt in contemporary writing to answer the challenge of animal ethics' (2010: 67). For McKay, the novella's 'experimental metafictional form brings the full potential of literary method to meet the ethical demands that animals place upon us' (67). One such demand involves the applicability of a discourse of animal rights. Donna Haraway, for instance, notes that Costello 'inhabits a radical language of animal rights [...] and she embraces all of its power to name extreme atrocity' (2008: 81). For Anat Pick, however, Coetzee's novel has 'helped reorient philosophical discussions in animal ethics away from utilitarian, reason, and rights-based approaches (that still occupy the center ground of the debate)' toward what she terms 'creaturely thinking' (2011: 7). Such thinking insists on a 'creaturely ethics' that 'does not depend on fulfilling any preliminary criteria of subjectivity and personhood' (193). Rather, says Pick, '[i]ts source lies in the recognition of the materiality and vulnerability of all living bodies, whether human or not, and in the absolute primacy of obligations over rights' (193).

The comparison between abattoirs and Nazi gas chambers is a controversial one, and Coetzee includes two fictionalized refutations of Costello's argument. The poet character Abraham Stern writes to Costello with the assertion: 'If Jews were treated like cattle, it does not follow that cattle are treated like Jews. The inversion insults the memory of the dead. It also trades on the horrors of the camps in a cheap way' (Coetzee, [2003] 2004: 94). The second refutation comes from a professor of philosophy, Thomas O'Hearne, who states the Cartesian position that: 'To animals, death is continuous with life' and thus 'to equate a butcher who slaughters a chicken with an executioner who kills a human being is a grave mistake' (109). The metafictional creation of the character of Costello and the dialogic inclusion of criticisms that counter her analogy are characteristic of the political and ethical disinterestedness of Coetzee's oeuvre. As McKay notes, 'Coetzee's fiction, nowhere more so than in *The Lives of Animals*, relentlessly does away with any clear-cut authority, moral or otherwise, and whether voiced by character or narrator' (2010: 69). Readers instead 'experience the effects of a competing set of discourses, which to be sure command varying degrees of power' (80). Still, it is Costello's opinion that is given primacy, and it is a view that echoes the speech delivered by Coetzee in Sydney (an edited version of which was published in the Australian newspaper *The Age*) which states that after the horrors of the Holocaust were revealed, humanity's self-reflexive cry should have been: 'What a terrible crime [...] to treat any living being like a unit in an industrial process!' (2007: n.p.). Furthermore, whilst giving voice to alternate perspectives on both the Holocaust and animal ethics, a core problem with Coetzee's analogy is the way in which it overlooks the socio-economic relations of labour and consumption relating to factory farming.

For Coetzee, the slaughtered animals are victims while humans, as homogenous actors, are the perpetrators. The emphasis in Costello's Holocaust analogy on a dichotomy of victim and perpetrator suggests that the workers in abattoirs and meat-eating consumers alike are akin to Nazis who, Costello says, 'had themselves become beasts' (Coetzee, [2003] 2004: 65) by unthinkingly adhering to a violent and discriminatory ideology. Yet, in noting the entangled 'histories of capitalist labor and nature' since the mid-nineteenth century, Shukin affirms that 'the labor of slaughter and the labor of consuming slaughter were (and still are) clearly divided along class, racial, and ethnic lines' (2009: 129, 103). For example, in the US (where Costello's lecture takes place), the industrial network of factory farming includes prison labour, where workers are disproportionately drawn from communities of colour at the sharp end of underemployment, poverty, and criminalization.[8] In establishing a simplified link between the industrial slaughter of animals and the Holocaust, then, Coetzee creates a false equivalence between the ideological violence of the Third Reich and the socio-economic violence of global factory farming practices. In so doing, *The Lives of Animals* and *Elizabeth Costello* fail to acknowledge the socio-economic conditions of factory farming that are structured by issues of ownership, labour, and consumption. For Costello, the 'horror [of the Holocaust] is that the killers refused to think themselves into the place of their victims, as did everyone else': the corresponding problem with the treatment of animals, then, is one merely of 'sympathy' (Coetzee, [2003] 2004: 79) and not a complex system of globalized food production, capitalist labour relations, and consumerism that relies on the exploitation of both workers and the bodies of nonhuman animals alongside the structural dependency of the vast majority of consumers upon this system.

Coetzee's writing has dominated analyses of literary depictions of animals reared for food. This has tended to limit discussion of the food industry in a manner that not only neglects the structural inequalities of production and consumption but also overlooks the treatment of nonhuman animals as sources of food within different historical geopolitical contexts that complicate Elizabeth Costello's Holocaust analogy. To expand upon the corpus of literature depicting the commodification of nonhuman animals for food, we can look to two novels by North American writers: *Griever: An American Monkey King in China* by Gerald Vizenor (Minnesota Chippewa) and Thomas King's *Truth and Bright Water*. *Griever* is comparable to Coetzee's writing to the extent that the slaughter of chickens is depicted as analogous to another form of human subjugation, namely the abuse of human rights in China. *Truth and Bright Water* includes references to bison in a manner that alludes to the history of settler colonial campaigns in North America to extinguish Indigenous forms of animal-based food production, making colonized societies reliant upon the industrial farming complex. Both novels follow trickster characters common across Native American and First Nations literature that are characterized by 'antisocial' behaviour, 'foolishness', 'promiscuity', and a 'creative cleverness' that 'keeps alive the possibility of transcending the social restrictions we regularly encounter' (Babcock-Abrahams, 1975: 147). The eponymous Griever in Vizenor's novel and Monroe Swimmer in King's are tricksters who are particularly interested in nonhuman animal life and stage artistic resurrections of chickens and bison respectively.

Griever is influenced by Vizenor's experience working at Tianjin University in China as a visiting Fulbright Professor in the 1980s and follows Griever de Hocus, a 'trickster teacher who liberated hundreds of chickens at a local street market and then vanished' (Vizenor, [1987] 1990: 19). Described as 'holosexual', Griever is a self-proclaimed trickster whose promiscuousness cuts across the animate and inanimate worlds: he 'seemed to love the whole world', we are told, including 'stones' and 'trees' (Vizenor, [1987] 1990: 21). This love underpins Griever's act of chicken liberation, which occurs early in the novel after he 'watched three chickens bleed to death [...]. In minutes the dead birds were boiled, plucked, paid, and carried naked from the market' (34). At first, Griever responds creatively by bringing the slaughtered chickens back to life through art: 'Griever opened his holster, drew the scroll, and with three coloured pens he resurrected the dead chickens. [...] He turned the scroll [...] and painted a proud white cock leading all the caged hens to freedom' (34). With his scroll in hand, Griever becomes the embodiment of the proud cockerel and approaches the market stall demanding that the chickens be released.

Although the act of liberation is for the most part a success, Griever is frustrated to see that '[s]everal birds scurried through the crowd with their heads down, back to the cages' (53). It is a moment that foreshadows the text's wider critique of Communist rule in China alongside a disillusionment at the possibility for freedom from totalitarianism. As Timothy R. Fox maintains,

> The release of caged birds in the novel is a symbolic prelude to what would later be Griever's most courageous act of liberation, when he frees condemned prisoners from public execution. Most of those who flee are gunned down by soldiers, but the group's only real political prisoner remains, waiting for her captors to return.
>
> (2009: 78)

The failure to achieve total liberation for both the chickens and prisoners marks, according to Fox, Vizenor's cynicism with China's 'bureaucrat-dominated cities' populated by people unable to envision a world beyond 'the hierarchies of historical dominance' (86). The novel instead ends with the suggestion that 'the next revolution' will emerge out of the 'marvelous world of tricksters' inhabiting the country's provinces (Vizenor, [1987] 1990: 234, 235).

Where Coetzee's Costello references the Holocaust to make a statement about the treatment of animals, and Vizenor's Griever confronts animal cruelty to ultimately raise awareness about human rights abuses in China, King's *Truth and Bright Water* alludes to the way in which settler colonialism saw the rearing of livestock for slaughter intricately bound up with the near extinction of the American bison. In Sioux history, as Estes explains, the American bison (referred to colloquially as buffalo) held a significant position in the figure of 'Pte Ska Win (the White Calf Buffalo Woman), who made the first treaty with the human and nonhuman worlds. To be a good relative is to honour that instruction' (2019: 109). Systematic over-hunting of bison by the US military was a central pillar of settler colonial campaigns to 'shatter the will' (110) of Indigenous nations, to dispossess them of their lands, and to establish monocultural farming and food industries (predominately cattle). The well-documented extirpation of bison numbers in North America from the tens of millions to fewer than a thousand by 1891 was, as the Anishinaabe writer and activist Winona LaDuke explains, 'part of military policy' tied directly to land dispossession, the extension of the railroads, 'the expansion of the cattle and beef empires', and ultimately 'the industrialization of American agriculture' ([1999] 2015: 141).[9] Prior to European settlement, the sustainable hunting of bison by Native Americans, according to Joshua Schuster, provided a necessary food source as well as 'bones used for tools, sinews for sewing, pelts used for clothing and housing, and bladders used to carry water' (2017: 102). After the extirpation of the bison, governmental programmes were initiated to feed Native communities dispossessed of their lands. LaDuke asserts that these programmes became 'a new commercial opportunity for the fledgling western cattle industries': the Indian Department purchased the beef used to feed Native Americans from ranchers raising livestock on stolen land; this 'intergenerational distortion of subsistence, and its replacement with industrialized dependency, continues today' ([1999] 2015: 142). As such, the near extinction of the bison in North America provides a salient example of the settler colonial decimation of native animal species not by accident but by design. The dominance of industrialized food industries in North America was predicated on policies expressly designed to isolate Indigenous peoples and deprive them of independence outside of the capitalist agricultural system.

In *Truth and Bright Water*, the artist and trickster character Monroe Swimmer seeks to repopulate the prairies on the US–Canada border with bison.[10] Rather than acting as a conservation project akin to the creation of National Parks in Africa or the whale-watching industry, however, Swimmer's is a project defined by its symbolic revival of the species as an alternative to touristic spectacle. Swimmer makes bison using papier-mâché fixed into the ground with stakes. By way of an explanation for this project, Swimmer announces that: 'If you want the herds to return, you have to understand magic. [...] Realism will only take you so far' (King, 1999: 198). In her reading of King's *The Truth About Stories* (2003), McHugh argues that King's concern with the 'extinction' of Native, 'nomadic lifeways' appears 'at the expense of how [such lifeways] are experienced across species lines' (2019: 160). Yet, in the earlier *Truth and Bright Water*, the ersatz bison are part of what Swimmer calls his 'restoration work' (King, 1999: 48), which also includes stealing back Indigenous bodily remains and artefacts from museums and painting an abandoned Catholic church the colour of grass and sky so that it disappears from the landscape. Thus, the inclusion of bison in Swimmer's definition of 'restoration' points to a concern with the ways in which human *and* nonhuman forms of endangerment are intertwined.

The novel's teenage narrator (who is referred to as Tecumseh, the name of a Shawnee chief) takes up employment with Swimmer as his assistant and describes how the papier-mâché bison on the prairies are 'all facing the river' (198), the body of water that acts as the border between the town of Truth in Montana and the Canadian reservation of Bright Water. As part of this formation, Swimmer includes 'a small buffalo by itself [...] looking back towards the church', commenting that, 'If the baby doesn't make it back to the herd in time, the coyotes will find it. [...] It's sad. [...] But it happens all the time' (198). This is left as an ominously ambiguous statement, but it can be read as an allusion to the history of the residential school system in Canada, which involved the government-funded, mandatory placement of First Nations children in Christian boarding schools for the purposes of 'assimilation'. It has since been reported widely that Canadian residential schools were the sites of systemic child abuse and 'cultural genocide'. In this way, the small, isolated buffalo looking toward the church stands in for all First Nations children removed from their families and subjected to acts of physical and sexual abuse, while the government and missionaries are represented by the predatory coyotes.[11] This reading is reinforced when Tecumseh asks Swimmer whether he plans to stay in Truth and Bright Water and Swimmer announces that his next project will be to paint 'an old residential school [that is] for sale over near Medicine River' (248).

The presence of Swimmer's papier-mâché bison is counterpointed by the real bison introduced to the annual Indian Days festival as a spectacle to 'bring in the tourists' (89). Tecumseh's father and uncle stage a bison hunting performance in which Tecumseh and his cousin Lum ride motorbikes around a paddock to corral the animals and shoot them with paintball guns: a 'White man's wet dream' (151), says Lum. After hitting a female bison with his paintball gun, however, Tecumseh experiences a passing moment of kinship: 'She swings her head from side to side as if she's scolding me, and in that moment, she reminds me of my grandmother' (150–151). The novel's denouement sees the Indigenous members of the town abandon the various forms of 'performative Native-ness' they feel impelled to engage in to generate money during the Indian Days festival and instead congregate in the prairies, the very site of Swimmer's creative 'restoration' of the landscape and the bison. They are drawn together by a bonfire that Swimmer has started in order to enact a 'giveaway' ceremony common to the Native Blackfoot and Plains Cree nations, whereby artefacts that Swimmer has acquired, such as a 'brass turtle' (242), a 'Navajo rug', and a 'small bronze sculpture of an Indian running alongside an elk' (243), are gifted to individuals. In this way, Swimmer's 'restoration work' marks an imaginative, community-driven approach to both species revival and cultural regeneration that stands in direct conflict with the exploitation of people and nonhuman animals for the purposes of touristic spectacle.

The allusions in *Truth and Bright Water* to hunting bison as being the 'White man's wet dream', and thus a necessary means of generating revenue through tourism for Indigenous communities, brings us to a discussion of the hunting of animals as game. This extends our exploration of the view of nonhuman animals as lifeforms to be killed or reared to produce commodities and cheap food. In game hunting, the animal's body is also disassembled and used as a resource, in part for food but also as a taxidermied trophy and specimen of scientific study. In the following section we will analyse the relationship between game hunting and the establishment of European natural history institutions for the study of animals during the era of high imperialism. This will involve a discussion of colonial texts set in East Africa (modern-day Kenya) by H. Rider Haggard and Karen Blixen that reveal the role of hunting for sport and science in the European imperial imaginary. To conclude, we will turn to Yomi Ṣode's contemporary poem 'Untitled', which evinces a comparable manoeuvre to both Wylie's 'Where in the waste is the wisdom?' and Ellams's 'Fuck/Empire' in that it reverses the colonial gaze and offers the perspective of the racialized and colonized subject who, in this context, has been turned into an encased museum specimen.

Game Hunting

By the closing decades of the nineteenth century, British East Africa had gained the status of a 'hunter's paradise'. This status was initiated by biodiversity loss in England caused by the enclosure of the countryside and the rise of agricultural farming. Originally, the English upper classes sought new opportunities in both game hunting and trade in South Africa where, as we have already seen, elephants and their ivory were highly prized. By the closing decades of the nineteenth century, however, over-hunting by British and Boer settlers had decimated wildlife populations across Southern Africa. This coincided with the 1880s 'Scramble for Africa' and the subsequent settlement by white aristocrats in East Africa. Steinhart maintains that the colonization of East Africa was predicated on four key factors: the suppression of Indigenous, tribal hunting traditions; the settler ideology that game hunting was the preserve of upper-class, white 'gentlemen'; the view of 'wildlife as a form of property whose ownership and use were controlled and determined by law'; and 'the symbolic uses of the hunt as reaffirmation and demonstration of the social hierarchy that gave meaning to the lives of gentlemen hunters or sportsmen of the European tradition' (2006: 61–62). This, in turn, led to the 'settler destruction of wildlife habitat through fencing, clearing, and burning, as well as intense predation' and 'constituted white settlement as the single most important factor in the decline of game numbers during the first half of the twentieth century' (99). This assertion aligns with contemporary assessments, including the U.N.'s 2019 Global Assessment Report on Biodiversity and Ecosystem Services, that hunting and habitat destruction constitute two of the primary drivers of the sixth extinction.

Hunting in Colonial Literature

The prominence of game hunting in East Africa is addressed by the renowned Kenyan writer Ngũgĩ wa Thiong'o in *Moving the Centre*, in which he identifies 'at least three Africas' that exist 'for Western Europe' (1993: 132). First, there is 'the businessman's Africa' for the 'European hunter after profit', whereby the continent is seen only as the source of 'an abundance of raw materials and an abundance of human labour' (132). Second, there is the 'tourists' Africa' for the 'European hunter after pleasure' which is 'devoid of human beings' and is instead 'a vast animal landscape, ruled over by elephants, lions and leopards' (133). Last, there is 'the Africa in European fiction' (133). These three 'Africas' are interconnected: the 'European hunter after pleasure' is 'really the hunter for profit but on holiday', and European literature about Africa turns writers into spokespeople 'for the hunter for gold and the hunter for pleasure' (133, 135). Ngũgĩ's three categories emphasize how colonial-era East Africa is a location that stages the intertwined histories of habitat eradication, species depletion, and the structural dependency of formerly tribal, Indigenous societies on capitalist–imperialism.

An analysis of late nineteenth and early twentieth century colonial literature set in East Africa offers us an insight into the connections between hunting and conservation, illuminating a cultural shift from colonial evocations of human dominion over animals to more self-reflexive accounts that begin to query assumptions of superiority. The colonialist view of the colonized environment as abundant in exotic fauna to be captured, categorized, and displayed is evoked in Haggard's 1886 imperial adventure novel *She*. The narrative follows three white English men – Holly, Leo, and Job – as they venture into Eastern Africa and are captured by the fictional Amahagger tribe, a 'lost civilisation' of Black African cannibals ruled by the spectral white queen Ayesha who has discovered the secret to eternal life. Holly recounts their arrival in Africa as an encounter with a wild and untamed environment:

> Taking advantage of this favouring wind, we sailed merrily up the river for three or four hours. Once we came across a school of hippopotami, which rose, and bellowed dreadfully at us within ten or a dozen fathoms of the boat, much to Job's alarm, and, I will confess, to my own. [...] Leo wanted to fire at them, but I dissuaded him, fearing the consequences.
> (Haggard, [1886] 2001: 72)

In this instant we see a vision of East Africa that is emptied of people and populated solely by wildlife which is both potential quarry and a potential threat. Holly's account of the men's arrival continues with the description that they also 'saw hundreds of crocodiles basking on the muddy banks, and thousands upon thousands of waterfowl' (72). Viewing the animals as inexhaustible, and assuming an immediate dominance over these nonhuman inhabitants of the region, Holly recounts that they opened fire on the fowl:

> [A]mong them was a wild goose, which, in addition to the sharp curved spurs of its wings, had a spur about three-quarters of an inch long growing from the skull just between the eyes. We never shot another like it, so I do not know if it was a 'sport' or a distinct species. In the latter case this incident may interest naturalists. Job named it the Unicorn Goose.
> (72)

This brief encounter between the three men and the fauna of East Africa at the beginning of the narrative – whereby unfamiliar animals are killed before being given names in English – stages the 'epistemic violence' (Spivak [1988] 1994) of imperial conquest. The white, English hunters do not seek knowledge about the environment to which they are outsiders; rather, they dominate and domesticate that environment, naming and claiming any new species they find. It is a scene that reveals how natural science offered a veneer of respectability to colonial hunting practices since the cabinets and dioramas of newly emerging natural history museums in late-nineteenth-century Britain were reliant upon the quarry of hunters.

In his account of the three 'Africas' that exist for Westerners, Ngũgĩ singles out one text for an ignominious mention: Blixen's 1937 memoir *Out of*

Africa, he says, is 'one of the most dangerous books ever written about Africa' because the book's 'racism [...] is persuasively put forward as love. But it is the love of a man for a horse or a pet' (1993: 133). Ngũgĩ's focus is on Blixen's depiction of her cook Kamante, who is dehumanized as though he were 'a civilised dog that has lived long with human beings' (134). Where Blixen's sense of racial superiority is evident in her depiction of Kamante, her memoir also marks a shift from the late-nineteenth-century texts of high imperialism, such as Haggard's, in that there is a palpable anxiety about being alienated from the land that Blixen wishes to call her new home. In this way, *Out of Africa* provides a prime example of how, as Patrick Wolfe remarks,

> [T]he erasure of indigeneity conflicts with the assertion of settler nationalism. On the one hand, settler society required the practical elimination of the natives in order to establish itself on their territory. On the symbolic level, however, settler society subsequently sought to recuperate indigeneity in order to express its difference – and accordingly, its independence – from the mother country.
>
> (2006: 389)

In *Out of Africa*, we can discern how colonial human–animal relations and the suppression of colonized populations combined as a fraught but fundamental part of the construction of settler colonial notions of belonging. As Abdulrazak Gurnah maintains, the memoir is characteristic of '[t]he ambivalence in settler writing' which 'derives from [...] two sources, the tribal imperatives of the imperialist narrative' – in the sense of there being a bounded white, settler 'tribe' or community to which one *belongs* – and 'the yearning for a wholesome self – which, paradoxically, depends on turning the European into the native' (2000: 277).

The settler colonial will to 'become native' is predicated in *Out of Africa* on ecological dynamics, particularly the act of game hunting. We see this in Blixen's mythologization of her close friend and lover, the renowned professional hunter Denys Finch-Hatton who died in a plane crash in 1931. After settling in Kenya in 1910 and eventually becoming a professional hunter, Finch-Hatton – along with Blixen's husband Baron Bror von Blixen-Finecke – became crucial to the 'transformation of sport hunting from Kenya's leading pastime to its leading service industry' and garnered a reputation as 'the most glamorous of the white hunter breed' (Steinhart, 2006: 107, 133). In Blixen's account of his death, Finch-Hatton is turned into a symbol of the possibility to forge a symbiotic, spiritual, and emotional attachment with the Kenyan flora and fauna, erasing in the process the significant levels of habitat eradication and defaunation caused by the very acts of trophy hunting that he helped professionalize and popularize:

> Denys had watched and followed all the ways of the Africa highlands, and better than any other white man he had known their soil and seasons, the

> vegetation and the wild animals, the winds and smells. [...] He had taken in the country, and in his eyes and his mind it had been changed, marked by his own individuality, and made part of him. Now [in death] Africa received him, and would change him, and make him one with herself.
>
> ([1937] 2001: 305)

Crucially, however, Finch-Hatton's belonging in East Africa is only fully achieved in death, contributing to the romanticized settler trope of being 'buried amidst the beautiful sights and loyal African servants who had surrounded and served them in life' (Steinhart, 2006: 101). Where *Out of Africa* presents the white, male hunter as the embodiment of a dominant outsider able to become one with the colonized environment, other contemporaneous, European writers expressed anti-colonial positions. In his reading of Leonard Woolf's memoir *Growing* (1961), for example, Derek Ryan notes that Woolf describes meeting Baron Blixen-Finecke in Ceylon and witnessing trophy hunting as a 'charade' (2022: 39). Woolf explains how hunting guides would often shoot at the white tourist hunter's side, a detail that undercuts the European's supposed prowess; such activities, Woolf says, were no more than 'despicable butchery' (1961: 221). Thus, although Ryan acknowledges that Woolf 'was part of [the] imperialist machine', he asserts that the memoir shows that Woolf is also 'attentive to how the very act of hunting connects to a British history of exploiting animals for economic gain' (2022: 39).

Blixen's own self-conscious attempt to enunciate her connection to the land and fauna of Kenya is evinced early in *Out of Africa* when she writes, '[i]n the highlands you woke up in the morning and thought: Here I am, where I ought to be' ([1937] 2001: 14), asserting a notion of belonging in East Africa that is somehow predestined. Yet, we find this assertion faltering when Blixen later asks: 'If I know a song of Africa – I thought – of the giraffe, and the African new moon lying on her back, of the ploughs in the fields, and the sweaty faces of the coffee-pickers, does Africa know a song of me?' (76). This question is marked by a sense of alienation from a dispassionate natural world that is oblivious to the settlers' existence. Pointedly, Blixen articulates this through the construction of a duality: on one side stands the wealthy European settler, whilst on the other is the undifferentiated entirety of the African continent, where both the fauna and the Black African labourers dispossessed of their land are glimpsed only as part of a romanticized and homogenized environment spread out beneath the night sky.

Blixen's anxiety over her desire to become native is reinforced in her account of the arrival to the farm of the young antelope she names Lulu. Blixen imbues Lulu with the power to act as a bridge between the human and nonhuman worlds, between the 'civilized' European space of the house and the 'wild' African environment outside, writing that:

> [T]he free union between my house and the antelope was a rare, honourable thing. Lulu came in from the wild world to show that we were

Life 159

on good terms with it, and she made my house one with the African landscape, so that nobody could tell where the one stopped and the other began.

(73–74)

This account of their kinship is only possible by eliding the hierarchies of species, class, and race upon which Blixen's presence in Kenya is predicated. Indeed, the 'squatters' upon whose ancestral land Blixen is living would certainly be aware of the strictly policed boundaries demarcating the settler household and the Kenyan landscape. Ultimately, Lulu's mystical powers work only in one direction.

Hunting and Natural History

The game hunting that Finch-Hatton was instrumental in popularizing provided not only trophies for wealthy Europeans and American hunters but also a wide array of specimens to be displayed to the public in the natural history museums that flourished at the end of the nineteenth and beginning of the twentieth centuries. In turn, the emergence of natural history as a specialism, according to MacKenzie in *Empire of Nature*, 'reflected the accelerating urge to order the world of nature, which was itself both an impulse towards and a symptom of the developing yearning to order and classify human affairs through imperialism' (1988: 36). Here, MacKenzie highlights the important link between the 'classificatory power' (36) of Europeans and Americans to taxonomize different animal species and the categorization of different human groups in terms of immutable biological characteristics. Such forms of supposedly objective categorization based on biological data fuelled the Neo-Darwinist insistence that the 'command of a global natural world' (36), that included colonized peoples, was the preserve of majority white, imperial nations. It is to this very conjunction between scientific classification and the racist ideology of colonialism that Frantz Fanon refers in *Black Skin, White Masks* when he challenges the 'epidermal racial schema' ([1952] 2008: 92) underpinning his objectification by a white child who calls him a frightening 'Negro'. In this schema, Fanon states, '[t]he Negro is an animal' (93) and is thus 'prevent[ed] from participating' (94) in the white world that sets the parameters of the category of the human.

In finding himself both objectified and dehumanized, Fanon asserts that he was 'an object among other objects' (89). This pronouncement resonates throughout the poem 'Untitled' by the Nigerian-British writer Ṣode, which was commissioned by the curator Subhadra Das for the *Displays of Power* exhibition at London's Grant Museum of Zoology. As part of the exhibition, a video performance of the poem was screened in and amongst the museum's cabinets of skeletal and bodily animal remains: shot in black and white by the director Hydar Dewachi it shows a close-up of Ṣode's face as he stares out to confront the passing spectators.[12] The poem establishes a number of conflicting dichotomies across species, races, and temporalities: humans are seen 'capturing, stabbing' and 'gutting' wild animals; European hunters and scientists 'befriended' the speaker's 'ancestors who dared to climb, dared to stick their limbs in places no white man would think of doing' but without 'acknowledgement of their bravery'; and when the contemporary visitor gazes at the displayed specimens, 'objectification still hold[s] as firm as a rifle to firing shoulder, the exoticism still breath[es] heavy'. Characterizing each of these dichotomies is a different form of silence that forestalls a full sense of comprehension and understanding. In this way, Ṣode reimagines natural history museums not as spaces of scientific exploration and education but as institutions that effectively silence the interlinked stories of colonization, exploitation, and species extinction.

The speaker describes the space of the museum as 'holding trauma like a last breath' where the 'object, specimen, fossil, or animal' is 'obediently silent'. Rather than viewing the animal artefacts on display as inert and already dead, the language frames them as being in a permanent state of dying, forever experiencing the historic trauma that led to their presence in the very museum that disavows the conditions of their capture. Only the speaker, who is also situated as an exhibit, can hear the 'rattle of bones in drawers, wanting to return home'. The contemporary visitor encounters these artefacts with a sense 'of intrigue, of wonder, and danger'. Yet, the 'sun' that 'breaks into these places' and illuminates the 'source of this wonder' is contrasted with the metaphorical 'blinds' that are 'drawn on its historic bloodshed'. The imagery of the sun here describes both the literal light that floods the museum space each day and the figurative light of scientific illumination that museums represent. From the outset, then, the metaphors of light and dark work to emphasize the poem's critique of the museum space as objectifying the natural world in a manner that silences the brutal histories underpinning the presence of non-European specimens and artefacts in London, far from their country of origin. In particular, the speaker foregrounds the histories of game hunting and resource extraction that have been examined over the course of this chapter.

These different forms of bloodshed are glimpsed fleetingly as the speaker directs our attention to the various specimens, mimicking the experience of passing the display cases and being overwhelmed by what is exhibited. For instance, the role of game hunting is alluded to in the speaker's reference to an 'impala' that was 'shot then made into a trophy', as well as the other taxidermied animals with 'eyes following my steps'. Grappling with the question of education and illumination on the bloodshed that the museum leaves in the dark, the speaker asks: 'Do I explain they were killed for status to brandish on their own land because they could, because an empire just can, make the living extinct as a form of hobby, irrespective of time?'. Elsewhere, we are directed to the history of the ivory trade by the 'tusks made into piano keys that ache for each note a child absentmindedly presses'. Once again, the animal is caught somewhere between life and death: the elephant's tusk has been reterritorialized from its slaughtered body while the ache reinterprets the pleasing and gentle sound of the piano as signalling a traumatic afterlife.

In 'Untitled', then, Şode enacts a symbolic revival of dead animal specimens who haunt the museum space, unable to find peace. The glass display case that provides clarity for the visitor becomes a cage for the displayed specimen, a paradoxical condition that is underscored when the speaker describes the 'glass containing the wailing, a wailing the privileged are tone deaf in hearing'. The speaker in turn 'star[es] at these objects' but is caught between the realms of spectator and specimen, noting that he feels 'as though it's me' behind the glass. It is an assertion that reminds us of Fanon's account of the 'white gaze' 'dissecting' and 'imprisoning' him within the biological schema that classifies Black people as a lower evolutionary 'phase' to white men ([1952] 2008: 95, 92, 108). The imagery and language of 'Untitled' also recalls the depiction of the elephant tusk in Ellams's 'Fuck/Empire': in both poems, disassembled and objectified animal remains are imaginatively awakened into a spectral world between the living and the dead, carrying with them the silenced stories of their slaughter for either sport, science, or religious shrines. The spectral revivals envisioned within the space of these two poems offer a point of contrast to new initiatives in conservation that seek to fully resurrect biological life, in some cases by using cloning and the DNA of long-extinct species. It is to these initiatives that we will turn next.

Revival

The international conservation movement is, paradoxically, bound up with the colonial commodification and exploitation of nonhuman life. It emerged during the interwar years out of British settler colonial efforts to both sustain an elitist pastime of game hunting and stymie the smuggling of valuable ivory to East African territories ruled by Britain's European rival, Italy. In the decades following the Second World War, the conservation of game for the purposes of controlled hunting gave way to the preservation of wildlife for posterity, which also served the purposes of tourism. In outlining this trajectory, Steinhart has noted that the 'international, imperial movement for the preservation of nature' worked on two main beliefs: first, that 'the best guardians of nature were the imperial and colonial ruling classes [...] now transformed and reincarnated as champions of game preservation'; and second, 'that the best instrument for preservation lay in the creation of nature and wildlife sanctuaries modelled on the aristocratic hunting parks of eighteenth-century Britain' (2006: 174). The formation of National Parks under the auspices of the Society for the Preservation of Fauna of the Empire, and the subsequent rise of safari tourism (aided by advancements in air travel), not only criminalized African hunters as poachers but led 'directly to [...] the ultimate destruction of the African hunting tradition in Kenya' (149). In this way, Steinhart states, any possibility for Indigenous Africans (such as Kikuyu, Kamba, and Wata communities) of establishing 'an independent life outside the global economy had been shattered by the 1950s conservation-inspired anti-poaching campaign' (205).

Although the 1970s–1990s saw various community-based challenges to the formation of National Parks (partly in response to the historical expulsion of Indigenous peoples from their ancestral lands), dominant forms of wildlife preservation today have expanded upon the National Parks-blueprint of 'fortress' conservation through fencing and commodification that simultaneously keeps some of the world's poorest communities dependent on tourism and global capitalism.[13] According to Bram Büscher and Robert Fletcher, mainstream conservationism is 'fundamentally capitalist and steeped in nature-people dichotomies, especially through its foundational emphasis on protected areas and continued infatuation with (images of) wilderness and "pristine" natures' (2020: 8). For this reason, they say, mainstream conservationist solutions are

> increasingly focused on the idea that conserved nature can be turned into in situ 'natural capital' so that the creativity of the pursuit of profit can effectively and efficiently be linked to the protection of nature and the 'environmental services' it provides.
>
> (3)

The contemporary climate crisis, however, has led to the emergence of more radical forms of conservation that challenge this status quo – namely 'new conservationism', 'neoprotectionism', and 'convivial conservation'.

Initiated by the article 'Conservation in the Anthropocene' (Kareiva et al., 2012), 'new conservationism' rejects the 'fortress' ideology that nature should remain 'untouched'. Instead, it sees the possible advantages of generating corporation-led solutions that address biodiversity loss in a manner that also tackles poverty across nations in the Global South through sustainable development initiatives. In assessing this position, however, Büscher and Fletcher point to the 'paradox in this advocacy that capitalist mechanisms are promoted to address problems that are in large part caused by capitalist development itself' (29). 'Neoprotectionism', by contrast, proposes limits on population, consumption, and economic growth as part of the systematic separation of humans from nature, essentially 'demand[ing] another resurgence and expansion of fortress-style protection' (33). One of the most radical examples of this perspective comes from Edward O. Wilson's *Half-Earth*, in which he argues that 'only by committing half of the planet's surface to nature can we hope to save the immensity of life-forms that compose it' (2016: 3). In challenging both new conservationism and neoprotectionism, Büscher and Fletcher advocate for their own concept of 'convivial conservation'. Informed by postcolonial and Indigenous perspectives, this proposal 'moves away from capital-inspired ways of rendering visible the value of nature' and instead emphasizes 'broader structures of sharing the wealth that nature provides'

(2020: 175). This includes exchanging the touristic spectacle of nature with a meaningful engagement with '"everyday nature", in all its splendour *and* mundaneness' (171, original emphasis). It also promotes reparations and the return of land to Indigenous peoples, as well as a basic income paid to individuals living in or around conservation areas that would provide them with 'options for livelihoods that will always need to include use of and interaction with biodiversity and resources' (188). Thus, where new conservationism invests in more human intervention through corporate funding, and neoprotectionism calls for less human intervention through the dramatic expansion of protected areas, convivial conservation looks to decolonial, democratic, and broadly socialist solutions that concern the well-being of both endangered nonhumans *and* marginalized and dispossessed human communities.

In terms of species endangerment and extinction, two of the dominant initiatives that have emerged since the beginning of the twenty-first century – de-extinction and rewilding – can be understood broadly as iterations of new conservationism and neoprotectionism respectively. The former relies predominantly on the private funding of scientific research into the revival of individual species, while the latter invests in the idea that nonhuman animals should be able to thrive in dynamic, self-willed spaces without human management. For advocates of rewilding, as George Monbiot remarks, 'nature consists not just of a collection of species but also of their ever-shifting relationships with each other and with the physical environment' (2014: 9). As this suggests, a key difference between these two approaches to conservation is that rewilding focuses on the ecosystem while de-extinction concentrates on individual species.[14]

A number of novels have emerged since the turn of the millennium that tackle the ethical, political, and practical implications of de-extinction science, notably Julia Leigh's *The Hunter*, Henrietta Rose-Innes's *Green Lion*, Kim Stanley Robinson's *2312* (2012), and Donna Mazza's *Fauna* (2020). Set in Australia, *Fauna* depicts a speculative future in which genome sequencing is used for the development of human life, rather than for conservation purposes, while *2312* is set largely across terraformed planets in the solar system.[15] As two novels that focus specifically on defaunation in settler colonies, and thus deal directly with the connections between capitalist–imperialism and de-extinction science, we will concentrate here on *The Hunter*, which envisions the patenting of thylacine DNA in Australia, and *Green Lion*, which depicts a fictionalized South African initiative to resurrect the black-maned lion.[16] A comparative analysis reveals how both novels place issues of species endangerment and extinction within a longer history of settler colonial ecocide.

De-extinction

Across America, Europe, Australia, and Japan, a range of de-extinction projects have emerged since the turn of the twenty-first century to bring back aurochs, woolly mammoths, the Pyrenean ibex, the gastric-brooding frog, the quagga, the Tasmanian tiger, the Caribbean monk seal, the golden lion tamarin, and the passenger pigeon. Some of these projects, such as the 'Lazarus frog' and ibex initiatives, use frozen cells that were collected before the species went extinct, the same process used in 1996 when scientists cloned Dolly the Sheep. Many others, however, are unable to rely upon existing cells and so are forced to reconstruct DNA sequences from preserved fossils, which can be up to 700,000 years old. As Beth Shapiro explains in *How to Clone a Mammoth: The Science of De-Extinction*, a reconfigured genome sequence can be used to discover the extinct animal's closest living relative. In the case of the woolly mammoth, for example, this is the Asian elephant. 'We identify differences between the elephant genome sequence and the mammoth genome sequence', writes Shapiro, 'and we design experiments to tweak the elephant genome, changing a few of the DNA bases at a time, until the genome looks a lot more mammoth-like' (2015: 11–12). A cell that contains a mammoth-like genome can then be developed into an embryo and used to impregnate a female Asian elephant. This work has been pioneered by the Harvard-based geneticist George Church, whose multiplex automated genomic engineering (M.A.G.E) technology 'promises nothing short of the resurrection of any extinct species whose genome is known or can be reconstructed from fossil remains' (Dawson 2016: 74–57). Another prominent North American initiative is 'Revive and Restore', led by Stewart Brand and Ryan Phelan and informed by Brand's oft-quoted assertion that: 'We are as Gods and might as well get used to it' (1968: n.p.).

One headline-grabbing de-extinction project that aligns itself with the ethos of rewilding is Sergey Zimov's 'Pleistocene Park' initiative, which proposes to rewild an area in northeast Siberia using revived woolly mammoths. In theory, as Olga Ulturgasheva and Barbara Bodenhorn explain, the mammoth's grazing patterns are thought to offer the potential to return Pleistocene-era grasslands to the region in an effort to 'reflect sunlight and capture more carbon in its roots than today's flora' (2022: 42). Yet, they also note how the project's planning has occluded

> the voice of Siberian indigenous populations who have been living in this area for eons and who have never been consulted on how this type of ambitious dystopian endeavour unfolding in front of their eyes could impact their livelihoods and sense of security.
>
> (43)

It is not clear, for instance, how the reintroduction of woolly mammoths would impact the livelihoods of Indigenous communities in the Siberian tundra whose subsistence is dependent upon hunting and reindeer herding. Pleistocene Park is thus regarded as a project that could adversely change the habitats of the very fauna that these communities rely on for their survival, contributing to the already detrimental effects of the logging, oil, and gas industries in the region.

Alongside the growth in de-extinction initiatives, concerns have been raised over the question of whether we *should* do something just because we *can*. Shapiro has pioneered some of the foundational scientific breakthroughs of de-extinction, but she is also one of the most prominent voices calling for a consideration of the potential pitfalls. This includes the fact that the original *causes* of extinction – such as deforestation, ecosystem depletion, and over-hunting – remain significant problems on global and localized scales. This aligns with Ulturgasheva and Bodenhorn's criticism of de-extinction when they assert that

> environmental transformations on a geological epoch scale can never be confined to one isolated activity, such as the grazing habits of large mammals with hooves. One must recognize that myriad other factors influenced and intervened in the course of environmental change, factors that include such disruptions as the multiple forms of development that changed the chemical and organic composition of the soil, flora and fauna irreversibly.
>
> (43)

Additionally, Shapiro notes the difficulty of embarking on de-extinction for some species 'without causing unnecessary animal suffering' (2015: 194) through the use of captive-breeding; the concern that '[r]eintroducing the extinct species may upset the existing dynamics within that ecosystem' (199); the insistence on an animal's behaviour being part of nature at the expense of nurture (e.g. can an animal raised by Asian elephants truly be categorized as a woolly mammoth?); and the fact that it is impossible to recreate an exact replica of an extinct species. In response to concerns about de-extinction initiatives, Shapiro insists that 'the present focus on bringing back particular species – whether that means mammoths, dodos, passenger pigeons, or anything else – is misguided', asserting that 'de-extinction has a place in our scientific future, but not as an antidote to extinctions that have already occurred' (10). Rather, she believes that the technology is useful not to resurrect individual species but to

> resurrect some of their extinct traits. By engineering these extinct traits into living organisms, we can help living species adapt to a changing environment. We can re-establish interactions between species that were lost when one species went extinct. In doing so, we can revive and restore vulnerable ecosystems. This – the resurrection of ecological interactions – is, in my mind, the real value of de-extinction technology.
>
> (10)

Ultimately, for Shapiro, developments in de-extinction provide an opportunity to 'actively create a future that is really better than today, not just one that is less bad than what we anticipate' (207). While this perspective is distinct from those that look to reverse time, play God, or develop *Jurassic*

Park-style tourist spectacles, it nevertheless sits in tension with a wide range of scholars in the fields of biology, conservation, and environmental humanities who have rejected the techno-fix of de-extinction, focusing instead on the importance of mourning the loss of extinct species.

In a 2017 special issue of *Australian Zoologist* entitled 'Dangerous Ideas in Zoology', the environmental scientists Peter B. Banks and Dieter F. Hochuli advocate for the significance of extinct animals acting as 'martyr species', without which 'conservation will lose its ability to argue against some of the key threats to wildlife and hence lose its voice in the fight against human impacts on the natural world' (2017: 393). For this reason, they argue, 'de-extinction is a dangerous idea for conservation' since 'it can be used as an ultimate offset for any environmental impact, however false this hope might prove to be' (393). In the same issue, the Extinction Studies scholars Deborah Bird Rose and Thom van Dooren maintain that '[i]n our time of anthropogenic mass extinction, dwelling with extinction – taking it seriously, not rushing to overcome it – may actually be the more important political and ethical work' (2017: 376). In this way, defaunation is seen as an opportunity for reflection on exploitative human–animal relations currently driving extinction rates. De-extinction initiatives, on the other hand, are regarded as 'painful and fraught procedures that arguably have a very low chance of success in the long term' and do nothing to mitigate 'the widespread destruction of living systems on this planet' (377). These perspectives offer weight to the earlier view of the Environmental Ethics scholar Ben A. Minteer that 'there is great virtue in keeping extinct species extinct. Meditation on their loss reminds us of our fallibility and our finitude' and encourages us to 'accept our moral and technological limits in nature' (2014: 261).

For Ashley Dawson, de-extinction science 'offers a seductive but dangerously deluding techno-fix for an environmental crisis generated by the systematic contradictions of capitalism' (2016: 77). In addressing this particular strand of conservation, Dawson warns that,

> [N]eoliberal ideologies have come to permeate conservation to such an extent that discussions of biodiversity have become the site for the elaboration of what might be called *disaster biocapitalism*. Just as [...] disaster capitalism [...] seizes on political calamities to further its accumulative aims, this disaster biocapitalism takes the extinction crisis as an opportunity to rachet up the commodification of life itself.
>
> (80, original emphasis)

Indeed, he writes that lawyers in the US have already started to claim that the DNA of a revived mammoth would be eligible for patenting as it would be the product of 'human ingenuity'. In this way, Dawson maintains that '[d]e-extinction provides a mouth-watering opportunity for a new round of capital accumulation based on generating and acquiring intellectual property rights over living organisms' (77–78).

Life 167

Framing developments in de-extinction science in terms of disaster biocapitalism aligns with the work of Anthony Carrigan and Pallavi Rastogi, both of whom have examined the important role of literature (and particularly analysis of colonial and postcolonial literatures) in re-evaluating disaster studies. Carrigan states that 'mainstream disaster studies approaches' should be 'reconfigure[d]',

> emphasising the need to address not just the *agents* of 'natural' disasters (e.g. environmental phenomena such as hurricanes, earthquakes, and droughts), but also the social, political, and economic *processes* that put particular groups at risk and underpin the scale of disasters.
>
> (2015: 120)

Rastogi takes cues from Fredric Jameson and Neil Lazarus in her theorization of what she calls the 'Disaster Unconscious', which can be evinced specifically in postcolonial disaster fiction. She argues that a disaster unconscious 'not only anchors the literary narrative to disastrous events, which are often social, political and economic in nature, but also focuses readerly attention on the need to disseminate information about, as well as manage, catastrophe through narration' (2020: 5). These critics understand that ecological disasters and vulnerability to disasters are in large part caused by social, political, and economic forces that take, in Carrigan's words, 'a disproportionate toll on the world's poorest communities, many of which are still grappling with the legacies of Western colonialism and neocolonial practices' (2015: 117). Yet disasters such as tsunamis, earthquakes, droughts, floods, wildfires, and hurricanes are often conceptualized and treated as natural and isolated events. This, we argue, is also true for species extinction and endangerment, which is often (though not always) associated with individual examples of charismatic megafauna, such as the woolly mammoth, dodo, bison, and polar bears. In pursuing this claim, we follow Carrigan, Rastogi, and Dawson in their analyses of how neoliberal responses to ecological disaster reinforce the economic dependence of the world's poorest nations upon global capitalism. Focusing on de-extinction science, we can see how one of the dominant contemporary strategies for the revival of biodiversity prioritises isolated cases of species loss *without* necessarily remedying the social causes and consequences of extinctions. Rather, it potentially reinscribes colonial-capitalist structures by conceiving ecological disaster as an opportunity for further capital accumulation.

De-extinction and Settler Colonialism

In *The Hunter*, Leigh imagines a scenario where de-extinction science has been developed in Australia by a shadowy Australian biotech company interested in harvesting animal DNA as a precious resource to be extracted, patented, and used commercially. The narrative follows a mercenary known only by the initial M who has been hired by the company after reports of a Tasmanian tiger (or thylacine) sighting in a small community referred to as 'Tiger Town' (Leigh, 1999: 3). The town's name signals the commodification of the thylacine's image in an Australian state with a history of settler colonialism, deforestation by the logging industry, and the decimation of the very animal that it now celebrates in the name of tourism. Indeed, the image of the extinct animal now proliferates in Tasmania across 'postcards, dishtowels, and other tourist ephemera, and is used to brand marketing items ranging from locally produced wine to the Primary Industries and Water Department' (Fletcher, 2010: 53).[17] The thylacine's iconic status – and its importance to research into de-extinction science – is underpinned by the story of its extinction.

Tasmania (formerly Van Diemen's Land) became a British penal colony in 1803 and later a settler colony after the Van Diemen's Land Company imported capitalist agricultural practices. Early settlers designated Tasmanian tigers as pests, holding the now disputed belief that they were a threat to their sheep, meaning that its disappearance is due to both habitat eradication and over-hunting. As Amy Fletcher affirms, 'the Company blamed the thylacine for significant livestock, and thus financial, losses [...] and established the first tiger bounty scheme in 1830' (2010: 52). This bounty, combined with those paid out by farmers' societies and the government, meant that Tasmanian tigers were hunted with the expressed aim of wiping them out. The species was critically endangered by 1910. In 1936, the Tasmanian government proclaimed the thylacine protected as part of the Animals and Birds Protection Act. The move proved to be belated, however, and just 59 days later the last known Tasmanian tiger died of old age on September 7 at the Beaumaris Private Zoo in Hobart.[18] With no more sightings in the wild, the Tasmanian tiger was officially declared extinct in 1986.[19] This declaration also signalled the end of an entire taxonomic family as the thylacine was the only species of Thylacinidae to survive beyond the Late Miocene era (which ended around 5 million years ago). As Carol Freeman has noted, in the case of the last thylacine, 'it is not just the species, nor the genus that is lost, it is the same as losing the whole Canid family – wolves, dogs, jackals and foxes' (2013: 201). September 7 has since been marked as Australia's National Threatened Species Day. Despite this annual day of reflection on the need to prevent further biodiversity loss, Australia holds the 'unenviable position as the world's capital for mammal extinction', with over 10 percent of the country's land mammals having been declared extinct since European settlement in the late eighteenth century.[20] 'All of these extinctions of Australian mammals', write the environmental scientists Banks and Hochuli, 'are in some way linked to human involvement, whether by introducing alien species, removing habitat, changing land use or burning regimes', meaning that 'Australia has an acute sense of extinction guilt' (2017: 391).

The thylacine's status as a symbol of species loss in Australia has meant that it has become central to de-extinction debates. Between 1999 and 2005, the thylacine's iconic status as a flagship symbol of extinction and animal conservation underpinned an initiative at the Australian Museum to try to bring the species back to life using DNA samples taken from a single specimen. In 2022, research into thylacine de-extinction began again when a team based at the University of Melbourne were awarded $5 million (€3.4 million) funding by the Wilson Family Trust to develop the TIGRR lab. This lab plans to develop the means of using deep de-extinction technologies to bring the thylacine back from the dead by using the mouse-like dunnart as the animal's living surrogate. In the US in August 2022, Colossal Biosciences, which launched only a year earlier, also announced its own thylacine de-extinction initiative using the M.A.G.E. technology of George Church.

In *The Hunter*, M has been employed not only to confirm the thylacine sighting in Tiger Town, but also to track and kill the animal, and to return to the mainland of Australia with its blood and reproductive organs. As he is privy only to what little information he needs to complete his task, M's story indicates little of the company's intentions beyond the following evocative reference:

> [W]hat he had retrieved so far had earnt them, how much? Hundreds of millions, probably billions. The company needed him, in fact, was indebted to him. Who was more valuable to a biotech company than a hunter: sampler and ensurer of exclusivity. Inbred thylacine, dodo, moa, mammoth, bunyip, yeti, girls with telekinetic power, boys with an immunity to pain, the goose that laid the golden egg ... mutations all, this was now the stuff that dreams – and wars – were made of.
>
> (Leigh, 1999: 50)

This allusion to the novel's wider context, as Carol Freeman states, raises the question of 'what might happen if a thylacine survived into a postmodern world of international rivalry, terrorism and biowarfare' (191). Indeed, the choice of blood and ovaries as the precious biopirated resources, and the fact that M retrieves these before burning the remains of the body to leave no trace, suggests that the text is set in a world in which the patenting of genomes by 'biodisaster capitalists' has become a reality. In the reference to wars, Leigh indicates a dystopian world in which de-extinction science has been harnessed not for conservation but for motives that may in fact be globally destructive.

The Hunter also questions the validity of reviving species in a world where the rate of extinction has been caused in part by deforestation. The novel was written in the wake of the Tasmanian logging boom, which saw the forestry industry replace 62,831 hectares of native forest with plantations and farmland between 1996 and 2000. This rate of deforestation has seen Tasmania boast 'one of the highest rates of land clearing in the developed world' (Green, Ward, and McConnachie, 2007: 102). The town where M stays to begin his excursions into the forest was 'once a logging town' (Leigh, 1999: 4) and is marked by the decaying remnants of the industry. Upon arrival M discovers a 'dead town' of 'vacant concrete plots' and 'abandoned' demountables as 'people have picked up their houses and moved on' (4). In place of a 'small working farm' stands 'the wood-and-iron feed shed and stables' that have 'all but collapsed', while the paddocks are covered in weeds and '[t]hree car wrecks, all missing panels, sit out rusting and all about lie discarded tin drums' (5). Before M drinks the water 'it occurs to him that it might be poisoned by nearby properties; it might even have run through the log dump' (9). The spectre of community protest hangs over this widespread industrial decay in the form of 'a poster reading "Stop the Road to Nowhere"', a corner of which had 'peeled loose' (10). M absentmindedly 'presses it back against the wall' (10), a move that indicates his potential affinity with environmental groups despite his reasons for being there.[21]

Tasmania's deforestation practices link contemporary economic deprivation with both defaunation and the historical dispossession and genocide of Aboriginal Tasmanians. According to Penny Green, Tony Ward, and Kirsten McConnachie even when logging is sanctioned by government concessions 'legally defined property rights are based on the expropriation of land from its indigenous inhabitants' (2007: 96). Leigh's narrative alludes to this confluence in the following passage:

> One day [M's] attention is caught by a ring of blackened stones and he imagines they might have been laid by the local Aboriginal people, in the years before they, the fullbloods, were almost driven to extinction. He remembers reading that the government had once tried to make another island, De Witt, an Aboriginal sanctuary – anything to redress their embarrassing demise. It was a tiny and forbidding rock of a place, shunned by all. And, naturally, the experiment failed. Then in 1936, the year the last thylacine died in captivity […], it was suggested that De Witt island could be put to use – any tigers to be rounded up and sent away … Something tempts M to pick up one of the smooth stones and balance it in his palm, and something again tempts him to put it back.
> (1999: 57)

M's encounter with the stones reveals Leigh's awareness that the ideology of settler colonial progress that demonized the Tasmanian tiger and replaced the forest with plantations and farms is the very same ideology that dehumanized and extinguished Aboriginal Tasmanians, known collectively as Palawa, during what is known as the country's Black War of 1828–1835.[22] The stones are one of the novel's only markers of an Aboriginal presence on the island, and the way in which M picks one up but then returns it is an ambivalent moment of disruption and repair. It is not clear what is driving M's actions in this fleeting moment, but it is a move that alludes to an alternative response to ecocidal and genocidal disaster that is not driven by the rapacious commodification of the nonhuman world in the name of wealth accumulation or warfare.

De-extinction and Tourism

In *Green Lion*, Rose-Innes also presents de-extinction science as being tied to a capitalist–anthropocentric insistence on the commodification of iconic extinct animals.[23] The central theme of de-extinction is signalled by the novel's title: the Green Lion is an 'ancient symbol' used in alchemy to make the Philosopher's Stone in order to 'bring things back to life' (Rose-Innes, 2015: 56). In this tradition, the lion symbolizes vitriol (or sulphate) used to purify matter and produce gold. We are introduced to this symbolism via the character of Mark, an estranged childhood friend of the protagonist Con. Mark is revealed as being obsessed with the Green Lion symbol: as an adolescent he created a life-sized version, dyeing the fur of one of the decaying lion trophies from his grandfather's hunting collection and forcing an old tennis ball into its mouth.

It is this childhood fascination that underpins Mark's decision to take a low-paid job at the Lion House, a conservation and captive breeding centre that has been built on the site of an abandoned Victorian-era zoo. Pointedly, it is also situated next to the Rhodes Memorial, where a bust of the British colonist Cecil Rhodes sits at the top of a stone staircase that is flanked by eight bronze sculptures of lions. When Con visits the centre, he finds his friend's hand-painted poster of the mythical Green Lion in the corner:

> A large lion standing up on its hind legs like a dog doing a trick. A golden sun caught in its jaws, bleeding golden blood. The lion's coat and mane were mossy green. Con recognised the image: it was copied off the cover of the little alchemical book that Mark had had in his rucksack. Something out of a medieval manuscript, perhaps.
>
> (111)

Con recalls that beneath the image a block of text included the affirmation that in devouring the sun the Green Lion '*could rejuvenate, revive withered plants, create golems. It could make the dead rise*' (112, original emphasis). The symbol comes to encapsulate Mark's passion for 'drag[ging] each and every animal back from the brink' (107) and saving endangered species by whatever means.

Con discovers that the Lion House has a 'focus on extinctions' but with 'a positive spin: animals brought back from death' (69). This amounts to a new programme to resurrect the extinct black-maned lion by breeding Dimitri, who was bought from a Russian circus, with the female Sekhmet, rescued from a canned hunting safari park in Namibia. Both Dmitri and Sekhmet carry the rare 'ancestral features' of black-maned lions: 'The size, the black mane, the ruff going down the belly' (21). The centre's director, Amina, affirms that

> there were Cape lions all over Europe, even after they were shot out here. In zoos, circuses. […] The genes are still circulating out there, but

diluted. The idea is to find individual specimens that have black-maned traits, breed them back. Like they did with quaggas.

(21)

Amina also reveals that funding for the breeding programme and the centre comes from 'the Parks Department, government high-ups – it's a big deal' (21). The impetus, however, is not to tackle biodiversity loss by reviving depleted ecosystems; rather, Amina explains that these officials 'don't want us to turn away the tourists' (21). The programme is thus informed by de-extinction as spectacle and as a means of generating revenue through tourism. Rather than ascribe to the Lion House's reliance on captive breeding and touristic spectacle, we discover that Mark had joined forces with a local group of animal welfare activists who wished to free the lions. In attempting to do so, however, Mark is attacked by Dmitri and hospitalized, leading to the male lion being put down.

We see an emphasis on touristic spectacle when Con first enters the Lion House and discovers a plaque that reads: '*Back from Extinction! Come and meet our breeding pair, Dmitri and Sekhmet – the first black-maned lions in the Cape since 1858*'. The plaque stands alongside a series of 'educational posters, documenting the usual: climate change and the countrywide drought, species loss, habitat decimation, the importance of keeping the fragile Table Mountain ecosystem closed off to people' (17, original emphasis). The scene displays a juxtaposition of the spectacular and the mundane: de-extinction is presented in the hyperbolic language of the circus show, engraved onto a permanent plaque for added gravitas; environmental catastrophe, on the other hand, is signalled in the form of mundane and ephemeral posters that monotonously list 'the usual' warnings, allowing them to become known, normalized, and ultimately disregarded. This juxtaposition foregrounds the novel's depiction of a damaging disconnect between de-extinction science and long-term solutions for tackling the vast, interconnected forms of 'slow violence' (Nixon, 2011) that make up our contemporary environmental crises.

The novel's conclusion draws together a number of the concerns that have been central to this chapter as a whole, namely the commodification of animal species, the prioritization of charismatic megafauna (such as elephants, whales, and lions), the ethical concerns raised by de-extinction, and the relationship between colonialism, game hunting, and conservationism. In opposition to a biocapitalist commodification of species, Rose-Innes invests in a response to defaunation that sits between spectacle and education, drawing on the positives of both. In the final chapter, the Lion House becomes the new Green Lion Centre, no longer focused on revenue generation through tourism but instead 'devoted to the interdisciplinary conjunction of Arts and Natural Sciences, under the joint auspices of the Departments of Environment, Recreation and Culture' (283). Gone is the captive breeding of charismatic megafauna, and in its place is a commitment to teaching the next generation about a shared inter-species kinship using the taxidermied, Victorian-era trophies that had previously been left to decay in Mark's parents' house. This new approach sees 'taxidermied animals' as the 'perfect emblems' of the new Centre: 'Never particularly rigorous scientific documents, these ones are now almost wholly imagined creations' (284).

Ultimately, the journey of the trophies from a private settler-colonial collection to a communal and educational space actively challenges the hierarchy of lifeforms underpinning both mass extinction and de-extinction technologies: the trophies have been freed from the private enclosure of the 'graceful Victorian' (38) house and brought out into the public domain where 'children are encouraged to touch and experience: stroke the fur, put their fingers in glass eyes, pass their hands between the rows of teeth' (283). In this way, the new Centre emulates the belief in generating a non-anthropocentric kinship with the nonhuman world that is voiced by Mossie from the activist group. When introducing Con to a ceremony the group holds that involves touching different animals, Mossie explains: 'To have the animal there. To touch it. Every person in that room – it helps them. It is something outside themselves. Their human lives' (185). The Centre's insistence on communal and interactive performance – akin to the creative resurrections performed by the trickster characters in Vizenor's *Griever* and King's *Truth and Bright Water* – marry Mossie's belief in sensory interaction with the *symbolic* restoration and revival of animals. In this way, Rose-Innes rejects both commercial forms of disaster biocapitalism and species revival as a source of touristic spectacle; instead, the final moments of *Green Lion* demonstrate an investment in community-driven forms of education that are based on an imaginative and affective awareness of a shared, inter-species animality.

Notes

1 'U.N. report: Nature's "unprecedented" decline; species extinction rates "accelerating"', May 6, 2019, https://www.un.org/sustainabledevelopment/blog/2019/05/nature-decline-unprecedented-report/ [accessed May 30, 2023]. The report states: 'The average abundance of native species in most major land-based habitats has fallen by at least 20%, mostly since 1900. More than 40% of amphibian species, almost 33% of reef-forming corals and more than a third of all marine mammals are threatened. The picture is less clear for insect species, but available evidence supports a tentative estimate of 10% being threatened. At least 680 vertebrate species had been driven to extinction since the 16th century and more than 9% of all domesticated breeds of mammals used for food and agriculture had become extinct by 2016, with at least 1,000 more breeds still threatened.'

2 See https://idlenomore.ca/campaigns-actions/ [accessed May 30, 2023].

3 For a literary depiction of how Asian elephants have also been the source of ivory, see Tania James's *The Tusk That Did the Damage* (2015). Additionally, Asian elephants have been essential to the creation of resources extracted from nature – especially timber – but their value in this context is contingent on their being alive. As Jonathan Saha argues, elephants used in the Burmese timber trade were treated as 'meaty machines to be captured, trained, worked, bought, sold and

experimented upon', and it was elephants that 'made possible the export of teak, a wood that due to the colony's dominance of the world market became synonymous with Burma'. In this context, elephant bodies are thus an asset that needed to be 'looked after, cared for, studied and even understood' (2017: 172). It is for this reason that Saha views elephants used in the timber trade as 'undead capital': they 'can be considered both living (valued for their agential capacities) and dead (demanding the labour of others to produce value)' (174).

4 See https://www.sanparks.org/parks/addo/ [accessed May 30, 2023].
5 In 2021, the museum announced plans to repatriate the carved tusk back to Benin as part of a wider initiative that includes artefacts from across Africa and Australia (see Feilden, 2021).
6 See Ross (2019).
7 See also Liu, et al. (2006).
8 According to Jason Browne, '[t]here are currently over 70 factories in California's 33 prisons alone' where prisoners 'operate dairies, farms, and slaughterhouses' (2007: 44) alongside other forms of work such as manufacturing and wood production. In addition, the American meat-packing industry is heavily reliant on immigrant labour, particularly Latino workers who are often met with anti-immigrant prejudice and the unfounded belief that they will be a disruptive burden on the local community (see also Artz et al., 2010). As well as the low pay and discrimination, meat-packing labour brings with it dehumanizing working conditions and damaging effects to workers' health and well-being. A report by Oxfam America found that the refrigerated conditions of meat-packing plants exacerbates repetitive strain injuries, with 86 percent of workers suffering hand and wrist pain and a rate of carpal tunnel syndrome seven times higher than workers in other industries. Those interviewed also reported having to wear diapers due to the near impossibility of taking breaks (see Oxfam America, 'Lives on the Line: The High Human Cost of Chicken', https://www.oxfamamerica.org/livesontheline/) [accessed May 30, 2023]. Research into the health effects of exposure to the slaughtering process has also revealed an elevated risk of lung and hematologic cancers in workers from across America, Europe, and Australasia (McLean and Pearce: 2004).
9 According to the IUCN Red List, the American bison at the time of writing is designated as 'near threatened' with stable numbers of roughly twelve thousand. The European bison is also currently designated as 'near threatened' but with its numbers increasing: https://www.iucnredlist.org/search?query=bison&searchType=species [accessed May 30, 2023]. See also the 'Wilder Blean' project that seeks to conserve a rewilded habitat for European bison in Kent, UK.
10 While King describes himself as a writer of Cherokee and Greek descent and has, throughout his career, committed himself to writing fiction and non-fiction about the impact of settler colonialism on First Nations communities, his ancestral links to the Cherokee nation have been questioned.
11 For a literary account of the legacy of residential schools see Tomson Highway's *Kiss of the Fur Queen* (1998) and Norma Dunning's poem 'Eskimo Pie II' in *Eskimo Pie: A Poetics of Inuit Identity* (2020). In 2021, the scale of unmarked graves found at the sites of residential schools was uncovered and reported on internationally (see https://www.bbc.co.uk/news/world-us-canada-57592243 [accessed May 30, 2023]). This reporting led to a formal apology by Pope Francis in 2022.
12 Şode's performance of the poem is available to view via Dewachi's website, from which all references here are taken: https://www.hydardewachi.com/untitled-2019-a-poem-by-yomi-sode/ [accessed May 30, 2023].
13 For a discussion of the relationship between conservation and the dispossession of land from Indigenous communities, see Dowie (2011). For an account of

Life 175

conservation practices that include Indigenous peoples and local communities, see Dawson, Londo, and Survival International (2023).

14 For a further discussion of rewilding, see Pettorelli, Durrant, and du Toit (2019) and Jepson and Blythe (2022).
15 For an analysis of *2312*, see Heise (2016), pp. 213–15.
16 In her 'Author's Note' to the novel, Rose-Innes explains that the narrative was inspired by unsuccessful attempts by the Tygerberg zookeeper John Spence to bring back black-maned lions and by the 'Quagga Project'. The 'Quagga Project' has led experiments by biochemistry researchers based at the University of California and the San Diego Zoo since 1984. It has been successful in breeding zebras with quagga-like stripes that, as Rose-Innes notes, can be seen 'roaming the slopes below Devil's Peak [in Cape Town] not far from the ruined Victorian Zoo' (2015: 291). To read more about this project, see https://quaggaproject.org/ [accessed May 30, 2023]. The genome sequencing is also detailed in Higuchi et al. (1984), pp. 282–284.
17 In 2005 Australia's *The Bulletin* promoted its 125th birthday by offering a $1.25 million prize for photographic evidence of a living specimen, but no submissions were authenticated (see Freeman, 2013: 191 n.5).
18 Until 2022, it was commonly thought that the last known thylacine was a male called Benjamin, of which there are photographs and film footage. The details of Benjamin's death added an especially emotive dimension to the ending of the species due to the fact that he died of neglect, having been accidentally locked out of his enclosure and exposed to freezing temperatures. Following research by Robert Paddle and Kathryn Medlock, it has now been confirmed that Benjamin was the penultimate thylacine. The last of the species was an elderly female whose name is unknown (see 'Thylacine mystery solved in TMAG collections: https://www.tmag.tas.gov.au/whats_on/newsselect/2022articles/thylacine_mystery_solved_in_tmag_collections [accessed May 30, 2023]).
19 See Fletcher (2010), p.53, and Heise (2016), p.45.
20 'Australia confirms extinction of 13 more species, including first reptile since colonisation', *The Guardian*, Wednesday March 3, 2021, https://www.theguardian.com/science/2021/mar/03/australia-confirms-extinction-of-13-more-species-including-first-reptile-since-colonisation [accessed May 30, 2023]. In response to the report that, since European colonization, 'more than 10% of the 320 land mammals known to have lived in Australia in 1788 are extinct', the Australian government published a ten-year 'Threatened Species Strategy' (http://www.environment.gov.au/biodiversity/threatened/publications/threatened-species-strategy-2021-2031 [accessed May 30, 2023]). This plan, however, was instantly criticized by environmental campaigners who have cited research by Brendan A. Wintle, et al. which shows that 'allocated spending' is only '15% of what is needed to avoid extinctions and recover threatened species' (2019: 3, 1). The research focusses on the Australian context but asserts that '[t]here is empirical evidence that the more a country spends on conservation, the fewer species it loses' (4). In May 2021, it was also reported that the Australian government attempted to prevent the publication of Wintle et al.'s 'Spending to Save' paper on conservation under-funding. Due to this pressure, the researchers removed all specific references to the ten-year 'Threatened Species' programme and assured the government that they would not discuss the paper's findings with the media (see 'Environment department tried to bury research that found huge underspend on Australian threatened species', *The Guardian*, Thursday May 13, 2021, https://www.theguardian.com/environment/2021/may/14/environment-department-tried-to-bury-research-that-found-huge-underspend-on-australian-threatened-species [accessed May 30, 2023].
21 While logging on the island is government-sanctioned, the industry situates Tasmania within a global network of 'illegal and unsustainable legal logging' that 'contributes to deforestation (directly and by opening forests up to other

destructive activities), destroying the world's greatest reservoirs of biodiversity, threatening species such as the great apes in equatorial Africa and orangutans in Borneo, and hastening climate change' (Green, Ward, and McConnachie, 2007: 95). The Tasmanian industry specifically has involved 'clear-felling and napalm' to remove 'all saleable timber' before 'destroying the remainder to make way for short-rotation tree crops', all of which 'has been carried out with the enthusiastic complicity of successive Tasmanian governments' (101). This has included the 'sanctioned killing of endangered and protected species such as the wombat and ring-tailed possum' and a 'failure to map forest types that are rare and endangered because it complicates decision making in the forest practices system' (104), a process that led to the accidental felling in 2003 of Australia's largest tree. At the heart of this story is the private forestry company Gunns Ltd., which rose to prominence to control 'over 85% of the state's logging' and in the process became 'the world's largest hardwood woodchip exporter' (101). During this period of success, and despite government concessions, the company's corporate wealth did not trickle down to the population and Tasmania 'remains the poorest of Australia's eight states and territories' (101). After charges of insider trading, a costly, controversial, and ultimately futile plan to build a pulp mill in Tamar Valley, and over a decade of sustained pressure from protesters and conservationists, Gunns went into administration in 2012 owing the banks $515 million. See 'Timeline: The rise and fall of Gunns': https://www.abc.net.au/news/2012-09-25/gunns-timber-company-rise-fall-timeline/4235708 [accessed May 30, 2023].

22 Palawa numbered between 4,000 and 15,000 at the time of British settlement. Early settlers, soldiers, and convicts were met with Indigenous resistance over the dispossession of land, the over-hunting of wild game, and later the rape, abduction, and murder of Aborigines. This led to the Black War when the British settler state-sanctioned martial law that ended in the genocide of Aboriginal Tasmanians. Although Aboriginal Tasmanians and their property were protected from 1805 under British law, colonial administrators rarely punished settlers for terrorizing and killing Aborigines and, as Benjamin Madley notes, '"heathen" Aborigines could not be sworn into British courts and were thus barred from giving testimony or serving as jurors' (2008: 89), effectively excluding them from the legal system. Those who were spared death during the Black War were incarcerated in detention camps at Wybalenna and Finders Island and subjected to '[i]mpure water, inadequate clothing, insufficient blankets, and poor shelter [which] precipitated lethal respiratory illnesses, including influenza, tuberculosis, and pneumonia' (101–02). Thus, the conditions faced by those Aboriginal Tasmanians who survived the Black War were at best inhospitable and at worse lethal. See also Turnbull (1948) and Ryan (1996).

23 For further analysis of *Green Lion* see Olsen (2022) and Simon (2023).

Bibliography

Armstrong, Philip. 2002. "The Postcolonial Animal." *Society & Animals* 10, no. 4: 413–419.

Armstrong, Philip. 2008. *What Animals Mean in the Fiction of Modernity*. London: Routledge.

Artz, Georgeanne, *et al.* 2010. "Is It a Jungle Out There? Meat Packing, Immigrants, and Rural Communities." *Journal of Agricultural and Resource Economics* 35, no. 2 (August): 299–315.

Babcock-Abrahams, Barbara. 1975. "'A Tolerated Margin of Mess': The Trickster and His Tales Reconsidered." *Journal of the Folklore Institute* 11, no. 3 (March): 147–186.

Banks, Peter B., and Dieter F. Hochuli. 2017. "Extinction, De-extinction and Conservation: A Dangerous Mix of Ideas." *Australian Zoologist* 38, no. 3, special issue: Dangerous Ideas in Zoology: 390–394. doi:10.7882/AZ.2016.012.

Bird Rose, Deborah, Thom van Dooren, and Matthew Chrulew. 2017. "Introduction: Telling Extinction Stories." In *Extinction Studies: Stories of Time, Death, and Generations*, edited by Bird Rose, van Dooren, and Chrulew, 1–17. New York: Colombia University Press.

Blixen, Karen. [1937] 2001. *Out of Africa*. London: Penguin.

Brand, Stewart. 1968. *Whole Earth Catalog* (Fall): https://monoskop.org/images/0/09/Brand_Stewart_Whole_Earth_Catalog_Fall_1968.pdf [accessed 2023].

Browne, Jason. 2007. "Rooted in Slavery: Prison Labor Exploitation." *Race, Poverty & the Environment* 14, no. 1, special issue: Just Jobs? Organizing for Economic Justice (Spring): 42–44.

Büscher, Bram, and Robert Fletcher. 2020. *The Conservation Revolution: Radical Ideas for Saving Nature Beyond the Anthropocene*. London: Verso.

Carrigan, Anthony. 2015. "Towards a Postcolonial Disaster Studies." In *Global Ecologies and the Environmental Humanities*, edited by Elizabeth DeLoughrey, Jill Didur, and Anthony Carrigan, 117–139. London: Routledge.

Coetzee, J.M. 1999. *The Lives of Animals*. London: Profile Books.

Coetzee, J.M. [2003] 2004. *Elizabeth Costello*. London: Vintage.

Coetzee, J.M. 2007. "Animals can't speak for themselves – it's up to us to do it." *The Age* 22 (February): https://www.theage.com.au/national/animals-cant-speak-for-themselves-its-up-to-us-to-do-it-20070222-ge49zt.html [accessed 2023].

Conrad, Joseph. [1899] 2007. *Heart of Darkness*. London: Penguin.

Dawson, Ashley. 2016. *Extinction: A Radical History*. London: OR Books.

Dawson, Ashley, Fiore Longo, and Survival International, eds. 2023. *Decolonize Conservation: Global Voices for Indigenous Self-Determination, Land, and a World in Common*. Brooklyn, NY: Common Notions.

Dirzo, Rodolfo, *et al*. 2014. "Defaunation in the Anthropocene." *Science* 345, no. 6195: 401–406.

Dowie, Mark. 2011. *Conservation Refugees: The Hundred-Year Conflict Between Global Conservation and Native Peoples*. London: MIT Press.

Edwardson, Rachel Nutaaq Ayałhuq Naŋinaaq. 2022. "She'll Do What She Needs to Do." In *Risky Futures: Climate, Geopolitics and Local Realities in the Uncertain Circumpolar North*, ed. by Olga Ulturgasheva and Barbara Bodenhorn, 89–102. Oxford: Berghahn Books.

Ellams, Inua. 2020. *The Actual*. London: Penned in the Margins.

Estes, Nick. 2019. *Our History is the Future: Standing Rock versus the Dakota Access Pipeline, and the Long Tradition of Indigenous Resistance*. London: Verso.

Fanon, Frantz. [1952] 2008. *Black Skin, White Masks*. Translated by Richard Philcox. New York: Grove Press.

Feilden, Eloise. 2021. "Manchester Museum makes moves towards repatriation and diversity", *Museums Association* (April 1): https://www.museumsassociation.org/museums-journal/news/2021/04/manchester-museum-makes-moves-towards-repatriation-and-diversity/ [accessed April 24, 2023].

Feinberg, Harvey M., and Marion Johnson. 1982. "The West African Ivory Trade during the Eighteenth Century: The '… and Ivory' Complex." *The International Journal of African Historical Studies* 15, no. 3: 435–453.

Fletcher, Amy. 2010. "Genuine fakes: Cloning extinct species as science and spectacle." *Politics and the Life Sciences* 29, no. 1 (March): 48–60. doi:10.2990/29_1_4.

Fox, Timothy R. 2009. "Realizing Fantastic Trickster Liberations in Gerald Vizenor's *Griever: An American Monkey King in China.*" *Journal of the Fantastic in the Arts* 20, no. 1: 70–90.

Freeman, Carol. 2013. "The last image: Julia Leigh's *The Hunter* as film." In *Animal Death*, edited by Jay Johnston and Fiona Probyn-Rapsey, 189–204. Sydney: Sydney University Press.

Green, Penny, Tony Ward, and Kirsten McConnachie. 2007. "Logging and Legality: Environmental Crime, Civil Society, and the State." *Social Justice* 34, no. 2, special issue: Beyond Transnational Crime: 94–110.

Gurnah, Abdulrazak. 2000. "Settler writing in Kenya: 'Nomenclature is an uncertain science in these wild parts'." In *Modernism and Empire*, edited by Howard Booth and Nigel Rigby, 275–291. Manchester: Manchester University Press.

Haggard, H. Rider. [1886] 2001. *She*. London: Penguin.

Haraway, Donna. 2008. *When Species Meet*. London: University of Minnesota Press.

Heise, Ursula K. 2016. *Imagining Extinction: The Cultural Meanings of Endangered Species*. London: University of Chicago Press.

Higuchi, Russell, *et al.* 1984. "DNA sequences from the quagga, an extinct member of the horse family." *Nature* 312 (November): 282–284.

Holgate, Ben. 2019. *Climate and Crises: Magical Realism as Environmental Discourse*. Abingdon: Routledge.

Huggan, Graham, and Helen Tiffin. [2010] 2015. *Postcolonial Ecocriticism: Literature: Animals, Environment*. London: Routledge.

Huggan, Graham. 2018. *Colonialism, Culture, Whales*. London: Bloomsbury Academic.

Hulme, Keri. [1986] 1988. *Te Kaihau: The Windeater*. London: Sceptre.

Hulme, Keri, and John Bryson. 1994. "Keri Hulme in conversation with John Bryson." *Antipodes* 8, no. 2 (December): 131–135.

Ihimaera, Witi. [1987] 2005. *The Whale Rider*. Essex: Heinemann.

Jones, Ryan Tucker, and Angela Wanhalla. 2019. "Introduction." *RCC Perspectives* 5, special issue: New Histories of Pacific Whaling: 5–8. https://www.jstor.org/stable/26850615.

Kareiva, Peter, *et al.* 2012. "Conservation in the Anthropocene: Beyond Solitude and Fragility." *Breakthrough Journal* 2 (Fall): https://thebreakthrough.org/journal/issue-2/conservation-in-the-anthropocene [accessed 2023].

King, Thomas. 1999. *Truth and Bright Water*. New York: Grove Press.

Kolbert, Elizabeth. 2014. *The Sixth Extinction: An Unnatural History*. London: Bloomsbury.

LaDuke, Winona. [1999] 2015. *All Our Relations: Native Struggles for Land and Life*. Chicago: Haymarket Books.

Leigh, Julia. 1999. *The Hunter*. London: Faber & Faber.

Liu, Yi-Ping, *et al.* 2006. "Multiple maternal origins of chickens: Out of the Asian jungles." *Molecular Phylogenetics and Evolution* 38, no. 1 (January): 12–19.

MacKenzie, John M. 1988. *The Empire of Nature: Hunting, Conservation and British Imperialism*. Manchester: Manchester University Press.

Madley, Benjamin. 2008. "From Terror to Genocide: Britain's Tasmanian Penal Colony and Australia's History Wars." *Journal of British Studies* 47, no. 1 (January): 77–106.

Marzec, Robert P. 2019. "The Monstrous and the Secure: Reading Conrad in the Anthropocene." In *Conrad and Nature: Essays*, edited by Lissa Schneider-Rebozo, Jeffrey Mathes McCarthy, and John G. Peters, 68–89. London: Routledge.

McHugh, Susan. 2019. *Love in a Time of Slaughters: Human-Animal Stories Against Genocide and Extinction*. Pennsylvania: Penn State University Press.

McKay, Robert. 2010. "Metafiction, Vegetarianism, and the Literary Performance of Animal Ethics in J.M. Coetzee's *The Lives of Animals*." *Safundi: The Journal of South African and American Studies* 11, no. 1–2: 67–85. doi:10.1080/17533170903458504.

McLean, Dave, and Neil Pearce. 2004. "Cancer among meat industry workers." *Scandinavian Journal of Work, Environment & Health* 30, no. 6 (December): 425–437.

Melville, Herman. [1851] 2003. *Moby Dick or, The Whale*. Penguin: London.

Minteer, Ben A. 2014. "Is It Right to Reverse Extinction?" *Nature* 509 (May): 261.

Monbiot, George. 2014. *Feral*. London: Penguin.

Murphy, Ryan Francis. 2013. "Exterminating the Elephant in *Heart of Darkness*." *The Conradian* 38, no. 2 (Autumn): 1–17.

Nixon, Rob. 2011. *Slow Violence and the Environmentalism of the Poor*. Cambridge, MA: Harvard University Press.

Oak Taylor, Jesse. 2019. "Wilderness after Nature: Conrad, Empire and the Anthropocene." In *Conrad and Nature: Essays*, edited by Lissa Schneider-Rebozo, Jeffrey Mathes McCarthy, and John G. Peters, 21–42. London: Routledge.

Olsen, Ida M. 2022. "Extinct and Undying Species: Animal Fetishism in *Green Lion* and *How the Dead Dream*." *Studies in the Novel* 54, no. 4: 426–444. doi:10.1353/sdn.2022.0032.

Patel, Raj, and Jason W. Moore. 2018. *A History of the World in Seven Cheap Things: A Guide to Capitalism, Nature, and the Future of the Planet*. London: Verso.

Pick, Anat. 2011. *Creaturely Poetics: Animality and Vulnerability in Literature and Film*. New York: Colombia University Press.

Rastogi, Pallavi. 2020. *Postcolonial Disaster: Narrating Disaster in the Twenty-First Century*. Evanston, Illinois: Northwestern University Press.

Rose-Innes, Henrietta. 2015. *Green Lion*. London: Aardvark Bureau.

Ross, D. 2019. "Consciousness, Language, and the Possibility of Non-human Personhood: Reflections on Elephants." *Journal of Consciousness Studies* 26, no. 3–4: 227–251.

Ryan, Derek. 2022. *Bloomsbury, Beasts and British Modernist Literature*. Cambridge: Cambridge University Press.

Ryan, Lyndall. 1996. *The Aboriginal Tasmanians*, 2nd edition. St. Leonards: Allen & Unwin.

Saha, Jonathan. 2017. "Colonizing Elephants: Animal Agency, Undead Capital and Imperial Science in British Burma." *British Journal for the History of Science*: 169–189. doi:10.1017/bjt.2017.6.

Schuster, Joshua. 2017. "Sustainability after extinction: On last animals and future bison." *Literature and Sustainability: Concept, Text and Culture*, edited by Adeline Johns-Putra, John Parham, and Louise Squire, 97–114. Manchester: Manchester University Press.

Shannon, Laurie. 2011. "Greasy Citizens and Tallow-Catches." In "Editor's Column: Literature in the Ages of Wood, Tallow, Coal, Whale Oil, Gasoline, Atomic Power, and Other Energy Sources." *PMLA* 126, no. 2 (March): 311–313.

Shapiro, Beth. 2015. *How to Clone a Mammoth: The Science of De-Extinction.* Oxford: Princeton University Press.

Shoemaker, Nancy. 2005. "Whale Meat in American History, Environmental History." *Environmental History* 10, no. 2 (April): 269–294.

Shukin, Nicole. 2009. *Animal Capital: Rendering Life in Biopolitical Times.* Minnesota: University of Minnesota Press.

Simon, Judith. 2023. "Sekhmet and the Shaman: Extinction, Ferality and Trans-species Connections in Henrietta Rose-Innes' *Green Lion.*" *English Studies in Africa* (April): 1–16. doi:10.1080/00138398.2023.2193473.

Sinha, Suvadip, and Amit R. Baishya, eds. 2020. "Introduction: Postcolonial Animalities." In *Postcolonial Animalities*, edited by Suvadip Sinha and Amit R. Baishya, 1–25. Routledge: Abingdon.

Ṣode, Yomi. 2019. "Untitled." https://www.hydardewachi.com/untitled-2019-a-poem-by-yomi-sode/ [accessed 2023].

Somerville, Keith. 2016. *Ivory: Power and Poaching in Africa.* London: C. Hurst & Co.

Spivak, Gayatri. [1988], 1994. "Can the subaltern speak?" In *Colonial Discourse and Post-Colonial Theory: A Reader*, edited by Patrick Williams and Laura Crisman, 66–111. New York: Colombia University Press.

Steinhart, Edward I. 2006. *Black Poachers, White Hunters: A Social History of Hunting in Colonial Kenya.* Ohio: Ohio University Press.

Steinwand, Jonathan. 2011. "What the whales would tell us: Cetacean communication in novels by Witi Ihimaera, Linda Hogan, Zakes Mda, and Amitav Ghosh." In *Postcolonial Ecologies: Literatures of the Environment*, edited by Elizabeth DeLoughrey and George B. Handley, 182–199. Oxford: Oxford University Press.

Thompsell, Angela. 2015. *Hunting Africa: British Sport, African Knowledge and the Nature of Empire.* Basingstoke: Palgrave Macmillan.

Turnbull, Clive. 1948. *Black War: The Extermination of the Tasmanian Aborigines.* Melbourne: Sun Books.

Ulturgasheva, Olga, and Barbara Bodenhorn. 2022. "Activating Cosmo-Geo-Analytics: Anthropocene, Arctics and Cryocide." In *Risky Futures: Climate, Geopolitics and Local Realities in the Uncertain Circumpolar North*, edited by Olga Ulturgasheva and Barbara Bodenhorn, 26–57. Oxford: Berghahn Books.

van Dooren, Thom, and Deborah Bird Rose. 2017. "Keeping Faith with the Dead: Mourning and De-extinction." *Australian Zoologist* 38, no. 3, special issue: Dangerous Ideas in Zoology: 375–378. doi:10.7882/AZ.2014.048.

Vizenor, Gerald. [1987] 1990. *Griever: An American Monkey King in China.* Minneapolis: University of Minnesota Press.

Wall Kimmerer, Robin. [2013] 2020. *Braiding Sweetgrass: Indigenous Wisdom, Scientific Knowledge and the Teachings of Plants.* London: Penguin.

wa Thiong'o, Ngũgĩ. 1993. *Moving the Centre: The Struggle for Cultural Freedoms.* Oxford: James Currey.

Wenzel, Jennifer. 2011. "Consumption for the Common Good? Commodity Biography Film in an Age of Postconsumerism." *Public Culture* 23, no. 3: 573–602. doi:10.1215/08992363-1336426.

Wilson, Edward O. 2016. *Half-Earth: Our Planet's Fight for Life.* London: Liveright.

Winston Blackmun, Barbara. 1997. "Icons and Emblems in Ivory: An Altar Tusk from the Palace of Old Benin." *Art Institute of Chicago Museum Studies* 23, no. 2, special issue: African Art at The Art Institute of Chicago: 148–163 and 197–198.

Wintle, Brendan A., et al. 2019. "Spending to save: What will it cost to half Australia's extinction crisis?" *Conservation Letters* 12e12682: 1–7. doi:10.1111/conl.12682.

Wolfe, Cary. 2003. *Animal Rites: Animal Culture, the Discourse of Species, and Posthumanist Theory*, Foreword by W.J.T. Mitchell. London: University of Chicago Press.

Wolfe, Patrick. 2006. "Settler colonialism and the elimination of the native." *Journal of Genocide Research* 8, no. 4 (December): 387–409. doi:10.1080/14623520601056240.

Woolf, Leonard. 1961. *Growing: An Autobiography of the Years 1904–1911*. New York: Harcourt Brace Jovanovich.

Wylie, Dan. 2006. "Why Write a Poem About Elephants?" *Mosaic* 39, no. 4: 27–46.

Wylie, Dan. 2013. *Slow Fires*, with etchings by Roxandra Dardagan Britz. Fourthwall Books.

Zapf, Hubert. 2017. *Literature as Cultural Ecology: Sustainable Texts*. London: Bloomsbury Academic.

Conclusion

Over the course of four thematic chapters – Earth, Water, Air, and Life – this book has analysed prose, poems, and plays from and about regions of intense ecological despoliation. This has involved reading widely, transnationally, and trans-historically as a means of attending to both the localized and global impacts of deforestation, land dispossession, drilling and mining, rapidly transforming ecosystems, pollution, and the catastrophic depletion of biodiversity. What emerges is an investment in the importance of global literature and literary studies in understanding how the activities of dominant human groups – and not human civilization as an undifferentiated whole – are responsible for the polycrises of the climate and ecological emergencies. Going further, many of the texts that have been examined here give a voice to silenced or marginalized experiences and worldviews that, for centuries, have prioritized ecologically sustainable ways of being-in-the-world in direct contrast to the practices of industrial-scale resource extraction, commodification, and ecocide that have been globalized by the spread of capitalist–imperialism from the fifteenth century through to the present day. Such worldviews are emphatically not those of the 'disappearing' or 'ecological Indian' kind; rather, they are defined by an experiential intimacy with rapidly changing environments and a recognition that all lifeforms are dependent upon complex ecosystems for survival, which often informs a collective anti-colonial and anti-capitalist political consciousness. In the words of Arundhati Roy, the marginalized and historically persecuted communities out of which these voices emerge are not 'keepers of our past', but 'may really be the guides to our future' (2010: n.p.).

It is undeniable that the burning of fossil fuels is the primary activity that has drastically disrupted the relationship between biotic and abiotic components of the planet's ecosystems, creating an increasingly uninhabitable environment for the Earth's human and nonhuman populations. One of the central strands that has run through much of this book is the way in which the petroleum industry represents the most dominant, contemporary form of resource extraction in a long history of extractivism that has been contingent upon the exploitation of people, fauna, and flora. In 'Earth' we examined novels and plays that chart the development of global capitalism, connecting

DOI: 10.4324/9780429353352-6

transatlantic slavery and the spread of plantation economies in the Caribbean to the proliferation of diamond and gold mining in nineteenth-century South Africa and oil mining in Scotland in the twentieth century. The continuing dominance of the petroleum industry in the twentieth- and twenty-first centuries was then attended to in the chapter 'Water' by looking to poetry by anti-oil activists from the Niger Delta and by Alaskan Native writers. Bringing these geographically distanced regions into conversation, moreover, allowed for a discussion of the relationship between the burning of fossil fuels and the release of greenhouse gases into the Earth's atmosphere. The Niger Delta was returned to in 'Air' due to the shared preoccupation with atmospheric pollution being caused by gas flaring practices across a range of contemporary novels by Nigerian, Cameroonian, and British writers. The centrality of oil extraction across these texts and contexts was linked in 'Air' to a concern with corporate culpability for pollution caused by the manufacture and use of pesticides, an issue captured most urgently in Indian-set novels and poems influenced by the fatal gas leak at the Union Carbide pesticide plant in Bhopal. Across each of these chapters, we showed how the sustainability of interconnected climatic elements is integral to the future survival of the biosphere. Through a reading of prose and poetry set across Africa, Australasia, and North America in 'Life', we explored how the 'sixth extinction' is underpinned by the treatment of nonhuman lifeforms as repositories of resources to be extracted, quarry to be hunted, or pests to be exterminated to make way for agriculture. And while we began the book by mapping the roots and routes of global capitalism, we ended by tracing the growth of the international conservation movement that, today, has been criticized for recirculating the commodification of nature and nonhuman animals.

As this suggests, our analyses here see prose, poetry, and plays as significant resources in the fight for an equitably sustainable world, counteracting sceptical perspectives on the ability of literature to dramatize ecological crises that transcend temporalities and locations. We saw in the Introduction how one of the most well-known examples of this scepticism comes from Amitav Ghosh's *The Great Derangement*, in which he focuses on the novel form to argue that dominant literary conventions render it unable to represent the interrelated catastrophes of ecological breakdown that span geographical regions, languages, historical periods, and nonhuman existence. In response to Ghosh, Robert Spencer and Anastasia Valassopoulos assert that searching for the climate change novel 'makes as little sense as asking, where is the novel of capitalism, or the novel about patriarchy? There are numerous works about climate change but there is no climate change novel' (2021: 205). They go on to note that Ghosh's own attempt to produce a climate change novel in *Gun Island* (2019) sees him try 'to compensate for all the mistakes and omissions' that he 'wrongly attributes to "serious fiction"', and ultimately 'ends up failing to satisfy' due to its 'misguided bagginess' and 'undisguised evangelism' (205). Our analysis of literature, from a wide range of periods and locations, has demonstrated just some of the texts that are not necessarily *about* the climate emergency but that have emerged out of global locations and historical eras of intensity concerning human-induced threats to the lithosphere, hydrosphere, cryosphere, atmosphere, and biosphere.

In drawing this book to a close, we will reflect on one particular form of storytelling that is seen by some as the best literary resource we have for raising awareness about the climate emergency, namely the eco-dystopian form (which has also been labelled 'cli-fi' or, more broadly, environmental apocalypticism). The 'language of disaster', write Rowland Hughes and Pat Wheeler, offers novelists 'the most compelling […] means of persuading [their] audience, not only of the devastation being wreaked upon global ecosystems, but of the human consequences of that devastation' (2013: 2). In assessing the eco-dystopian form, we will first set out some of the reasons for its centrality in environmental and climate justice discourse as a mode of writing that provides a subjective and affective dimension to environmental science and has the capacity to reach mainstream audiences. Second, we will examine some of the critical perspectives on the limitations of eco-dystopian storytelling, including views that it further marginalizes the voices of oppressed communities and renders environmental despoliation as exceptional to, rather than embedded in, the development of global capitalism.

To finish, we will reflect upon what can be thought of as the 'Janus-faced' quality of eco-dystopian storytelling in relation to the topic of climate migration. By 'Janus-faced' we mean that eco-dystopian visions of the Earth's future have the potential to inspire supranational cooperation and planning for mitigation but that such speculative visions are also taken up as a means of framing the climate emergency in terms of national security and the reinforcement of borders. We will assess how an environmental apocalypticism is evident in fiction that contributes to calls for an end to the fossil fuel-burning status quo *and* in 'green nationalism', which mobilizes concerns for the environment to blame 'innocents and victims, to the extent that, in its most vicious form, it wants more of them to go out of existence' (Malm and the Zetkin Collective, 2021: 154). In the latter, 'the ecological crisis is not denied but enlisted as a reason to fortify borders and keep aliens out' (154–55), representing the convergence of environmentalism with a neo-Malthusian logic of migration and population controls. In examining this issue, we do not seek to stymie eco-dystopian imaginaries that might be capable of generating greater awareness of the ways in which environmental breakdown will catastrophically transform the globe. Rather, we will discuss the eco-dystopian form here in the hope that it will open up further questions about the relationship between global literature and the environment for our readers to pursue.

Eco-Dystopias

In his seminal book *The Environmental Imagination*, Lawrence Buell asserts that '[a]pocalypse is the single most powerful master metaphor that the contemporary environmental imagination has at its disposal' (1995: 285). This, he says, is because 'the rhetoric of apocalypticism implies that the fate of the world hinges on the arousal of the imagination to a sense of crisis' and projects a disastrous future for 'a civilisation that refuses to transform itself according to the doctrine of the web [of interdependence]' (285). This view underpins the widespread focus in the environmental humanities on dystopian narratives that project readers forward in time to a world transformed by extreme weather conditions. The term 'cli-fi' was coined in 2007 by the climate activist Dan Bloom to suggest that such narratives were becoming a sub-genre in and of themselves.[1] As the pun suggests, Bloom's neologism names an off-shoot of Science Fiction (SF) whereby many SF conventions – speculative warnings of the underside of utopian planning, the dominance of technology over society, post-apocalyptic visions of a world gone wrong – are adopted for stories that respond specifically to the scientific predictions of environmental catastrophe. The connections between cli-fi and SF, according to Andrea Whiteley et al., 'are amplified through the latter's ability to portray futures at planetary scales [...] and make connections between global threats and individual lives', which has been 'a pointed weakness in the environmental movement' (2016: 29). Indeed, where environmental activism has historically worked to bring mainstream attention to the scientific data concerning such phenomena as global warming, deforestation, rising sea levels, mass ice melt, air pollution, and species extinction, literature situates these warnings within society in a manner that 'can elucidate the complexities of the problem in ways far removed from temperature charts and other scientific ways of understanding climate change' (34).

In her overview of cli-fi novels, Adeline Johns-Putra offers two broad categories that can be discerned between narratives set in the present day and those set in an imagined future. In the former, 'climate change emerges as a complex political problem demanding just as complex solutions' whilst also figuring as 'a profoundly personal ethical dilemma' and 'the prime cause of psychological anxiety and delusion' (2016: 269). Examples that Johns-Putra cites include T.C. Boyle's *A Friend of the Earth* (2000), John Wray's *Lowboy* (2009), Ian McEwan's *Solar* (2010), and Kim Stanley Robinson's 'Science in the Capital' trilogy (2004, 2005, 2007). In future-set cli-fi, by comparison, 'climate change is depicted not just as an internal or psychological problem' but is dramatized 'for its external effects, often as part of an overall collapse including technological over-reliance, economic instability, and increased social division' (269). Texts such as Jeanette Winterson's *The Stone Gods* (1997), Maggie Gee's *The Ice People* (1998), Cormac McCarthy's *The Road* (2006), and Margaret Atwood's 'MaddAdam' trilogy (2003, 2009, 2013) emphasize 'physical dramas' that emerge as a consequence of climate breakdown instead of 'emotional or mental ones' (2016: 269). In such novels, 'the difficulty of survival becomes a dominant theme' alongside 'the importance of intergenerational obligation in order to survive climate devastation' (269).[2]

The advocacy for eco-dystopian narratives has coincided with a range of critical perspectives that see the privileging of an apocalyptic future as potentially eliding the past and present-day drivers of climate polycrises across the globe. For example, the speculative, apocalyptic imaginary so central to eco-dystopias has been assessed by Ghosh when he writes that

> cli-fi is made up mostly of disaster stories set in the future, and that, to me, is exactly the rub. The future is but one aspect of the Anthropocene: this era also includes the recent past, and, most significantly, the present.
> (2016: 72)

For Ghosh, a core problem with speculative fictions of climate breakdown lies in the fact that 'the Anthropocene [...] is not an imagined "other" world apart from ours; nor is it located in another "time" or another "dimension"' (72–73). This view aligns with that of Elizabeth DeLoughrey who, in her reading of works by the Māori writer Keri Hulme, warns that the dystopian form has the potential to make ecological disaster seem alien. By comparison, in Hulme's work DeLoughrey sees an avowed eschewal of 'an apocalyptic narrative that would position humans outside the "natural" world, or narrate change in nonhuman nature (such as flooding) as extraordinary, which is to say exceptional to human experience' (2015: 363).

The Nigerian-South African critic Philip Aghoghovwia also addresses the potential for apocalyptic narratives to frame climate breakdown as exceptional, as though climate change were a singular, external *thing* akin to an invading extra-terrestrial army looking to wipe out humanity. 'Prevailing iterations of the Anthropocene', argues Aghoghovwia, 'tend to elide the specificities of site-based, local events of climate change, presenting human-induced changes of the earth's climate in abstract terms by means of scientific modelling and speculative projections' (2021: 34). In place of such apocalyptic predictions, Aghoghovwia advocates for what he calls an 'apocalyptic realism' that can attend to the fact that, in regions such as the Niger Delta, 'the apocalyptic future projected as a possible or imminent occurrence is already a quotidian reality' (34). An apocalyptic realism, he says, is able to 'frame climate change as events, rather than abstract processes, putting environmental issues in graphic contexts rather than discursive abstractions' (45).

The problems that Ghosh, DeLoughrey, and Aghoghovwia identify are associated with the view elsewhere that environmental apocalypticism has the potential to render the fossil fuel industry as a hidden referent whilst de-historicizing ecological disasters from the global spread of capitalist–imperial relations. For Andreas Malm, cli-fi 'has so far failed conspicuously on one score: rarely, if ever, does it broach the cause of the problem', meaning that 'the act of extracting and burning fossil fuels is no more visible than in any other contemporary literature' (2017: 126). The fact that 'cli-fi floats above the material base of the fossil economy', he says, means that it is a literary form that has a 'limited capacity for illuminating the causes of present and future heat, in the worst case even serving to naturalize it' (126). Critics with a particular interest in the long-standing effects of ecological despoliation upon formerly colonized and Indigenous societies have also raised problems with an over-reliance on an environmental apocalypticism. For the Potawatomi scholar Kyle Whyte, for example, when 'dystopian or postapocalyptic narratives of climate crises' are adopted to depict 'humans in horrific science-fiction scenarios', '[s]uch narratives can erase Indigenous peoples' perspectives on the connections between climate change and colonial violence' (2018: 225). These perspectives update a longer-standing evaluation of SF offered by Noah Berlatsky. In an article for *The Atlantic*, Berlatsky notes that, 'with its alien invasions, evil empires, authoritarian dystopia, and new lands discovered and pacified, [...] sci-fi is often obsessed with colonialism and imperial adventure' (2014: n.p.). Although such narratives, he says, can force imperial and post-imperial nations to question their justifications for colonial violence, they also have the potential to 'erase those who are at the business end of imperial terror, positing white European colonizers as the threatened victims in a genocidal race war' (n.p.).

This brings us back to the problems faced by adopting the universalizing concept of the Anthropocene, whereby humans are framed as an undifferentiated actor wreaking havoc on the natural world. In the eco-dystopian imaginary, it is too easy for this Anthropocene discourse to be turned on its head, and for an undifferentiated humanity to be seen as the universal victim of climate breakdown despite the unevenness in both culpability and the present-day burdens of ecological despoliation across the globe. If such unevenness is elided in mainstream understandings of present and future impacts of the climate crisis, and if the capitalist–imperial causes of climate breakdown are omitted, there is the potential for socio-political responses to the climate emergency to bolster existing forms of national isolationism and protectionism. Such a predicament leads us to a consideration of the following question: what if eco-dystopias 'transfix their audience with horror, command attention and shock people out of a position of comfortable apathy' (Hughes and Wheeler, 2013: 2) but in a manner that gives more oxygen to the anti-migrant narratives already being peddled by political parties across wealthy nations of the Global North? One means of responding to this question is to interrogate the logics underpinning forms of national isolationism and to turn to eco-dystopian narratives that directly confront issues of climate-induced migration.

Hostile Environments: Eco-Dystopianism and Migration

We have seen in this book how environmental polycrises are placing unprecedented pressure on the livelihoods of the world's poorest and most vulnerable societies, creating/exacerbating civil wars over resources as well as causing mass internal and global migration.[3] Current predictions estimate that climate breakdown could lead to the migration of over two hundred million people by 2050 (Clement et al., 2021), and the term 'climate refugee' is already proliferating across mainstream media reporting on instances of displacement due to such extreme conditions as flooding, drought, and wildfires. At the same time, however, there is currently no legal means by which asylum can be claimed by someone displaced due to ecological circumstances. 'The absence of a definition and legal provisions for those displaced by climate and environmental issues', writes Lydia Ayame Hiraide, 'means that people already vulnerable to environmental catastrophe may find difficulty accessing adequate protection and support to resettle elsewhere' (2023: 271).[4]

The response to this forecast from a progressive standpoint dedicated to human rights and social equality would be for individual nation-states to work together, to commit to alternatives to fossil fuel use, and for the wealthier nations most responsible for the climate emergency to provide sanctuary to people left dispossessed of their homelands by the effects of global warming. Such a stance has been voiced by the postcolonial historian Dipesh Chakrabarty, who argues that the global impact of ecological breakdown points us intellectually to 'a universal that arises from a shared sense of catastrophe' (2009: 222). Similarly, Spencer and Valassopoulos maintain:

> If the increasing concentration of carbon dioxide and other greenhouse gases irrevocably alters the atmosphere and therefore the future of all life on Earth, then the ideology of 'every man for himself' is immediately proved false and new forms of collective responsibility become urgently necessary. Something similar could be said about migration. Nothing demonstrates the obsolescence or at least the invidiousness of borders and the offensive arbitrariness of state-sanctioned distinctions between citizens and non-citizens more than the spectacle of refugees herded into camps, incarcerated in cages, tortured and enslaved in Libya or callously abandoned to their deaths in the Mediterranean.
>
> (2021: 100)

The politics driving resurgences in nationalism across Europe and America, however, suggest that, in the short to mid-term at least, climate breakdown will be deployed as a justification for governments across the Global North to strengthen their border controls, arguing that 'outsiders' imperil the future survival of the nation-state. Thus, as Neel Ahuja notes, 'understanding migration in an era of climate change' will not require 'a new universal vision of human history'; rather, what will be necessary is a comprehension of how 'the types of mobility networks available to people who experience weather disasters have everything to do with the outcomes of how environmental violence grafts on to the existing violences of racism, colonialism, and capitalism' (2021: 130).

Indeed, the increased militarization of borders and the policing of migrants is already being fuelled by the fallacious arguments that two of the key drivers of the climate emergency are overpopulation across the Global South and migration from periphery/semi-periphery nations to core nations.

These perspectives have their roots in the American environmental movement of the 1960s and 70s, and especially in the writing of neo-Malthusian environmentalists Paul R. Ehrlich (author of *The Population Bomb*, published in 1968) and Garratt Hardin. Through a reading of Hardin's reactionary article 'Living on a Lifeboat' (1974), one of the authors of this book, Matthew Whittle, has elsewhere defined the confluence of anti-migrant sentiment, concerns with overpopulation, and environmentalism as 'lifeboat nationalism' (Whittle, 2021). This term names the way in which wealthy nation-states in the Global North adopt the imagery of the already-full lifeboat to justify denying sanctuary to people fleeing regions that have been rendered inhospitable by the effects of global warming and unsustainable resource extraction.

The reality, however, is that population growth and migration are not responsible for the environmental polycrises that imperil the globe today. Research by David Satterthwaite (a contributor to the IPCC) shows that it is wealthy countries with slowly rising or even declining populations that have the largest reliance on fossil fuels (Satterthwaite, 2009). Moreover, as Andreas Malm and the Zetkin Collective maintain,

> practically every country in the global South that had moved into the spiral of self-sustaining economic growth predicated on fossil fuels had first experienced a *decline* in fertility rates. The fires rose to the sky where demography had lost importance. They burned through the accumulation of capital, not procreation.
>
> (2021: 173)[5]

A fixation on population size promotes a neo-Malthusian vision of the world that detracts from the culpability of the fossil fuel industry and places an emphasis on policing reproductive rights and global migration. Additionally, 'overly apocalyptic assertions of depopulation', argues Anthony Carrigan, can potentially 'play into the hands of disaster capitalists' (2011: 287), working to legitimize the integration of postcolonial regions more firmly into the very neoliberal economic structures that are exacerbating the climate crisis.

Along with the consumption of goods and services that need oil and coal for their production, distribution, and disposal, it is the military industrial complex that acts as one of the biggest contributors to the damaging levels of greenhouse gases in the Earth's atmosphere. In *The Nutmeg's Curse: Parables for a Planet in Crisis*, Ghosh recognizes that 'a country's ability to project military force is directly connected to the size of its carbon footprint', a fact that has 'been true since the early nineteenth century' (2021: 121). At the same time, Ghosh acknowledges the irony that, while it is the military industrial complex of the US and other wealthy nations that bears a large responsibility for the climate emergency, 'climate-related disasters have themselves become a contributing factor in the steep increase in military spending that is underway around the world' (129). This is indicative of the climate crisis being framed not in ecological terms but as a national security concern, breathing new life into the 'clash of civilizations' discourse that was integral to the US–UK 'War on Terror' at the beginning of the twenty-first century.[6]

If eco-dystopian visions of the future can be co-opted into the anti-migrant and national security discourses of 'green nationalism', what role can literature play in providing an affective, subjective, and experiential dimension to Environmental Science data in a manner that also challenges nationalist isolationism? We saw in our chapter 'Earth' how Octavia Butler's dystopian novels *Parable of the Sower* (1993) and *Parable of the Talents* (1998) depict climate breakdown as fuelling social divisions, nationalist and religious fundamentalism, and mass migration to other planets. To this we can add a number of contemporary, eco-dystopian novels that avowedly confront the invidious correlations between climate action, nationalist conceptions of belonging, and the scapegoating of migrants and refugees. From across Australia, America, Europe, and Asia, these include Alexis Wright's *The Swan Book* (2013), Omar El Akkad's *American War* (2017), Maja Lunde's *The End of the Ocean* (2017, originally published in Norway as *Blå*), Yoko Tawada's *Scattered All Over the Earth* (2018), and John Lanchester's *The Wall* (2019).

Of these, *The Swan Book* stands out as a novel that confronts us with the confluent experiences of climate-induced migration, colonial dispossession, and what Rob Nixon terms 'displacement without moving', which refers to 'the loss of land and resources [...] that leaves communities stranded in a place stripped of the very characteristics that made it inhabitable' (2011: 19). Central to the plot is the relationship between the young Aboriginal protagonist, Oblivia, and the white Italian refugee, Bella Donna, who are forced to live together on a swamp that has been turned into an Aboriginal detention centre run by the Army in Australia. Bella Donna explains to Oblivia that when 'wild weather storms, or the culmination of years of droughts, high temperature and winds' ([2013] 2006: 25) left Europe uninhabitable, the rich escaped in planes while the poor were left to drift 'among the other countless stateless millions of sea gypsies looking for somewhere to live' (23). To the Aboriginal community of the swamp, however, such treatment is not considered exceptional; these were '[c]onversations that meant nothing to overwhelmed swamp people who had always been told to forget the past by anyone thinking that they were born conquerors. They already knew what it was like to lose Country' (40). In this way, Wright's dystopian narrative eschews the trope of exceptionality: the twin violences of displacement and ecological despoliation have become an unremarkable occurrence to the Aboriginal inhabitants of the swamp, meaning that *The Swan Book* can be read as blending environmental apocalypticism with Aghoghovwia's concept of 'apocalyptic realism'.

Additionally, Wright blends human and nonhuman stories of dislocation together, foregrounding how any awareness of climate-induced migration must also be attentive to other-than-human lifeforms. When the detention centre is destroyed, and superstorms flood Australia's cities, Oblivia recounts her experience of forced migration through new lands 'half-destroyed by war' or 'slapped hard in the face by famine' (5). '[E]ven when I bring gifts to their door', she says, 'the local people, although hungry and tired, find the courage to reject a person from their paradise no matter how far they have travelled, simply for not belonging' (5). We know from the novel's outset that this is Oblivia's fate and yet in the denouement she returns to the decimated detention camp and nurses one of the black swans that are co-inhabitants of the swamp. Throughout the novel, the swans act as the central symbol of animal dislocation and extirpation, having been forced to migrate to new lands because of habitat eradication. The scene of inter-species communion at the novel's close is marked by Oblivia asking herself, 'How would she keep telling the swan another million times that the lake was gone, having to hold its beating heart closer to prevent its wings from spreading in a swim through the dust' (333). The fact that this question is left open means that *The Swan Book* stages a form of human–animal kinship, whereby survival is coterminous and not based on a conflict over space, whilst also actively resisting the notion that the labour of fighting for ecological recovery lies either with Indigenous communities or with those born into a world on fire.

Wright offers one example of how environmental apocalypticism can be adopted in a manner that is cognizant of both the colonial contexts of climate breakdown and the threat of exclusionary nationalisms rising with the seas. This demonstrates how we cannot rely only upon narrowly Western-centric eco-dystopian visions of a near-to-distant future after the worst effects of climate breakdown have begun to be felt across the wealthy nations of the Global North. Instead, as we have done throughout this book, we must read globally, for it is in the textual spaces of novels, poems, and plays from/set in postcolonial and Indigenous regions where new and equitable forms of sociality across national/continental borders can be envisioned. We must also be alert to the co-option of environmental apocalypticism by the exclusionary discourses of 'green nationalism', meaning that an advocacy for the marginalized voices of dislocated people seeking asylum must be a core preoccupation in the environmental humanities.

It is through literature, moreover, that the epistemologies, grassroots activist movements, and environmental ethics of historically persecuted, Indigenous peoples can be represented in a manner that frames climate breakdown as the latest and most globally impactful iteration of capitalist–imperial eco-, geno-, and epistemicide. Acknowledging this upends the colonial and racist hierarchies that treat human and more-than-human persons of frontier regions as mere testing zones, as disposable, or even as already disposed of. Indeed, one of the great criticisms of the painfully slow response to the climate and ecological emergencies by global superpowers is that they have been able to ignore environmental polycrises *because* they have thus far been least and last affected. The writers and writing we have explored here counteract the extractive and exploitative logics of colonialism and capitalism, recognizing how the scandalous unevenness of the experience of capitalist modernity (a point foundational to the work of the Warwick Research Collective) registers globally in both spatial and temporal terms. They depict the development of capitalist modernity *not* in terms that cast Indigenous and (formerly) colonized peoples as primitive, backwards, and as somehow representative of a living past, but as leading writers of the future of the planet as a multiply constituted and connected whole. This approach calls for further analyses of distinct and disparate literatures directed towards a *shared* responsibility to protect and preserve global environments if we are to establish socially equitable and ecologically sustainable futures.

Notes

1 For an account of the 'rise of cli-fi', see Glass (2013).
2 For a relatively expansive list and description of cli-fi novels, plays, and poetry, see also Trexler and Johns-Putra (2011) and Burnett (2018).
3 See Parenti (2011), Miller (2017), and Ahuja (2021).
4 In place of 'climate refugee', Hiraide advocates for adopting the terminology 'ecologically displaced persons'. Doing so, she says, would mean that 'the environmental cause of internal displacement is established without the burden of racialisation, xenophobia, and division. Such discussions enable audiences to cultivate compassion, sympathy, and empathy for the current and potential victims of ecological change' (276).
5 This assertion is based on research conducted by Stephenson et al. (2010).
6 For a discussion of the relationship between climate change and national security policy, see Whittle (2023).

Bibliography

Aghoghovwia, Philip. 2021. "Anthropocene Arts: Apocalyptic Realism and the Post-Oil Imaginary in the Niger Delta." In *Climate Realism: The Aesthetics of Weather and Atmosphere in the Anthropocene*, edited by Lynn Badia, Marija Centinić, and Jeff Diamanti, 33–46. London: Routledge.

Ahuja, Neel. 2021. *Planetary Specters: Race, Migration, and Climate Change in the Twenty-First Century*. Chapel Hill: University of North Carolina Press.

Berlatsky, Noah. 2014. "Why Sci-Fi Keeps Imagining the Subjugation of White People." *The Atlantic*, April 25: https://www.theatlantic.com/entertainment/archive/2014/04/why-sci-fi-keeps-imagining-the-enslavement-of-white-people/361173 [accessed May 25, 2023].

Buell, Lawrence. 1995. *The Environmental Imagination: Thoreau, Nature Writing, and the Formation of American Culture*. London: Harvard University Press.

Burnett, Lucy. 2018. "Firing the climate canon—a literary critique of the genre of climate change." *Green Letters* 22, no. 2: 161–180. doi:10.1080/14688417.2018.1472027.

Carrigan, Anthony. 2011. "'Out of This Great Tragedy Will Come a World Class Tourism Destination': Disaster, Ecology, and Post-Tsunami Tourism Development in Sri Lanka." In *Postcolonial Ecologies: Literatures of the Environment*, edited by Elizabeth DeLoughrey and George B. Handley, 273–290. Oxford: Oxford University Press.

Chakrabarty, Dipesh. 2009. "The Climate of History: Four Theses." *Critical Inquiry* 35, no. 2: 197–222.
Clement, Viviane, *et al.* 2021. *Groundswell Part 2: Acting on Internal Climate Migration.* Washington D.C.: World Bank.
DeLoughrey, Elizabeth. 2015. "Ordinary Futures: Interspecies Worldings in the Anthropocene." In *Global Ecologies and the Environmental Humanities,* edited by Elizabeth DeLoughrey, Jill Didur, and Anthony Carrigan, 352–372. London: Routledge.
Ghosh, Amitav. 2016. *The Great Derangement.* London: University of Chicago Press.
Ghosh, Amitav. 2021. *The Nutmeg's Curse: Parables for a Planet in Crisis.* London: John Murray.
Glass, Rodge. 2013. "Global warning: The rise of 'cli-fi'." *The Guardian*, May 31: https://www.theguardian.com/books/2013/may/31/global-warning-rise-cli-fi [accessed May 28, 2023].
Hiraide, Lydia Ayame. 2023. "Climate refugees: A useful concept? Towards an alternative vocabulary of ecological displacement." *Politics* 43, no. 2: 267–282. https://doi.org/10.1177/02633957221077257.
Hughes, Rowland, and Pat Wheeler. 2013. "Introduction: Eco-Dystopias: Nature and the Dystopian Imagination." *Critical Survey* 25, no. 2: 1–6.
Johns-Putra, Adeline. 2016. "Climate change in literature and literary studies: From cli-fi, climate change theater and ecopoetry to ecocriticism and climate change criticism." *WIREs Clim Change* 7: 266–282. doi:10.1002/wcc.385.
Malm, Andreas. 2017. "'This is the Hell That I Have Heard Of': Some Dialectical Images in Fossil Fuel Fiction." *Forum for Modern Language Studies* 53, no. 2: 121–141. doi:10.1093/fmls/cqw090.
Malm, Andreas, and the Zetkin Collective. 2021. *White Skin, Black Fuel: On the Danger of Fossil Fascism.* London: Verso.
Miller, Todd. 2017. *Storming the Wall: Climate Change, Migration, and Homeland Security.* San Francisco: City Lights.
Nixon, Rob. 2011. *Slow Violence and the Environmentalism of the Poor.* Cambridge, MA: Harvard University Press.
Parenti, Christian. 2011. *Tropic of Chaos: Climate Change and the New Geography of Violence.* New York: Nation Books.
Roy, Arundhati. 2010. "The Trickledown Revolution." *Outlook*, September 20: https://www.outlookindia.com/magazine/story/the-trickledown-revolution/267040 [accessed May 25, 2023].
Satterthwaite, David. 2009. "The implications of population growth and urbanization for climate change." *Environment and Urbanization* 21, no. 2: 545–567.
Stephenson, Judith, *et al.* 2010. "Population Dynamics and Climate Change: What Are the Links?" *Journal of Public Health* 32, no. 2 (June): 150–156. https://doi.org/10.1093/pubmed/fdq038.
Trexler, Adam, and Adeline Johns-Putra. 2011. "Climate change in literature and literary criticism". *Wiley Interdisciplinary Reviews: Climate Change*, no. 2: 185–200.
Whiteley, Andrea, *et al.* 2016. "Climate Change Imaginaries: Examining Expectation Narratives in Cli-Fi Novels." *Bulletin of Science, Technology & Society* 36, no. 1: 28–37. doi:10.1177/0270467615622845.
Whittle, Matthew. 2021. "Hostile Environments, Climate Justice, and the Politics of the Lifeboat." *Moving Worlds: A Journal of Transcultural Writings* 20, no. 2, special issue: Postcolonial Futures: 83–98.

Whittle, Matthew. 2023. "The narrative practices of Hostile Environments: The story of the nation-as-family and the story of security." *Frontiers in Human Dynamics: Refugees and Conflict* 5 (April): open access. https://doi.org/10.3389/fhumd.2023.11441861.

Whyte, Kyle. 2018. "Indigenous Science (Fiction) for the Anthropocene: Ancestral Dystopias and Fantasies of Climate Change Crises." *Environment and Planning E: Nature and Space* 1, no. 1–2: 224–242. https://doi.org/10.1177/2514848618777621.

Wright, Alexis. [2013] 2016. *The Swan Book*. St Ives: Constable.

Glossary of Key Terms

Animal studies an interdisciplinary field of academic study focusing on human–animal relations (see also *ecocentrism; environmental humanities; kinship; speciesism*).

Anthropocene the proposed geological epoch that is characterized by the changes brought about to the earth's climate, geology, and ecosystems by human activity (see also *billion Black Anthropocenes; Capitalocene; Cthulucene; Holocene; Plantationocene*).

Anthropocentrism a perspective that sees humans as separate from, and more valuable than, other forms of life (see also *Cartesianism; ecocentrism; environmental humanities; kinship*).

Atmosphere a component of the Earth's climate system comprising layers of gas (see also *biosphere; cryosphere; hydrosphere; lithosphere*).

Bhopal disaster a fatal gas leak at a pesticide plant in the Indian city of Bhopal in 1984.

Billion black Anthropocenes a term coined by Kathryn Yusoff that conceptualizes the history of colonialism and transatlantic slavery as core drivers of the Anthropocene (see also *Anthropocene; Capitalocene; Cthulucene; Holocene; Plantationocene*).

Biosphere a component of the Earth's climate system that comprises all living things (see also *atmosphere; cryosphere; hydrosphere; lithosphere*).

Capitalist–imperialism a term denoting the expansion of European empires as an advanced and globalized stage of economic development.

Capitalocene a term devised by Andreas Malm and Alf Hornborg, and popularized by Jason W. Moore, that interprets the economic relations of capitalism as the main driver of human impacts on the Earth's ecosystems (see also *Anthropocene; billion Black Anthropocenes; Cthulucene; Holocene; Plantationocene*).

Carbon sink ecosystems capable of absorbing and storing carbon dioxide from the atmosphere in large quantities – e.g. rainforests, oceans, and peatlands.

Cartesianism the view proposed by René Descartes that humans are the only living organism with thought and self-consciousness; all other organisms operate like machines (see also *animal studies; anthropocentricism; ecocentrism; speciesism*).

Charismatic megafauna a collective term for large, popular, and photogenic mammals such as whales, elephants, and polar bears that dominate the imagery of environmentalism (see also *conservationism*).

Cli-fi a neologism coined by Dan Bloom for 'climate-fiction' that adopts many of the tropes associated with Science Fiction to dramatize the effects of climate change (see also *eco-dystopian literature; environmental apocalypticism*).

Climate justice a socio-political ideology that recognizes the unequal effects of climate breakdown and insists that any climate action must be rooted in social, political, and economic equality (see also *climate refugee; eco-apartheid; environmental racism*).

Climate refugee a term for people displaced due to the effects of climate crises. This is, however, not a legally recognized term (see also *climate justice; eco-apartheid; environmental racism*).

Conservationism a commitment to the preservation of nature (see also *eco-tourism*).

Cryosphere a component of the Earth's climate system comprising frozen ocean waters that make up ice and permafrost (see also *atmosphere; biosphere; hydrosphere; lithosphere*).

Cthulucene Donna Haraway's term for a new ecological epoch and ethical endeavour based on multispecies kinship, to follow the Anthropocene (see also *Anthropocene; billion Black Anthropocenes; Capitalocene; Holocene; Plantationocene*).

Decolonization the process whereby nation-states gain political, economic, and social independence from a colonizing country (see also *neo-colonialism; Pan-Africanism*).

De-extinction scientific research into the revival of extinct animals using DNA acquired either from fossils or from living specimens taken prior to extinction (see also *defaunation; sixth extinction*).

Defaunation a term devised by Rodolfo Dirzo et al. that places the crisis of species extinction alongside deforestation (see also *de-extinction; deforestation; sixth extinction*).

Deforestation the systematic clearing of trees from densely forested areas such as the Amazon rainforest, typically as part of the logging industry (see also *de-extinction; defaunation; sixth extinction*).

Eco-apartheid a term that denotes (i) the separation of humans from the natural world, or (ii) the structural inequities within and between societies that determine the benefits and burdens relating to fossil fuel extraction and use (see also *climate justice; climate refugee; environmental racism*).

Ecocentrism a view that values the natural environment and all living organisms (see also *animal studies; anthropocentrism; Cartesianism environmental humanities*).

Ecocide the mass destruction of ecosystems by human activities.
Ecocriticism a methodological approach to analysing the relationship between humans and the environment in literature, rooted in the interdisciplinary field of the environmental humanities (see also *animal studies; environmental humanities*).
Eco-dystopian literature a sub-genre of dystopian fiction interested specifically in imagining the world after the worst effects of climate breakdown have occurred (see also *eco-poetry; environmental apocalypticism*).
Eco-poetry a form of poetry that is preoccupied with nature and the environment (see also *eco-dystopian literature; environmental apocalypticism*).
Eco-tourism touristic activities focused on natural environments, often directed towards charismatic megafauna and linked to conservation initiatives – e.g. whale-watching (see also *charismatic megafauna; conservationism*).
Environmental apocalypticism a means of envisioning societies after the impacts of the climate emergency have occurred in order to inspire transformative social and political change in the present (see also *eco-dystopian literature; eco-poetry*).
Environmental humanities an interdisciplinary field of academic study focusing on the connections between human cultures and the environment (see also *ecocriticism*).
Environmental racism denotes the treatment of non-white societies and regions as frontier zones for resource extraction and/or sites of waste disposal (see also *climate justice; climate refugee; eco-apartheid; frontier zone*).
Epistemicide the marginalization, silencing, and/or destruction of systems of knowledge (see *epistemic violence*).
Epistemic violence coined by Gayatri Spivak to name the varied activities of dominant human groups that cause epistemicide (see also *epistemicide*).
Extractivism the industrial-scale removal of natural materials for use as resources, primarily through mining and drilling (see also *fossil fuels; greenhouse gases*).
First Nations a collective term for the Indigenous nations of Canada (see also *Indigenous; settler colonialism*).
Fossil fuels natural materials containing carbon and hydrogen that are formed from decomposed plants and animals – primarily oil, coal, and natural gas – and extracted from the Earth's crust and used for energy (see also *extractivism; greenhouse gases*).
Frontier zone a territory combining the exploitation of labour, extraction of resources, and production of waste. Usually dominated by the extraction of natural materials, including for food, energy and raw materials. (see also *eco-apartheid; environmental racism; extractivism; fossil fuels*).
Gas flaring the burning of methane from natural gases that are extracted along with oil during the drilling process (see also *extractivism; fossil fuels*).

Glossary of Key Terms

Geo-engineering the large-scale use of technology to mitigate against the effects of climate change by intervening in the Earth's ecosystems.

Golden spike an agreed-upon marker in stratigraphic material (e.g. rocks and ice) for geological change, often defining shifts in geological epochs (see also *Anthropocene; Holocene; Orbis spike*).

Greenhouse gases gases released from the burning of fossil fuels – primarily carbon dioxide and methane – that remain in the Earth's atmosphere and trap in heat from solar radiation (see also *extractivism; fossil fuels*).

Green nationalism the co-option of climate action initiatives in nationalist ideologies and political policies (see also *neo-Malthusianism*).

Green Revolution the U.S. and World Bank-funded marketing of pesticides, fertilizers, high-yield-variety seeds, and irrigation to South America and South-East Asia at the beginning of the Cold War era.

Heterotemporality the idea that world time is not homogenous, universal, or unified, but multiply conceptualized and experienced so that, for example, movement forwards and backwards through time is possible, even simultaneously.

Holocene the current geological epoch that began 11,700 years ago following the end of the Ice Age (see also *Anthropocene; billion Black Anthropocenes; Capitalocene; Cthulucene; Plantationocene*).

Humus the organic matter in soil that is made up of decomposed animals and plants, deriving from the Latin for 'ground'.

Hydrosphere a component of the Earth's climate system comprising water (see also *atmosphere; biosphere; cryosphere; lithosphere*).

Indigenous collective term for societies inhabiting a land prior to European colonization (see also *First Nations; Native American; Māori; settler colonialism*).

Kinship when rooted in Indigenous epistemologies, a term that refers to the connections between humans and the natural world, including plants, animals, the land, waterways, and the sky (see also *epistemicide; First Nations; Indigenous; lifeways; Native American; Māori*).

Lifeways term used in association with Indigenous belief systems to encompass the idea of human life lived responsibly alongside, with, and through the spirit worlds of local bioregions. The term combines the holistic contexts of Indigenous cosmologies, stories, worldviews, kinship, language, governance, environmental knowledge, etc. (see also *epistemicide; First Nations; Indigenous; Native American; Māori*).

Lithosphere a component of the Earth's climate system that comprises the crust and upper mantle layer (see also *atmosphere; biosphere; cryosphere; hydrosphere*).

Māori collective term for Indigenous communities inhabiting Aotearoa New Zealand prior to European colonization (see also *First Nations; Indigenous; Native American; settler colonialism*).

Maroons term to describe escaped African and African-descendant enslaved people in the Americas, Caribbean, and Indian Ocean.

Mercantilism economic philosophy based on trade and export, which formed the primary economic policy for dominant European nations across the fifteenth to eighteenth centuries.

Monocultural farming an agricultural process that involves mass-cultivation of one specific type of crop (or 'monocultural plantation'), or one specific species or breed of animal (e.g. the cheviot sheep).

More-than-human a theoretical, ecocentric term to denote biological connections between organisms, also known as 'other-than-human' (see also *anthropocentrism; ecocentrism*).

Native American a collective (and contested) term for the Indigenous nations of the US (see also *First Nations; Indigenous; Māori; settler colonialism*).

Neo-colonialism the continuing influence of industrialized, imperial, or post-imperial countries on the economic and political policies of formerly colonized, independent nations, rooted in Kwame Nkrumah's *Neo-colonialism: The Last Stage of Imperialism* (see also *capitalist–imperialism; decolonization; Pan-Africanism*).

Neo-Malthusianism the belief that population and migration controls are a key means of ensuring that the Earth remains habitable for human survival, rooted in the writing of the late-eighteenth-century English cleric Thomas Robert Malthus (see also *green nationalism*).

Orbis spike coined by Simon Lewis and Mark A. Maslin to name the 'golden spike' that marks a rapid dip in global levels of atmospheric CO_2 following the colonization of the Americas, with the lowest point recorded being in 1610 (derived from the Latin for 'world'). Suggested by Lewis and Maslin as the beginning of the Anthropocene (see also *Anthropocene; billion Black Anthropocenes; Capitalocene; golden spike; Holocene; Plantationocene; Cthulucene*).

Pan-Africanism a political/cultural ideology based on collaboration between independent African nation-states and the African diaspora, in opposition to European colonialism and neo-colonialism (see also *decolonization; neo-colonialism*).

Personhood when used in animal studies, a term denoting the extension of human rights to non-human animals, especially those that demonstrate the capacity for independent thought and culture (see also *animal studies; charismatic megafauna; ecocentrism*).

Petrocapitalism/imperialism a specific form of capitalism/imperialism that is tied to the profits generated through the extraction and commodification of crude oil (see also *capitalist–imperialism; extractivism; fossil fuels; greenhouse gases*).

Petro-fiction/drama/poetry,

or petro literature forms of literature that focus on the extraction and use of oil and its environmental impacts (see also *extractivism; fossil fuels; greenhouse gases*).

Petromodernity the socio-economic reliance on the extraction and consumption of oil (see also *extractivism; fossil fuels; greenhouse gases*).

Plantationocene an alternative to 'Anthropocene' positing that climate breakdown began with the shift to monocultural plantation farming that required the industrial-scale transportation of people, non-human animals, and foodstuffs as part of the transatlantic slave trade (see also *billion Black Anthropocenes; Capitalocene; Cthulucene; Holocene; monocultural farming*).

Plantocracy the dominant class of plantation and slave-owners in the Caribbean.

Rewilding a conservationist belief in the need to restore areas of nature to an uncultivated state, free of human intervention (see also *conservationism*).

Romanticism a movement in literature, originating in the eighteenth century, interested in the relationship between humans and the natural world (see also *eco-poetry*).

Settler colonialism a specific form of colonial domination whereby the colonizers seek to claim a territory as their national home, administer it from within, and displace or exterminate Indigenous societies to become the ruling and/or majority population (see also *Indigenous*).

Sixth extinction a term denoting how the contemporary rate of species extinction has been seen only five times in the Earth's history; the extinction of the dinosaurs constitutes the fifth global extinction event (see also *defaunation; de-extinction*).

Slow violence coined by Rob Nixon to name slow-moving, attritional, and unspectacular forms of violence committed by dominant human groups on the Earth's ecosystems.

Speciesism the anthropocentric belief that non-human animals are inferior to humans (see also *animal studies; anthropocentricism; Cartesianism; ecocentrism; kinship*).

Two-Eyed Seeing (*Etuaptmumk*) the advocation for a combination of traditional, Indigenous knowledges about the environment with 'Western' environmental scientific research (see also *Indigenous*).

World-ecology (from Jason Moore) theorizes that the pursuit of the endless accumulation of wealth in global capitalism is made possible by the production of nature (and humans as part of nature) in a web of life (see also *capitalist–imperialism; world-systems theory*).

World-systems theory (from Immanuel Wallerstein) conceptualizes the dynamic interconnectedness of global, capitalist economic systems that leads to the formation of core (industrial/post-industrial), semi-periphery (industrializing), and periphery (underdeveloped) nations (see also *capitalist–imperialism; world-ecology*).

Suggested Further Reading

Abberley, Will, et al. 2022. *Modern British Nature Writing, 1789–2020*. Cambridge: Cambridge University Press.
Adams, Jonathan S., and Thomas O. McShane. 1992. *The Myth of Wild Africa: Conservation without Illusion*. London: University of California Press.
Adams, William, and Martin Mulligan. 2003. *Decolonizing Nature: Strategies for Conservation in a Post-Colonial Era*. London: Routledge.
Aghoghovwia, Philip. 2022. *Violent Ecotropes: Petroculture in the Niger Delta*. Cape Town: HSRC Press.
Animal Studies Group. 2006. *Killing Animals*. Chicago: University of Illinois Press.
Aron, Adam R. 2023. *The Climate Crisis: Science, Impacts, Policy, Psychology, Justice, Social Movements*. Cambridge: Cambridge University Press.
Baker, Timothy C. 2022. *New Forms of Environmental Writing: Gleaning and Fragmentation*. London: Bloomsbury Academic.
Bezan, Sarah, and Robert McKay. 2022. *Animal Remains*. London: Routledge.
Boast, Hannah. 2020. *Hydrofictions: Water, Power and Politics in Israeli and Palestinian Literature*. Edinburgh: Edinburgh University Press.
Bonneuil, Christophe, and Jean-Baptiste Fressoz. 2017. *The Shock of the Anthropocene*. London: Verso.
Bracke, Astrid. 2018. *Climate Crisis and the 21st-Century British Novel*. London: Bloomsbury.
Braverman, Iris, ed. 2022. *Laws of the Seas: Interdisciplinary Currents*. London: Routledge.
Buck, Holly Jean. 2019. *After Geoengineering: Climate Tragedy, Repair, and Restoration*. London: Verso.
Buck, Holly Jean. 2021. *Ending Fossil Fuels: Why Net Zero is Not Enough*. London: Verso.
Caminero-Santangelo, Byron, and Garth Myers, eds. 2011. *Environment at the Margins: Literary and Environmental Studies in Africa*. Athens, Ohio: Ohio University Press.
Carrigan, Anthony. 2011. *Postcolonial Tourism: Literature, Culture and Environment*. London: Routledge.
Clark, Timothy. 2010. "Some Climate Change Ironies: Deconstruction, Environmental Politics and the Closure of Ecocriticism." *Oxford Literary Review* 32, no. 1: 131–149. http://www.jstor.org/stable/44030826.
Clark, Timothy. 2012. *The Cambridge Introduction to Literature and the Environment*. Cambridge: Cambridge University Press.

Clark, Timothy. 2015. *Ecocriticism on the Edge: The Anthropocene as a Threshold Concept*. London: Bloomsbury Academic.
Clark, Timothy. 2019. *The Value of Ecocriticism*. Cambridge: Cambridge University Press.
Daggett, Cara. 2018. "Petro-masculinity: Fossil Fuels and Authoritarian Desire." *Millennium* 47, no. 1: 25–44. https://doi.org/10.1177/0305829818775817.
Dawson, Ashley. 2020. *People's Power: Reclaiming the Energy Commons*. London: OR Books.
Deneholz Morse, Deborah, and Martin A. Danahay, eds. 2007. *Victorian Animal Dreams: Representations of Animals in Victorian Literature and Culture*. Aldershot: Ashgate.
Dimock, Wai Chee. 2020. *Weak Planet: Literature and Assisted Survival*. Chicago: University of Chicago Press.
Evans, Mel. 2015. *Artwash: Big Oil and the Arts*. London: Pluto Press.
Ferdinand, Malcolm. 2019. *Decolonial Ecology: Thinking from the Caribbean World*, trans. by Anthony Paul Smith. Cambridge: Polity Press.
Fiskio, Janet. 2021. *Climate Change, Literature, and Environmental Justice: Poetics of Dissent and Repair*. Cambridge: Cambridge University Press.
Gadgil, Madhav, and Ramachandra Guha. 1995. *Ecology and Equity: The Use and Abuse of Nature in Contemporary India*. London: Routledge.
Garrard, Greg, Alex Goodbody, George B. Handley, and Stephanie Posthumus. 2019. *Climate Change Scepticism: A Transnational Ecocritical Analysis*. London: Bloomsbury Academic.
Guha, Ramachandra, and J. Martinez-Alier. 1997. *Varieties of Environmentalism: Essays North and South*. London: Earthscan.
Guha, Ramachandra. 2000. *Environmentalism: A Global History*. London: Longman.
Hamouchene, Hamza, and Katie Sandwell. 2023. *Dismantling Green Colonialism: Energy and Climate Justice in the Arab Region*. London: Pluto Press.
Haraway, Donna. 2003. *The Companion Species Manifesto: Dogs, People, and Significant Otherness*. Chicago: Prickly Paradigm Press.
Hernandez, Jessica. 2022. *Fresh Banana Leaves: Healing Indigenous Landscapes Through Indigenous Science*. Berkley, California: North Atlantic Books.
Krenak, Ailton. 2020. *Ideas to Postpone the End of the World*, trans. by Anthony Doyle. Anansi International.
Lawrence Hyatt, Vera, and Rex Nettleford, eds. 1995. *Race, Discourse, and the Origin of the Americas*. London: Smithsonian Institute Press.
Maathai, Wangari. 2006. *Unbowed: A Memoir*. London: Arrow Books.
McDonald, David A. ed. 2002. *Environmental Justice in South Africa*. Ohio: Ohio University Press.
McFarland, Sarah E. 2021. *Ecocollapse Fiction and the Cultures of Human Extinction*. London: Bloomsbury Academic.
Mortimer-Sandilands, Catriona, and Bruce Erickson, eds. 2010. *Queer Ecologies: Sex, Nature, Politics, Desire*. Bloomington and Indianapolis: Indiana University Press.
Morton, Timothy. 2007. *Ecology Without Nature: Rethinking Environmental Aesthetics*. Cambridge MA: Harvard University Press.
Morton, Timothy. 2018. *Being Ecological*. London: Pelican.
Nagai, Kaori. 2020. *Imperial Beast Fables: Animals, Cosmopolitanism, and the British Empire*. Basingstoke: Palgrave Macmillan.

Nyberg, Daniel, Christopher Wright, and Vanessa Bowden. 2022. *Organising Responses to Climate Change: The Politics of Mitigation, Adaptation and Suffering.* Cambridge: Cambridge University Press.

Nyman, Jopi. 2003. *Postcolonial Animal Tales from Kipling to Coetzee.* New Delhi: Atlantic Publishers.

Oppermann, Serpil, and Serenella Iovino, eds. 2016. *Environmental Humanities: Voices from the Anthropocene.* London: Rowman and Littlefield.

Parham, John, and Louise Westling, eds. 2017. *A Global History of Literature and the Environment.* Cambridge: Cambridge University Press.

Roos, Bonnie, and Alex Hunt, eds. 2010. *Postcolonial Green: Environmental Politics and World Narratives.* London: University of Virginia Press.

Siperstein, Stephen, Shane Hall, and Stephanie LeManager, eds. 2016. *Teaching Climate Change in the Humanities.* London: Routledge.

Solnit, Rebecca, and Thelma Young Lutunatabua, eds. 2023. *Not Too Late: Changing the Climate Story from Despair to Possibility.* Chicago, IL: Haymarket Books.

Spiegel, Marjorie. 1996. *The Dreaded Comparison: Human and Animal Slavery.* New York: Mirror Books.

Subramanian, Meera. 2015. *Elemental India: The Natural World at a Time of Crisis and Opportunity.* Noida, Delhi: HarperCollins India.

Szeman, Imre, Jennifer Wenzel, and Patricia Yaeger. 2017. *Fueling Culture: 101 Words for Energy and Environment.* New York: Fordham University Press.

Tobias, Michael Charles, and Jane Grey Morrison. 2017. *Anthrozoology: Embracing Co-Existence in the Anthropocene.* Cham, Switzerland: Springer Nature.

Tsing, Anna Lowenhaupt. 2021. *The Mushroom at the End of the World: On the Possibility of Life in Capitalist Ruins.* Oxford: Princeton University Press.

Van Dooren, Thom. 2016. *Flight Ways: Life and Loss at the Edge of Extinction.* New York: Columbia University Press.

Wainwright, Joel, and Geoff Mann. 2018. *Climate Leviathan: A Political Theory of Our Planetary Future.* London: Verso.

Index

Aboriginal Australians 190
Aboriginal Tasmanians 170, 176n22; see also Tasmania
Abrahams, Peter, see Mine Boy
Achebe, Chinua 9, 136
Addo Elephant National Park 136
Africa 28, 64, 75–6, 107, 112–113, 123, 138, 158–9, 174n5, 183; air pollution in 104, 106, 124n7; colonisation of 29, 32; decolonization of 57; deforestation in 137; dirge literature of 81; eco-apartheid in 122–3; effect of geo-engineering upon 24n10; hunting in 133–6, 139, 155, 161; Indigenous knowledges of 21, 43, 46, 70; neocolonialism in 22, 112; oil production in 77–8, 104, 114, 123n5; pesticide use in 121; presidents of 57; represented in Anglo-American literature 4, 156–7; slavery from 30–1, 34, 38, 43, 47–8, 55, 71n2; species loss in 10, 130,136, 176n21; trade unions of 58, 71n6; see also British East Africa; Kenya; Niger Delta; Nigeria; Scramble for Africa; South Africa
African American literature 33
African Charter, the 123
Agary, Kaine 99n1
Aghoghovwia, Philip 76, 82, 86, 190
agriculture; see farm, farming
Ahuja, Neel 123, 188, 192n3
air pollution 22, 51, 52, 59, 78, 103–5, 108, 111, 122–3, 123n1, 123n2, 124n7, 129, 130, 185
Akpik, Fannie Kuutuuq 91
Alaska 10, 22, 46, 75, 86–99, 183; see also Inuit cultures and communities; Iñupiat cultures and communities

Alaskan Native Claims Settlement Act 91
Amazon (corporation) 3
Amazon rainforest 29
American War (El Akkad, Omar) 190
Americas, the 14, 21, 30, 31, 33, 47, 48; see also New World, the; North America; United States of America, US
Amnesty International 105
Angola 69, 112
animal studies 10, 11, 132
Anthropocene, the 6, 7, 12–18, 24n12, 24n14, 31, 32, 103, 162, 186, 187; see also Crutzen, Paul; Yusoff, Kathryn
Anthropocene Working Group 14; see also Anthropocene, the
anti-capitalism 131, 182
anti-colonialism 18, 21, 29, 32, 57, 58, 70, 131, 158, 182
anti-racism 32, 53, 57–8; see also racism; slave rebellion
Aotearoa New Zealand 10, 133, 142–4
apartheid 53, 54, 71n3
Arawak 30
Arctic 22, 75–6, 86–98, 99n4, 99n5, 183; ice melt 129, 130, 183, 185; see also Alaska; Inuit cultures and communities; Iñupiat cultures and communities
Armitage, Simon 98
Armstrong, Philip 132, 141
Asia 30, 87, 190; Cold War politics and 114; eco-apartheid in 122; effect of geo-engineering upon 24n10; the Green Revolution in 115; indentured labour from 44; ivory trade and 134–5, 173n3; pesticide use in 121;

represented in Anglo-American literature 4;
Asian elephant 164–5, 173n3
Atlantic Ocean 30
atmosphere 1–2, 103, 184; the Anthropocene and the 103; chemical leaks and the 121; eco-apartheid and the 104; gas flaring and the 78; greenhouse gases and the 183, 188, 189; Green Revolution and the 22; Inuit cosmology and the 91; oil spills and the 105
Attridge, Derek 8
Atwood, Margaret, *see* 'MaddAdam' trilogy
Australasia: factory farming in 174n8; species loss in 10, 183; *see also* Aoetearoa New Zealand; Australia; Tasmania
Australia 163, 167–69, 175n20, 190–1; colonisation of 131; deforestation in 176n21; mining in 49; species loss in 134, 168, 175n20; de-extinction projects in 163, 166, 167, 169
autobiography 31–2

Bacigalupi, Paolo 9; *The Windup Girl* 71n7
ballad poetry 118
Banda, Hastings 57
Barad, Karen 39
Bassey, Nnimmo 21, 74, 78, 82–5; 'I will not dance to your beat' 84–5; *We Thought It Was Oil But It Was Blood* 82–3
Benin, British invasion of 139, 174 n.5
Bera, Baribor 79
Bessora, *see Petroleum*
'Bhopal' (Avaes Mohammad) 22, 104, 115, 118–119, 121, 126n23
Bhopal disaster, the 22, 104, 114–115, 116–119, 120–21, 125 n.19, 125n21, 183
Bhopal: A Prayer for Rain 125n20
biodiversity 163, 166, 167; loss of 2, 62, 78, 105, 129–30, 154–5, 162, 168, 172, 175n21, 182
biosphere 1–2, 183, 184
bird 90, 91–4, 118, 124n17, 129, 148, 168; arctic loon 91–2; chicken 133, 148, 149, 151–2; cormorant 92–3, 94; grouse 62; moa 143; kiwi 143; passenger pigeon 130, 164, 165; pheasant 62; weka 143

Bird Rose, Deborah 132, 166
bison (buffalo) 133, 151, 152, 153–54
Black War (Tasmania) 170, 176n22
Blixen, Karen 154; *Out of Africa* 23, 133, 156–59
Bloom, Dan 185
blue humanities 74
Bodenhorn, Barbara 87, 95, 164, 165
Bontemps, Arna 16, 32–33, 37–41; *Black Thunder, Gabriel's Revolt: Virginia, 1800* 21, 28, 32–3, 37–41, 45–6, 70; *Drums at Dusk* 37; *Story of the Negro* 37; *Popo and Fifina* 37
Brazil 29, 46, 69
Brecht, Bertolt 60, 61
Bristol Bay 92–4, 99n8, 99n9; *see also* okpik, dg nanouk
British East Africa 133, 135, 154–6, 158, 161; *see also* Kenya
Buell, Lawrence 184–5
Burma *see* Myanmar
Büscher, Bram 162
Butler, Octavia 33, 41–47; *Parable of the Sower* 21, 28, 32, 41–3, 44, 46–7, 70, 190; *Parable of the Talents* 21, 28, 32, 41, 43–7, 70, 190

Calvino, Italo, *see* 'The Petrol Pump'
Canada 46, 49, 62, 75, 87, 96, 153
Capitalocene 15–16, 17, 18, 29, 31; *see also* Malm, Andreas; Moore, Jason
Carbon Dreams (Susan M. Gaines) 71n7
carbon sinks 2, 29, 129
Caribbean 28, 33, 34, 37, 48, 57; 62, 183; colonisation of 14, 30–1, 47; deforestation in 36, 70; novels 43; slavery in 42–4, 183
Carrigan, Anthony 120, 124n14, 167, 189
Carson, Rachel, *see Silent Spring*
Cartesianism 145, 149
Casanova, Pascale 24n9
cattle 29, 54, 55, 57, 149, 152; cows 68, 83
Césaire, Aimé 35
Ceylon, trophy hunting in 158
Chakrabarty, Dipesh 188
Chamoiseau, Patrick, *see Texaco*
charismatic megafauna 133, 141, 148, 167, 172
China 29, 87, 151, 152; air pollution in 123, 126n25; book publishing in 24n4; Communism in 115, 151–2; the Green

Revolution and 124n15; human rights in 151–2
Christianity 32, 42, 51
Chrulew, Matthew 132
Church, George 164, 169
Cities of Salt (Abdelrahman Munif) 76
class 3, 12, 15, 19, 20, 159; African-American class struggle 33; activism and 111–112, 124n11; conservationism and 161; eco-apartheid and 22, 108–10, 123; factory farming and 150; hunting and 61, 63, 137, 155; the Industrial Revolution and 48; neocolonialism and 104; political theatre and 60–1; *see also* workers' unions
cli-fi, climate fiction 8, 185, 186, 192 n.1, 192n2
climate justice 18, 22, 104, 124n11, 184
climate refugee 187, 192n4
coal 19, 28, 49, 54, 62, 63, 68, 70, 75, 84, 189; the Anthropocene and 14, 16; British law against use of 103; the Industrial Revolution and 48; *see also* mines, mining
Coetzee, J. M. 152; *Elizabeth Costello* 22, 133, 148–51; *The Lives of Animals* 148, 149–51
Cold War, the 114, 115
Columbus, Christopher 14, 30, 31, 47, 48; *see also* New World, the
Comaroff, Jean 75–6, 77
Comaroff, John 75–6, 77
Congo Free State 135
Conrad, Joseph, *see Heart of Darkness*
conservationism 88, 131, 134, 153, 161, 166, 172, 174n13, 183; debates about 161–63; elephants and 133, 138; hunting and 155, 161–2; international conservation movement 23, 134, 161; ivory smuggling and 135–6; whales and 140–1; *see also* The International Union for the Conservation of Nature (IUCN) Red List
Convention on International Trade in Endangered Species (CITES) 136
COP27 6
corn 31, 37
Côte d'Ivoire 135
cotton 15, 31, 48
Covid-19 6, 95
Crimean War 62
crofts, crofters, crofting 63, 64, 67–9

Crutzen, Paul 12, 13, 15–17, 31; *see also* Anthropocene, the
cryosphere 1, 21, 74, 184; Indigenous awareness of changes to the 88; people of the 96–7; *see also* Arctic
Cthulucene, *see* Haraway, Donna
cyanide 57, 116
Cyclonopaedia (Reza Negarestani) 71n7

Dakota Access Pipeline 131
Damrosch, David 24n9
Davies, Jeremy 12, 13
Dawson, Ashley 164, 166, 167, 175n13
de-extinction 23, 134, 163–67, 171–73; *see also* extinction; sixth extinction, the
defaunation 130, 134, 166, 170, 172; *see also* extinction
deforestation 2, 21, 31, 33, 40, 45, 70, 129, 182, 185; the Amazon and 29; Australasia and 168–70, 175n21; colonialism and 28, 36, 47, 40, 137; monocultural farming and 29–30, 40; Scotland and 62; species loss and 130, 165
dehumanization 120, 157, 159; of colonized peoples 133; extractivist labour and 52, 55; factory farming and 174n8; of Indigenous populations 131, 170; plantation slavery and 43
Delahunt, Meaghan, *see The Red Book*
DeLoughrey, Elizabeth 43, 74, 186
Devi, Mahasweta, *see* 'Dhowli'
'Dhowli' (Mahasweta Devi) 125n18
Diemberger, Hildegard 88
Dimock, Wai Chee 7, 24n9
Diogenes of Sinope 52
Dirzo, Rodolfo 129–130
disaster (ecological) 9, 107, 170, 173, 188, 189; cli-fi and 184, 186; disaster biocapitalism 166–7, 169, 173; disaster capitalism 189; disaster studies 167; postcolonial disaster fiction 167; *see also* Bhopal disaster
disease 2, 14, 30, 31, 41, 51, 59, 63, 78, 105, 106, 109, 110
Dobee, Saturday 79
dodo, extinction of 130, 165, 167, 169
dog 52, 55, 120, 168
Dooren, Thom van 132, 166
Douglass, Frederick 31
drought 2, 167, 172, 188, 190; deforestation and 29; geo-engineering and 24n10; India and 115, 116

Duckert, Lowell 20, 74
Duffy, Carol Ann 98
Dunning, Norma, *see Eskimo Pie and the Poetics of Inuit Identity*
Dutch disease (economic theory) 77, 85
dystopia 21, 28, 41, 46, 148, 185–7, 190; de-extinction and 164, 169; *see also* eco-dystopian literature

Eaglestone, Robert 2
Earthworks 55
Eawo, Nordu 79
eco-apartheid 22, 104, 122–23
eco-dystopian literature 184–87, 190, 191; *see also* dystopia
eco-poetry 9, 77, 98–9, 99n1
eco-materialism 10–11
eco-tourism 133, 140; *see also* tourism
ecocriticism 9, 10, 11, 20, 74; postcolonial ecocriticism 120, 132
ecosystems 13, 23, 134, 163; the Anthropocene and 12; collapse of 23n1; destruction of 6, 30, 33, 47, 165, 182, 184; effect of Highland Clearances on 63–4; effect of mining on 50; effect of oil drilling on 91, 94, 98; Indigenous cosmologies and 20, 144; ocean ecosystems 142; protection/revival of 2, 172
education 4, 19
Edwardson, Rachel Nutaaq Ayałhuq Naŋinaaq 20, 91, 140
Egya, Sule Emmanuel 84, 110
Ehrlich, Paul R. 189
Omar, El Akkad, *see American War*
Ellams, Inua, *see* 'Fuck/Empire'
The End of the Ocean (Maja Lunde) 190
Enmakaje (Swarga) (Ambikasutan Mangad) 125n18
environmental racism 119, 120, 122; *see also* racism
The Epic of Gilgamesh 9
Equiano, Olauda 31
Eskimo Pie and the Poetics of Inuit Identity (Norma Dunning) 174n11
Estes, Nick 18, 131, 152
Etuaptmumk (Two-Eyed Seeing) 88
Expressway (Sina Queyras) 71n7
extinction 1, 6, 23n1, 94, 129–34, 153, 163, 165, 167, 173, 185; Australia and 168, 175n20, 191; Aboriginal Tasmanians and 170; buffalo (bison) and 133, 152–3; colonialism and 130–1, 160; cultural responses to 131; deforestation and 169; elephants and 136–7, 138; Extinction Studies 166; settler colonialism and 163, 168–9; slavery and 31; slow violence and 83; Tasmanian tiger and 168–9; whales and 140, 141, 147; *see also* de-extinction; sixth extinction, the
Extinction Rebellion 6

Fanon, Frantz 106, 124n7; *The Wretched of the Earth* 113; *Black Skin, White Masks* 159
farm, farming 5, 29, 54, 62, 65, 110, 111, 136, 155, 168, 169, 170; factory farming 148–50, 174n8; industrial farming complex 151; in literature 44, 55, 158, 170; monocultural farming 21, 29–30, 33, 59, 61–2, 70, 152; pesticide use in 114, 116, 121, 124n17, 125n18; and sustainability 5, 54, 132
Fauna (Donna Mazza) 163
feminism 21, 29, 53, 54, 57, 59, 70; ecofeminism 103
Ferber, Edna, *see Giant*
Fifth Pan-African Congress 57; *see also* Pan-Africanism
Finch-Hatton, Denys 157–58, 159
fire 2, 36, 189, 191; discovery and control of 15; gas flaring and 106–7, 108, 111; land clearance and 29, 36, 46; wildfires 3, 29, 167, 188
First Nations 20, 62, 75, 88, 151, 153, 174n10
fish 62, 76, 82, 92, 93, 105, 116, 143; shark 129, 143
fishing 62, 65, 66, 78, 95, 106, 142; Māori customs and 142; no-fish zones 5; sixth extinction and 129
Fletcher, Robert 162
flood 3, 9, 40, 167, 186, 188
food 14, 42–3, 23, 46, 52, 54, 59, 71n6, 93, 95, 130, 173n1; food production 28, 29, 50, 114, 116, 133, 141, 147–8, 150; food industry 22, 133, 134, 150–4, 173n1; food security 1, 87, 115; seafood 92
Ford, Henry 148
fossil fuels 1, 2, 3, 5, 9, 15, 69, 70, 71; the Anthropocene and 103; cli-fi and 186; consumption of/reliance on 9, 13–14, 22, 23, 49, 72, 74, 76, 89, 182–3, 184, 188, 189; geo-engineering and 24n10;

global warming and 141; polluting effects of 96, 98–9, 104–5
Friends of the Earth International 78
French revolution, the 34
A Friend of the Earth (T.C. Boyle) 185
'Fuck/Empire' (Inua Ellams) 22, 133, 139–140, 154, 161

Gaard, Greta 103, 123
Gaelic 64, 65
Gaia principle (James Lovelock) 18
Gaines, Susan M., *see Carbon Dreams*
Gandhi, Indira 115
Garko, Adam Usman 99n1
Garricks, Chiemeka 99n1
Garvey, Amy Ashwood 57
gas flaring 22, 68, 78, 85, 104–114, 123n4, 123n5, 124n6, 183
Gautreaux, Tim 71n7
Gbooko, Daniel 79
Gee, Maggie, *see The Ice People*
gender 3, 8, 12, 19, 20, 70, 108, 145; activism and 111–112, 124n11; eco-apartheid and 22, 104; marriage and 53; neocolonialism and 104; *see also* feminism
genocide 76, 78, 191; of Aboriginal Tasmanians 170–1, 176n22; the Anthropocene and 17, 31; Caribbean history and 30–1; colonialism and 14, 31, 130, 132; cultural genocide 153; sci-fi and 187; slavery and 37, 47
geo-engineering 13, 17, 24n10
Ghosh, Amitav 7, 8, 9, 60, 76; *The Great Derangement* 5, 6–7, 183, 186; *Gun Island* 183; *The Hungry Tide* 142; *The Nutmeg's Curse* 189
Giant (Edna Ferber) 71n7
Gilroy, Paul 122
Glen Grey Act (1894) 54
Global Assessment Report on Biodiversity and Ecosystem Services 129, 155
global warming 21, 22, 23n1, 74, 89, 90, 95, 96, 98–9, 103, 129, 185, 188, 189
globalization 1, 8, 9, 10, 11–12, 16, 182; colonialism and 47; of human foodstuffs 14, 150; neoliberalism and 65; and the whaling industry 141–2; world literature and 24n9
Gomba, Obari 21, 74; *The Ascent Stone* 80, 85

Grant Museum of Zoology 159
Great Acceleration 13, 14; *see also* Anthropocene
greenhouse gases 2, 13, 95, 103, 123n2, 183, 188, 189
green nationalism 184, 190, 191
Green Revolution, the 10, 22, 104, 114–115, 121, 124n15, 124n16
Griever: An American Monkey King in China (Gerald Vizenor) 22, 133, 151–2, 173
Gurnah, Abdulrazak 157

Habila, Helon 99n1; *Oil on Water* 22, 104, 106–8, 112, 113, 114
Haggard, H. Rider 154, 157; *She* 23, 133, 156; *King Solomon's Mines* 53
Haiti (San Domingo) 34–37, 39, 48; *see also* Hispaniola
Haitian revolution 32, 33, 34, 36–37
Haraway, Donna 16, 31, 39, 71n1, 149; Cthulucene, concept of 17–18
Harcharek, Jana Pausauraq 91
Hardin, Garratt 189
Hartman, Saidiya 41
Heart of Darkness (Joseph Conrad) 22, 53, 133, 136–137, 138, 140
Health of Mother Earth Foundation 78
Heise, Ursula K. 7, 131, 175n15, 175n19
heterotemporalities 28, 41, 46
Highland Clearances 59, 61, 62,
Highway, Tomson, *see Kiss of the Fur Queen*
Hispaniola 30, 48; *see also* Haiti
Hobbs Keckley, Elizabeth 31
Hogan, Linda, *see People of the Whale*
Høgsbjerg, Christian 32, 34
Holocaust, the 133, 150, 151, 152
Holocene 12, 13, 24n12, 31
Hornborg, Alf 15
horses 37, 41, 42
How Beautiful We Were (Imbolo Mbue) 22, 104, 112–114
Huggan, Graham 4, 37, 87, 120, 131, 132, 136, 147
Hughes, Langston 37
Hughes, Rowland 184, 187
Hulme, Keri 186; 'One Whale, Singing' 22, 133, 142, 145–147
human rights 188; discourse of 121, 122; abuses of 59, 151–2

Index 209

humus 17, 36, 39; *see also* soil; Haraway, Donna
The Hunter (Julia Leigh) 23, 134, 163, 167–70
hunting 64, 129, 132, 140, 154–61, 165, 169, 183; of bison 152–4; in the colonial era 23, 130, 133, 134–7, 139, 155–9, 161, 168, 176n22; in Indigenous societies 54, 92, 95, 152, 155, 164; and natural history 159–61; and slavery 31; for sport 59, 62, 133, 137, 138, 154, 157–8, 171–2; trophy hunting 10, 133–4, 137, 157–8, 160; of whales 140–1
hydrosphere 1, 2, 21, 74, 184

ice/icescapes 1, 65, 74, 75, 86, 129; the Anthropocene and 13; melting of 7, 21, 87, 88, 89, 90, 94–8, 129, 130, 185; Inuit knowledge of/reliance upon 88, 92, 95–9
Ice Age 12
The Ice People (Maggie Gee) 185
Idle No More 6, 131, 173n2
Ifowodo, Ogaga 21, 74; *The Oil Lamp* 80, 83–4
Ihimaera, Witi 9; *The Whale Rider* 22, 133, 142–145
Ikiriko, Ibiwari 21, 74; *Oily Tears of the Delta* 79–80
indentured labour 28, 44, 46, 54; *see also* slavery
India 10, 22, 44, 49, 104, 114–117, 121, 123, 124n15, 124n6, 124n18, 135; in literature 114–123, 124n22, 126n24, 126n25, 142, 183
Indigenous studies 10, 11, 20, 132
Industrial Revolution 14, 16, 48, 49
industrialization 14, 28, 48, 60, 141, 152; of agriculture 152–3; of oil extraction 94; of South Africa 49–50; and trade 133
infant mortality 78
International Union for the Conservation of Nature (IUCN) Red List, the 23n1, 136, 174n9
Inuit cultures and communities 20, 22, 88, 89, 91–3, 95, 140, 174n11, 183; writing 75, 77, 90, 98–9; whaling and 140
Iñupiat cultures and communities 20, 75, 89, 90, 91, 93, 94

Inyang, Udeme Eno 79, 80
ivory 22, 130, 133, 134–40, 147, 155, 160, 161, 173n3

Jacobs, Harriet 31
James, C.L.R. 16, 32–37; *Toussaint Louverture: The Story of the Only Successful Slave Revolt in History* 21 28, 32, 34–37, 39, 70; *The Black Jacobins* 32, 34, 36–37, 48
Jameson, Fredric 23, 167
Jamie, Kathleen, *see* 'The Reindeer Cave'
Jamieson, Robert Alan, *see Thin Wealth: A Novel from an Oil Decade*
Japan 23n4, 29, 163
Jews 55, 149
Johannesburg 54, 56, 57
Johns-Putra, Adeline 98, 185, 192n2

Kavenna, Joanna 71n7
Kenya 57, 133, 154, 158–9; hunting in 10, 134–5, 157–8, 161
Kenyatta, Jomo 57
Kimberley (New Rush) 49–53, 54, 59
Kimberley Process Certification Scheme (2000) 59
Kimmerer, Robin Wall 131
King Leopold II of Belgium 135
King, Thomas 174n10; *Truth and Bright Water* 22, 133, 151, 152–4, 173
Kiobel, Barinem 79
Kipling, Rudyard 17
kin, kinship 11, 17, 81, 130–1, 144–5, 154, 159, 173, 191
Kiss of the Fur Queen (Tomson Highway) 174n11
Klein, Naomi 18, 24n10
Koegler, Caroline 4
Kolbert, Elizabeth 129

labour 10, 16, 30, 49, 50, 52–3, 54–6, 64, 71, 113, 141, 148, 150, 155, 158, 174n8; agricultural 115, 125n17; in Britain 15; *see also* indentured labour; slavery
Labrador, Chief Charles 88
LaDuke, Winona 90–1, 152
Lancaster, John, *see The Wall*
Lazarus, Neil 167
Leigh, Julia, *see The Hunter*
LeMenager, Stephanie 3–4, 60
Levera, Paul 79
Lewis, Simon 13, 14, 16, 103
Lia, Simone 71n7

lion 130, 136, 155,163, 171–2, 175n16
The Lives of Others (Neel Mukherjee) 125n18
lithosphere 1, 2, 21, 28, 184
L'Ouverture, Toussaint 36, 37
Love in the Kingdom of Oil (Nawal El-Saadawi) 71n7
Lowboy (John Wray) 185
Lunde, Maja, *see The End of the Ocean*

Mabanckou, Alain 71n7
Macdonald, Graeme 29, 76; aesthetics of oil and 61; *The Cheviot, the Stag and the Black, Black Oil* and 60–1, 64–70, 75; petro-drama and 71; petro-fiction and 77, 83
MacKenzie, John M. 135, 159
'MaddAdam' trilogy (Margaret Atwood) 185
Madeira 29–30
Makonnen, T. Ras 57
Malm, Andreas 15, 24n6, 184, 186, 189
Mandela, Nelson 85
Mangad, Ambikasutan, *see Enmakaje* (Swarga)
Māori, 18, 186; environmental ethics of 133, 142–4,
Marikana Massacre 59
Marshall, Albert 88
Marshall, Murdena 88
Marxism 10, 16, 58; Pan-Africanism and 32; World literature and 24n9
Marzec, Robert P. 134, 148
Maslin, Mark A. 13, 14, 16, 103–4
Mazza, Donna, *see Fauna*
Mbue, Imbolo, *see How Beautiful We Were*
McCarthy, Cormac, *see The Road*
McEwan, Ian, *see Solar*
McGrath, John, 21, 29; *The Cheviot, the Stag and the Black, Black Oil* 59–71, 75; 'The Year of the Cheviot' 69
McHugh, Susan 132, 153
McKay, Robert 149, 150
McNeill, John R. 13, 14, 17
Mda, Zakes, *see The Whale Caller*
Melville, Herman, *see Moby Dick or, The Whale*
Mentz, Steve 74
Mexico 46, 115, 121, 124n15
Midnight's Children (Salman Rushdie) 126n24
Miéville, China 71n7
Milliard, Peter 57

mines, mining 21, 28, 68, 69, 70, 98, 182; coal mining 28, 49, 54, 68; British labour and 15; diamond mining 29, 49–52, 53–4, 59, 87, 183; gold mining 29, 48, 53–9, 93, 183; mineral mining 65; miners' strikes 57, 71n6; settler colonialism and 62; *see also* South Africa; oil extraction; worker's unions
Mine Boy (Peter Abrahams) 21, 29, 53–9, 70
Moby Dick or, The Whale (Herman Melville) 22, 133, 141
Mohammad, Avaes, *see* 'Bhopal'
Monbiot, George 62, 163
Moore, Jason 28–29, 30, 31, 48, 50, 55, 148; world-ecology, theory of 10, 11, 15–16, 35
more-than-human 17, 75, 93, 191, 199; *see also* other-than-human
Motion, Andrew 98
Movement for the Emancipation of the Niger Delta (MEND), the 6, 111–112
Movement for the Survival of Ogoni People (MOSOP), the 78; *see also* Saro-Wiwa, Ken; Ogoni
Mukherjee, Neel, *see The Lives of Others*
Mukherjee, Pablo 10–11, 116, 117, 120
Munif, Abdelrahman, *see Cities of Salt*
Munir, Laine 110, 111, 124n11
Myanmar (Burma) 49, 121; timber trade of 173n3

NASA 24n13
nation(s): African nations 22, 37, 57, 77, 114; colonizing nations 28, 51, 159, 187; core nations 29, 50, 76, 85, 188, 189; globalization and 12, 65; Indigenous nations 140, 151, 152, 154; literature and 3, 19; peripheral nations 49–50, 114, 117, 162, 167, 188; postcolonial theory and 10–11; semi-peripheral nations 49, 56, 188; threat of global warming to 6, 96; *see also* First Nations, nationalism; world-system, world-systems theory
National Institute for Space Research 29
National Parks 153, 161–2; *see also* Addo Elephant National Park
national security 184, 190, 192n6
National Threatened Species Day (Australia) 168
nationalism, 23, 190, 191; colonial expansion and 51; settler colonialism

and 157; postcolonial theory and 11; see also nation(s)
Native Land Act (1913) 54
nature writing 10, 98
natural history 134, 154; museums of 23, 140, 156, 159–61
Negarestani, Reza, see *Cyclonopaedia*
neocolonialism 22, 85, 98, 104, 112, 113, 132, 167
neo-Darwinism 159
neoliberalism 1, 64, 65, 120, 167, 189
neo-Malthusianism 184, 189
Neruda, Pablo, see 'Standard Oil Co.'
New World, the 14, 15, 17, 30–1, 36, 48; see also Americas, the; Caribbean
Ngozi, Chuma-Udeh 99n1
Niblett, Michael 29, 50, 60, 71
Niger Delta: anti-oil protest in the 111–112; gas flaring in the 104–111, 123n4, 183; oil extraction in the 22, 74–76, 78, 98, 186; petropoetry and the 21, 76–86, 98–9, 183; see also Movement for the Emancipation of the Niger Delta (MEND); Nigeria
Nigeria 10, 69, 98–9, 107, 109, 112, 123n4, 183; civil war in 81; gas flaring in 105–6, 108, 123n5; gender and 110, 124n11; neocolonialism in 22, 85, 104; oil extraction in 75, 77–8, 98; oil spills in 99n2; petropoetry and 80, 84–5, 99, 99n1; see also Niger Delta
Nigerian Oil Spill Monitor 99n2
Nixon, Rob 59, 117, 119, 120, 190; slow violence 7, 83, 124n13, 172
Nkrumah, Kwame 57
North America 6, 10, 87, 91, 130, 131, 133, 142, 151–3, 164, 183; see also United States of America, US; Canada
North Sea 60, 66
Nuate, Felix 79

Oak Taylor, Jesse 103, 136, 137
ocean acidification 129, 130
ocean circulations 1, 21, 95
oceanic literary studies 74
Ofiemun, Odia 99n1
Ogoni 75, 78–82, 85, 105;
Ogoni Nine, the 79, 80–1, 85; see also Saro-Wiwa, Ken
Oguyade, Ogaga 99n1
Oil! (Upton Sinclair) 71n7
Oil Encounter 76
oil extraction 22, 113, 183; in the Arctic 90–1; global warming and 89; ice melt and 87, 94; in the Niger Delta 104–6, 108, 110–111, 123n5
'OIL: From the bottom of the pit' (Peter Cizek, Phil Angers, Marc Tessier) 71n7
oil pollution 21, 22, 75, 183; in Alaska 90–1, 96–9; in the Niger Delta 78–9, 83–6; see also air pollution; oil spill
Oil Pollution Act (Alaska) 90, 99n7
oil spill 78, 99n2, 104–5; *Exxon Valdez* 90–1; see also oil pollution
Ojaide, Tanure 21, 74; *Delta Blues* 80–2, 83
Okara, Gabriel 99n1
Okpewho, Isidore 99n1
okpik, dg nanouk 22, 74, 87, 89–90, 92–3, 96–7, 99; 'If Oil is Drilled in Bristol Bay' 90, 92–3; 'Anthropocene Years' 90, 96–7
Okri, Ben 99n1
Oliver, Mary 9, 98
Orbis spike 14, 16
Orhero, Mathias Iroro 79, 80, 81
Osundare, Niyi 21, 74, 85–6; *The Eye of the Earth* 85–6
other-than-human 17, 18, 82, 87, 89, 92, 131, 191; see also more-than-human; personhood
Otobotekere, Christian 99n1
Out of Africa, see Blixen, Karen

Padmore, George 57
Pan-Africanism 21, 29, 32, 37, 59, 70; see also Fifth Pan-African Congress
Paris Agreement 6
Pass Laws 54, 71n3
Patel, Raj 29, 30, 31, 35, 50, 148
People of the Whale (Linda Hogan) 142
personhood 17, 31, 75, 93, 120, 133, 147, 149; see also more-than-human; other-than-human
pesticides 22, 104, 114–116, 119, 121–2, 124n12, 124n17, 125n18, 183; see also pests
pests 2, 30, 114, 116, 121, 130, 133, 168, 183; see also pesticides
petro-drama 21, 29, 60, 70, 71
petrofiction 76–7, 83; see also Ghosh, Amitav
'The Petrol Pump' (Italo Calvino) 71n7
Petroleum (Bessora) 71n7

petropoetry 21, 74, 76–7, 79–86, 90, 86, 96, 99, 104
plantation 16, 28, 31–2, 35, 37, 38, 40, 41, 43, 44, 45, 46; see also plantation economies; slavery
plantation economies 16, 28, 33, 36, 42–3, 46, 47–8, 70, 183; see also plantation; slavery
Plantationocene 15, 16, 17, 31, 71n1
polar bear 95, 167
Polwarth, Lord 67
Portuguese empire 29, 48, 130
postcolonialism, postcolonial studies 4, 10, 11, 20, 24n9, 87, 132, 162, 167, 188
postcolonial ecocriticism, see ecocriticism
Pratt, Mary Louise 92
PricewaterhouseCoopers 29
Prince, Mary 31
Prosser, Gabriel 33, 37, 40, 46
Prosser, Thomas 37
provision plots 28, 41, 42–4, 47; see also slavery

quagga, extinction of 130; de-extinction of 163–4, 172, 175n16
Queen Victoria 63
Queyras, Sina, see Expressway

race 3, 8, 12, 19, 53–9, 70, 71n4, 187; and activism 32, 33, 57–8, 124n11; and animal studies 133; and the Anthropocene 17, 31–2, 37–8; and development discourse 122; and eco-apartheid 22, 104, 111, 123; and factory farming 150; and hunting 137, 160; and Indigenous/postcolonial studies 11; and the mining industries 21, 50–1, 53–9; and neocolonialism 104, 132; and neo-Darwinism 159; and the Plantationocene 16; and sci-fi 187; and settler colonialism 137, 157–9; and world-systems theory 49; see also anti-racism; environmental racism; racism; slavery
Rachel Carson Centre for Environment and Society 105
racism 38–9, 45, 53, 58, 64, 82, 124n7, 136, 157, 159, 188, 191; see also anti-racism; environmental racism; race; slavery
Rastogi, Pallavi 167
Reagan, Ronald 45

The Red Book (Meaghan Delahunt) 22, 104, 115, 117–118, 121, 122, 125n22
'The Reindeer Cave' (Kathleen Jamie) 7
residential school system (Canada) 153, 174n11
rewilding 134, 163, 164, 174n9, 175n14
Rexford, Cathy Tagnak 22, 74, 87, 89–94, 99; 'Scripture According to Sila' 90, 91–2, 93, 94; 'Migration' 90, 96
Rhodes, Cecil 53, 171; DeBeers 54
The Road (Cormac McCarthy) 71n7, 185
Robinson, Kim Stanley, 24n7; 'Science in the Capital' trilogy 185; *2312* 163, 175n15
Rockefeller Foundation 114
Romanticism 9, 10, 19, 98, 99
Rose-Innes, Henrietta 9; *The Green Lion* 23, 134, 163, 171–3, 175n16, 176n23
Roy, Arundhati 182; *Capitalism: A Ghost Story* 125n18
Rushdie, Salman, see *Midnight's Children*
Russia 87, 96, 99n5, 105, 171

Sandford, Winifred, see *Windfall and Other Stories*
Saro-Wiwa, Ken 21, 74, 77–82, 84–5; *A Forest of Flowers* 71n7, 81; 'Keep Out of Prison' 79; *On A Darkling Plain* 81; *Silence Would Be Treason* 79, 82; *Sozaboy: A Novel in Rotten English* 81
Scattered All Over the Earth (Yoko Tawada) 190
Schreiner, Olive, see *Undine*
science fiction, sci-fi 8, 33, 185, 187
Scotland 10, 21, 28, 59–70, 183; Highlands of 59, 61–9
Scramble for Africa, the 87, 135, 155
seals 92, 95, 164
Second World War, the 57, 135, 161
settler colonialism 16, 18, 21, 23, 113, 131, 173; in Alaska 98; the Anthropocene and 24n14, 31–2;in Aotearoa New Zealand 142; discourse of 38, 157; Indigenous studies and 10; in Kenya 133, 155–9, 161; in North America 91, 151, 152–3; species extinction and 163, 167–8; in Tasmania 170, 176n22
7: 84 Theatre Company 62, 69, 70
Shapiro, Beth 164–5

sheep 55, 60, 61–3, 64, 67, 141, 168; Dolly the 164
Shell Oil 65, 78, 85, 105, 123n4, 123n5
Shiva, Vandana 104, 124n16
Shukin, Nicole 148, 150
Silent Spring (Rachel Carson) 114
Sinclair, Upton, *see Oil!*
Sinha, Indra 9, 116, 117, 125n19; *Animal's People* 22, 104, 115, 119–122, 126n24
sixth extinction, the 13, 22, 32, 129, 131, 132, 134, 155, 183
Skolstrejk för Klimatet (School Strike for Climate) 6
slave rebellion 21, 28, 32–41, 45–6, 70; *see also* anti-racism; slavery
slave trade 14, 30–2, 57, 71n2, 183; *see also* slavery
slavery 1, 14, 15, 16, 28–47, 48, 50, 55, 70, 136, 139, 188; abolition of 8, 44; narratives of 31, 32; *see also* indentured labour; plantation; provision plots; slave rebellion; slave trade
slow violence, *see* Nixon, Rob
smog 103, 121, 123, 126n25
Snyder, Gary 98
Society for the Preservation of Fauna of the Empire 161
Ṣode, Yomi, *see* 'Untitled'
soil 1, 21, 22, 28–40, 42, 45, 47, 50, 51, 55, 60, 62, 66, 68, 157, 165; erosion of 54, 59, 62, 116, 121; pollution of 78, 84, 114, 116, 121; *see also* plantation
Solar (Ian McEwan) 185
song 38, 60, 61, 80, 89, 138, 142, 144, 146, 158; birdsong 92–3, 94; folk song 65, 66–7, 82; mourning song 86; whalesong 146–7;
South Africa 21, 28, 49–59, 62, 70, 71n3, 71n4, 71n6, 123n5, 130, 131, 134, 135–136, 142, 155, 163, 183
Spain 30, 34, 47–8
speciesism 82, 136
Spencer, Robert 3, 7, 9, 34, 183, 188
Spivak, Gayatri 130; epistemic violence 130–131, 156
Sri Lanka (Ceylon) 49, 137, 158
'Standard Oil Co.' (Pablo Neruda) 71n7
steam power 13, 14, 15, 16, 21, 49, 51, 62, 70, 136
Steffen, Will 13, 14, 17
Steinhart, Edward I. 134, 135, 155, 157, 158, 161–2

Steinwand, Jonathan 141–142, 143, 144
Stevenson, Robert Louis, *see Treasure Island*
Stoermer, Eugene 13, 16
The Stone Gods (Jeanette Winterson) 185
storms 3, 40–1, 45–6, 86, 95, 190, 191
sugar, sugarcane 14, 21, 29–31, 34–8, 43, 48, 70
Sunderland, Duke and Duchess of 61
The Swan Book (Alexis Wright) 190–191
Szeman, Imre 3, 4, 24n5, 60, 71n7, 77

Taino 30, 48
Tangaroa 18, 142
Tasmania 49, 168–70, 175n21; *see also* Aboriginal Tasmanians
Tasmanian tiger (thylacine) 170; extinction of 130, 168, 175n18; de-extinction of 163, 164, 168–9
Tawada, Yoko, *see Scattered All Over the Earth*
testimony 19, 21, 31, 77, 84, 85, 176n22
Texaco (Patrick Chamoiseau) 71n7
The Tusk That Did the Damage (Tania James) 173n3
theatre 11, 34, 59–70; Epic theatre 60; political theatre 60, 69
Thin Wealth: A Novel from an Oil Decade (Robert Alan Jamieson) 71n7
Thunberg, Greta 6
Tiffin, Helen 37, 120, 131, 132, 136
Tiny Sunbirds Far Away (Christie Watson) 22, 104, 108–112
tobacco 31, 37, 43
tourism 59, 60, 63–9, 137, 138, 153–4, 155, 158, 161–3, 166, 168; de-extinction and 171–3; *see also* eco-tourism
translation 5, 11, 18, 121, 126n25
Treasure Island (Robert Louis Stevenson) 53
Tremain, Rose 71n7
Trump, Donald 15, 45
Tsing, Anna L. 16, 71n1

Ulturgasheva, Olga 87, 95, 164, 165
Union Carbide 104, 114, 116–122, 125n20, 183
Undine (Olive Schreiner) 21, 29, 49–53, 54, 59
'Untitled' (Yomi Ṣode) 23, 133, 154, 159–161, 174n12
United Nations (U.N.) 6, 122, 129, 155, 173n1

United States of America, US 28, 33, 37, 92, 125n19, 141, 153, 163, 166, 169, 188, 189, 190; and colonialism 87, 135, 152; and globalization 11; and the Green Revolution 104, 114, 115–17, 124n15; and pollution 112, 123; as dominating market 23n4, 29; as frontier 62, 70, 90, 91, 92; factory farming in 150, 174n8; literature from and about 7, 28, 31–3, 37–47, 65–7, 76, 98, 99, 113; President of the 15, 44–5; *see also* Americas, the; North America

urbanization 14, 28, 48, 50, 124n7, 141

Valassopoulos, Anastasia 3, 7, 9, 183, 188
Vizenor, Gerald, *see Griever: An American Monkey King in China*

wa Thiong'o, Ngũgĩ 156–7; *Moving the Centre* 155
The Wall (John Lancaster) 190
Wallerstein, Immanuel 49
Warwick Research Collective (WReC) 10, 24n9, 29, 192
Watson, Christie, *see Tiny Sunbirds Far Away*
Watt, James 13
Watt-Cloutier, Sheila 88
Wenzel, Jennifer 5, 7, 30, 35, 68, 136, 139
whale 19, 87, 92, 130, 140–7, 149, 153, 172; whaling 10, 22, 130, 133, 134, 140–4
The Whale Caller (Zakes Mda) 142
Whyte, Kyle 187
Wilson, Edward O. 162

Windfall and Other Stories (Winifred Sandford) 71n7
Wolfe, Cary 147
Wolfe, Patrick 157
Woolf, Leonard 158
woolly mammoth 167, 169; de-extinction of 163–6
Wordsworth, William 98
workers' unions 21, 29, 58, 59, 70, 71n6
World Bank, the 105,114, 115, 123n5
world-ecology, *see* Moore, Jason
World Health Organization (WHO) 103, 123n1
world literature, world-literature 10, 24n9, 19; *The Cheviot the Stag and the Black, Black Oil* as, 21, 29, 71
World Peoples Climate Conference 84
world-system, world-systems theory 14, 49, 60, 69, 76; *see also* nation(s); Wallerstein, Immanuel; Warwick Research Collective (WReC)
Wray, John, *see Lowboy*
Wright, Alexis, *see The Swan Book*
Wylie, Dan 134, 135–6, 140; 'Where in the waste is the wisdom?' 22, 133, 137–139, 154
Wynter, Sylvia 43–4, 46

Yaeger, Patricia 19
Yassin-Kassab, Robin 71n7
Yeibo, Ebi 99n1
Yusoff, Kathryn 24n14, 32, 38, 41, 48; billion Black Anthropocenes 16–17, 32; *A Billion Black Anthropocenes or None* 28, 31

Zimov, Sergey 164
zoo 168, 171, 175n16

For Product Safety Concerns and Information please contact our EU representative GPSR@taylorandfrancis.com
Taylor & Francis Verlag GmbH, Kaufingerstraße 24, 80331 München, Germany

www.ingramcontent.com/pod-product-compliance
Lightning Source LLC
Chambersburg PA
CBHW051357290426
44108CB00015B/2044